P9-DSV-824

BURN, BABY, BURN!

The Los Angeles Race Riot August, 1965

by Jerry Cohen
and William S. Murphy

Introduction by Robert Kirsch

E. P. DUTTON & CO., INC. NEW YORK 1966

BURN, BABY, BURN!

Published simultaneously in Canada by Clarke, Irwin & Company Limited, Toronto and Vancouver

Library of Congress Catalog Card Number: 66–21295

Fourth Printing October 1969

List of Illustrations

California's Governor Edmund G. (Pat) Brown visits riot area

Reverend Martin Luther King, Jr., expresses his views on the causes of the riot

A police officer explains to a woman how to locate a missing relative

Looters on the loose

The heart of Watts following the August holocaust

The Central Ave. district, showing the ruins of burned-out store buildings

A man hired to help clean the rubble from the devastated community

Looters running through the streets, carrying stolen or plundered merchandise

A detective checks for fingerprints in a house after a fire in September revealed a storehouse of stolen loot

INTRODUCTION

By Robert Kirsch

PERHAPS THE MOST striking lesson of the many which are implicit in the fire and violence that have become known as the Watts riots of mid-August, 1965, is that a ghetto need not look like one. South Central Los Angeles, a long corridor of Negro communities, which was the setting for the worst race riot in the history of this country, is no warren of moldering tenements, no grid of asphalt unrelieved by trees, lawns, gardens. From the vantage point of airliners making their east-to-west approach to the Los Angeles International Airport, the observer sees no difference between the bungalow homes, the garish sherbet-colored apartment houses, the markets and shopping districts of Watts, Willowbrook and the cities of South Gate or Inglewood. For the freeway driver, intent as he is likely to be on the perils of high-speed traffic, occasional glances reveal antennaed roofs rolling by.

Yet, this is where a seemingly routine arrest on a hot, humid summer night triggered the human storm whose elements were despair, hopelessness, disappointment. Some called these events nothing less than insurrection. Some said it was more a caste riot than a race riot. For the Negroes who had moved out of the ghettos into the lower-middle-class and middle-class communities of West Adams, Baldwin Hills, the Pico area were not involved. Indeed, some of the greatest bitterness was directed against them. It was widely believed that those who were reaping the advantages of a city whose conscience had been touched by the civil rights movement, who were in contact with that other Los Angeles, the Los Angeles of opportunity and mobility, of culture and education, had abandoned their brothers in South Central Los Angeles.

White Los Angeles knew even less about Watts. It was remote both geographically and psychologically, bounded by a tier of older, all-white cities along its eastern and western borders. South Central Los Angeles was until the riots a kind of forgotten archipelago in the garish basin of the region. Many residents, when the riots broke out, had to consult maps to find out where Watts and Willowbrook were. They found out soon enough. By freeway, Watts was minutes away and there was a sudden sense of vulnerability and fear.

This came after the sickening sadness and embarrassment that such a thing could occur in a place that prided itself on its race relations, on the absence of the sort of riots that had bruised Harlem and Chicago, Detroit and East St. Louis, the harsh and overt prejudice of some of the towns in the Deep South. For all the problems inherent in its pituitary growth, Los Angeles is maturing from boosterism to pride. Every city has a concern for its image. This restless, balkanized urban sprawl worships its image as a kind of household god: the casual, open way of life; the sense of frontier opportunity; toleration of differences, eccentricities.

These are qualities easily caricatured. But they exist and they have enabled some prodigious accomplishments. There are also other images, somewhat less attractive: a naïve worship of bigness for its own sake, a tendency toward simple solutions of complicated problems, a belief that newness and movement are proof against the worst difficulties besetting the older, more stabilized cities of the East. The Watts riots may (we must be tentative) have been Los Angeles' rites of passage as an American city.

This depends on whether we are willing to examine some of the hard truths that lie in the shards of Watts. If these were truths that concern Los Angeles alone, they would be important enough. But, they concern all of America.

"Let anything happen in the rest of the country," the novelist Idwal Jones wrote, "in Arkansas or Maine, and there is instant repercussion inside the borders of Southern California; it has become the national hot-bed and testing ground." Carey McWilliams called Southern California "a great laboratory of experimentation, a forcing ground, a place where ideas, practices and customs must prove their worth or be discarded."

People who come here in their thousands bring with them the experiences of their past. The Southern Negro sees in the uniform of a Los Angeles policeman a symbol that reminds him of a century of oppression. The policeman may be conditioned by his own background. This is a microcosm of America, good and bad, promising and frustrating. Another writer, the neglected but prescient Farnsworth Crowder, wrote almost fifty years ago: "Here American institutions sharpen into focus so startling as to give the effect, sometimes, of caricature. Here the socio-economic class conflict is vividly posed in burning silhouettes against the wall of factory and the hinterland. Here American scholarship and research are at their best; American cults and quasi-religions are at their shallow and shabby worst; here are America's indignant soap-boxers and pamphleteers, bigots surrendered to some over-simplified ideal, its scared reactionaries and its grim stand-patters; its baronial aristocracy, its patient poor, its sober, good-natured middle class; its promoters, racketeers, opportunists and politicians; its fagged-out oldsters and its brash raw youth . . . What America is, California is, with accents, in italics . . . National currents of thought, passion, aspirations and protest . . . have a way of boiling up in a chemistry of . . . unexpected crystallizations."

Southern California is also a projection into the future, a suggestion of what may be in store in the megalopoles of the seventies and eighties. It is no accident that such problems as smog, traffic, parking, water, education, a whole variety of challenges in urban ecology focused and sharpened here.

Suddenly the narrative you will read in these pages becomes more than a story of conflict and violence, of tragedy and contention. It becomes an allegory of the human condition in the middle twentieth century. We see in these pages the collision between dreams and reality, the uncomfortable but insistent proposition that there are more than two sides to issues, the strange failure of communication in an era that prides itself on mass, instant, electronic contact. Throughout those days, people asked perhaps innocently, "What else do *they* want?" They pointed to the examples of achievements by Negroes in Los Angeles, of conditions which they felt were better than any in other parts of the country. There were indeed dramatic individual success stories (three city councilmen, many judges, a postmaster, city commissioners, scientists, teachers, prosperous businessmen who were Negroes); and these were true. But not true enough. Statistics could be shown of higher unemployment, higher population density, poverty, inequities. There are such statistics in this book. More importantly, there are individual lives described. The faces come out of the crowd.

Dr. Martin Luther King, who came to Los Angeles because he sensed that here the nonviolent civil rights movement received its greatest blow, put it this way: "Progress whets the appetite for more progress." It was more than balm for a wounded city; it was a challenge to determine what constituted the basic needs and wants of a whole group of Americans. And its implications went beyond the Negro, touched the malaise of a whole society.

The answers we do not yet know. One civil rights activist, Louise Meriwether, who went to work the second day of the riot as the first Negro story analyst in a Hollywood studio, said, "We failed in Watts. We could not touch them. It wasn't political here. It was economic and social and in the end beyond us." Another CORE worker said, "It was easier for us in Los Angeles to go to Bogalusa or Selma than to bang our heads against Watts." For Los Angeles could salve its conscience, pour its support to the civil rights struggle in the South, while it failed to touch the deeper and more complex problems of the Watts-Willowbrook area.

In the Negro ghetto of its own city, the traditional Southern California solutions of growth, space and size just did not work. The same sort of pressures were building there as in the black ghettos of Harlem, Bedford-Stuyvesant, Chicago: the corroding dole, the sense of lost dignity, of missing identity. When the explanations came, when the bickering, blaming and justifications filled the air of this hyperventilated city (a psychiatrist mentioned the irony that the radio and television conversation shows are filled with talk that neither communicates nor provides catharsis), it became obvious that the semantic difficulties were almost insurmountable. Such a phrase as "police brutality" had completely different meanings for Chief Parker than it had for someone like Louis Lomax, the Negro historian and television commentator, who is one of the most eloquent spokesmen for the Negro in this community. Yet, even Lomax in his eloquence speaks two different languages when he addresses his white and Negro middle-class audiences and when he is talking to the people from Watts.

To a convention of the Negro Political Action Association, he says the white man, "has done wrong so long, he now thinks he's right to do wrong." Yet on his popular television show, he is anxious to communicate to the community as a whole in terms free of cant and bitterness. But on the Sunday night of the riots, like many Negro intellectuals, the ambivalence was most apparent in a monologue that started out abhorring the violence, and ended up in a strange attempt to translate the riot into a demonstration by the Negro community.

No one has the answers yet. Possibly because there are many answers, some of them relevant, others only a suggestion of what may be done. One of the former is that the way in which Los

Angeles has been absorbing its in-migration in the past broke down in the ghetto. Somehow large numbers of people have found jobs, housing, opportunity, upward mobility. Before Watts the failures were individual—men and women who were rejected, or minorities such as the Mexican-American, who were quiet and tractable and accepted their fate. This changed in Watts—a whole caste rebelled. And Los Angeles will never be the same.

In the days after the riots, there were other things we had to face about our city. Perhaps one was that it was no more a city than the Austro-Hungarian Empire was an empire. In the aftermath of the riots, Los Angeles seemed to crystallize into its components, "a collection of suburbs in search of a city," Willard Huntington Wright called it. Others have called it a city without a face.

We have to attempt to define the geographic and political reality. You may be confused by the fact that there were three separate police forces involved in the skein and tangle of the riots—the California Highway Patrol, the Los Angeles Police Department, the Los Angeles Sheriff's Office. You may wonder about the other cities referred to—Inglewood, Huntington Park, Torrance, Lynwood, Compton, Gardena. Even Angelenos are confused about it. To sort it out: First, there is Southern California, an immense geographical area, from the Mexican border on the south, two hundred miles to the Tehachapi Mountains on the north, from the Colorado River on the east to the Pacific Ocean on the west. Sometimes, Los Angeles and Southern California are used interchangeably, which is erroneous, but considering the attenuation of the region is understandable. At the center of this region is Los Angeles County, 4,000 square miles in size, the most populous and influential county of the ten that comprise Southern California.

More than ten million people live in Southern California, more than six million in Los Angeles County. Over 90 percent of the population of Southern California lives on about 15 percent of the land area, for most of it is desert or rugged mountain country. The populated area is mainly in a tangled necklace of towns and cities between the coastal ranges and the coast.

Los Angeles County is roughly in the center of Southern California, Los Angeles City spreads out like a four-spoked pop-art wheel from the center of Los Angeles County; the area of the riots is the south-central spoke of that wheel. But the City of Los Angeles is only the largest of the 70 cities in the county. There is no geographic unity. Its 457-square miles meander around a patchwork of towns and county strips, districts and neighborhoods, and even an occasional Federal enclave such as that of the Sawtelle Veterans Hospital, or a state enclave such as the University of California at Los Angeles. If most of the minority groups live within the city limits, their communities have little in common with the far reaches of West Los Angeles and the San Fernando Valley, or Pacific Palisades or San Pedro-Wilmington. Watts was once a separate little agricultural community, populated by Negroes from the beginning, but remote from the rest of the city. It grew up against the bastions of the independent cities that line it on east and west, and filled up as its people were turned back from expanding into white residential neighborhoods.

In this crazy quilt of jurisdictions, law enforcement may shift from the Los Angeles Police Department on one side of a street to the Los Angeles Sheriff's Department on the other side of the same street. The California Highway Patrol's area may stop suddenly as the officers are pursuing a traffic violator (which happened in the triggering incident).

It takes a specialist to explain the intricacies of these 70 city governments and the county government which operates city services in the unincorporated areas. The City of Los Angeles has more coherence in the efficiency of its services, such as the Police Department and Fire Department, than in its political structure. (It is no accident that Chief Parker emerges as a strong figure in the August riots; the elected city officials have much more difficulty in performing their tasks.) Municipal government has its weaknesses in an obsolete and complicated charter that puts real power into the 15-man City Council (and each councilman represents a district with its special character and needs and most often with only the vaguest loyalty to the city). The mayor reigns but hardly rules. The city charter, adopted in 1925, has 122,000 words, has been amended many times. The county charter, written in 1912, has only 14,000 words.

Mayor Samuel Yorty, a politically ambitious, personable man, spent his first term in an almost constant battle with the City Council. The major issue of those years was whether or not there would be a combined rubbish collection. The City Council had contracted with a private concern to provide separate pickup of tin cans and metal. The mayor finally won, but the long contention pointed up the difficulty of meeting large-scale city problems, even in those areas where the county or state did not have prior jurisdiction.

Negro representation on the council began only within the last five years. More prosperous and long-established districts managed to assert their claims before south-central Los Angeles. The neglect made itself felt in many ways. For most residents of the district, the only contact with city government was through the Police Department, and then largely in situations that involved trouble. A previously successful deputy auxiliary police program which was most effective in minority neighborhoods was discontinued when Chief Parker took over. After that, community relations contact began to deteriorate.

These are some of the matters that are covered in the narrative you are about to read. It is a remarkable piece of journalism, which comes close to deserving to be called history. Because of the research, the careful penetration to the eye of the human storm which was the Watts riots, you will find much that has

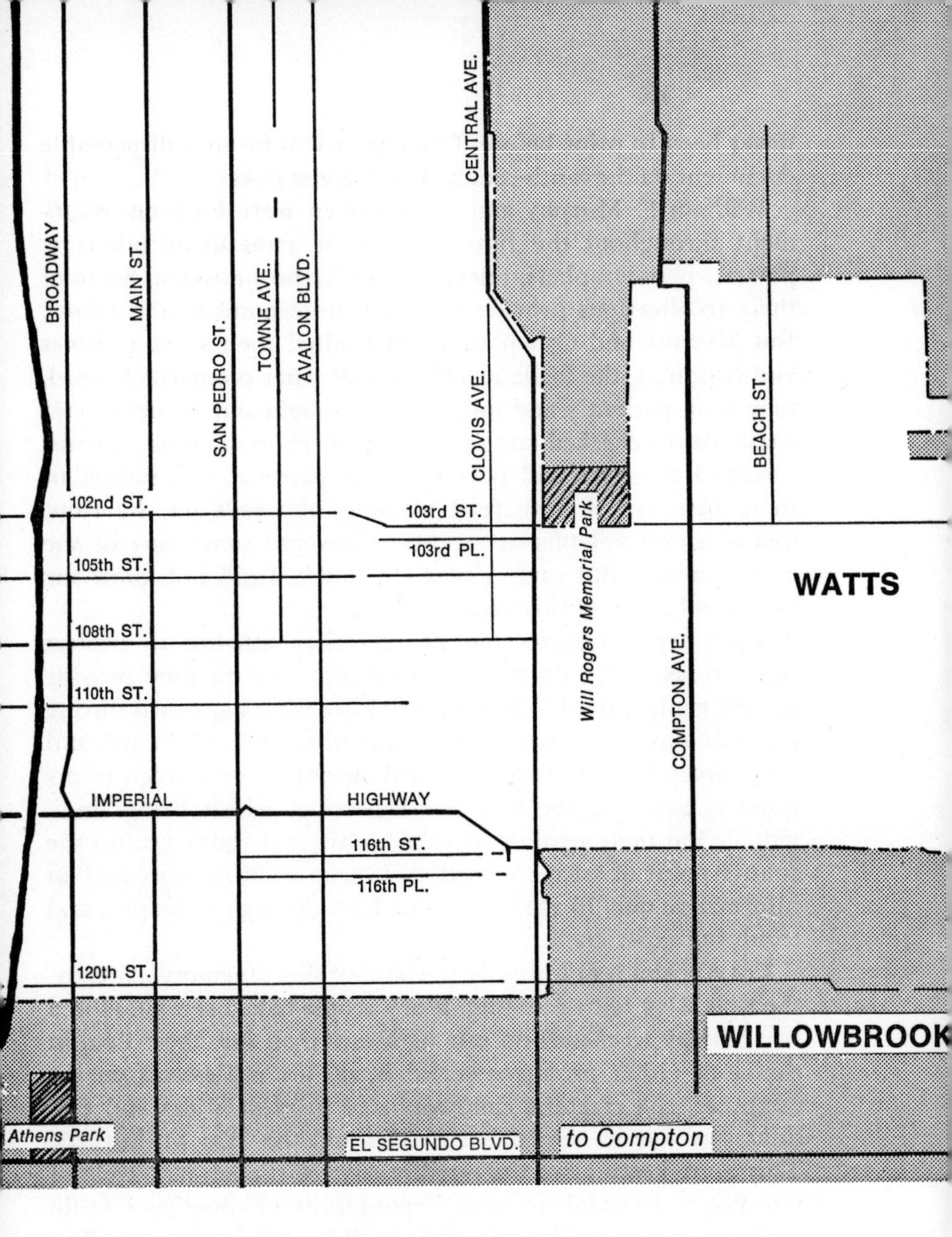

THE WATTS AREA

Los Angeles County

City of Los Angeles

Scale: 2800 feet = one inch

never been in print before. I believe it will be an indispensable document on the south-central Los Angeles riots.

William S. Murphy and Jerry Cohen were both on assignment throughout the riots. So were a great many other reporters, photographers, television and radio newsmen. Some of their recollections provide a vivid counterpoint to the events. But Murphy and Cohen have not limited their work to notes and clippings, the facile recollection of what occurred. Instead, they have patiently and methodically sought out witnesses and participants, checked and cross-checked reports and documents, recorded the lives and portrayed the personal experiences of those involved. I have read millions of words on the riots, including several official reports; I covered some part of the events myself. But until I read this book, I did not know the sweep and detail of this tragedy.

They are not advocates, nor do they attempt to protect reputations. They do not retail slogans, nor do they provide instant explanations. They seek to relate what happened during those six days, what came before and what came afterward, and they succeed in a remarkably lucid chronicle, one which to my mind is equal to the best war reporting, which brings individuals and their separate identities alive and viable against the counterpoint of great contention. It is an exciting story and an informative one. In reading it, one lives through a complex and troubling experience.

Los Angeles is notoriously the land of short memory. Already, the riots seem to be receding. More people have been killed in a few holiday weekends on our highways than lost their lives in the riots. Other problems crowd in on us: restlessness on the campuses, the creeping catastrophe of hillslide slides and erosions, the war in Vietnam, elections and the War on Poverty. This book keeps alive the terrible days of the adrenal cycle of violence and appeals to us as a community of conscience to do what we can to avoid the fearful possibility that is expressed in the McCone Commission report, " . . . the existing breach, if allowed to persist, could in time split our society irretrievably. So serious and so explosive is the situation that, unless it is checked, the August riots may seem by comparison to be only a curtain raiser for what could blow up one day in the future."

That is the challenge.

— ACKNOWLEDGMENTS

THE AUTHORS WISH to express their appreciation to the following members of the *Los Angeles Times* editorial staff for their suggestions and assistance during the period this book was being written:

Ray Rogers, H. Durant Osborne, Jack Jones, Art Berman, Paul Weeks, George Reasons, Robert Richardson, Eric Malnic, Philip Fradkin, Robert Jackson, Carroll (Spud) Corliss, Howard Hertel, Paul Beck, Ron Einstoss and Richard West. Several of these *Times* writers were eyewitnesses to various incidents which are described in the narrative. *Times* photographers Cal Montney, Jack Gaunt, Don Cormier and Joe Kennedy supplied illuminating accounts of their own personal experiences in the field from the time of the outbreak of the riot.

The authors also wish to thank Robert Kirsch, novelist and Book Editor of the *Los Angeles Times,* who read the manuscript, offered invaluable suggestions, and contributed the Introduction to this book.

We should also like to express our gratitude to the California Highway Patrol, the Los Angeles Sheriff's Department, the Los Angeles Fire Department and the California National Guard for invaluable aid in obtaining information to document this story.

Wherever accounts detailing the actions of members of the Los Angeles Police Department appear, these were obtained from testimony taken by the office of the Los Angeles District Attorney, the Los Angeles County Coroner and other sources of public record. The Los Angeles Police Department refused to allow the authors to interview any officers who participated in suppressing the riot, and declined to permit the examination of records which are normally available to accredited representatives of any news media.

PART ONE

1

ON FEBRUARY 23, 1965, the Federal Bureau of Investigation published a manual dealing with riots and their control. It is titled, appropriately enough, *Prevention and Control of Mobs and Riots.* It is available to any peace officer for the asking. Among the observations in this astonishingly prophetic little manual are these:

"Whenever a civil disturbance or riot occurs, there are always certain factors or developments which have prepared the way. . . . Some kind of provocation triggers the violence. This precipitating incident, even though it might have been completely imaginary, becomes exaggerated through rumor and magnified out of proportion to its actual importance.

"Full-scale rioting begins when one or two of these isolated clashes take hold and instigate mob action. . . . We must bear in mind that frustration breeds aggression on the part of any group. A frustrated minority may resort to aggression just as a frustrated majority group may. . . . When the tension has built up, when the frustration has existed long enough, when rumor has done its work—the conditions are ripe.

"When irritations on both sides have become common, when the potential opponents are in close proximity, and when there is enough bad feeling, the ingredients are available. Every little clash must be regarded as a spark that can start the conflagration."

In Los Angeles, during the early evening of August 11, 1965, the conditions were ripe. The ingredients were available. Rumor would do its work. And the spark was there.

Only the presence of Marquette, Ronald and Rena Frye was required—and a twenty-year-old woman barber named Joyce Ann Gaines.

They would be present soon enough as this extraordinarily hot, uncommonly humid mid-August day neared a close.

The screwdriver, an innocent-appearing mixture, has a relatively short barroom history, having attained its popularity in the post-World War II years. It has neither the tradition of, say, the mint julep, nor the kick of the martini. But it is serviceable, and for many persons this combination of vodka and orange juice can be highly volatile. Just how many screwdrivers are needed to intoxicate a man depends on his size, biochemistry and drinking habits.

Marquette and Ronald Frye were both young men and, by their own admissions, neither was an experienced drinker. Marquette was twenty-one; his stepbrother Ronald, to whom he is unrelated by blood, was twenty-two.

A question was to arise later regarding the exact number of screwdrivers they consumed on the afternoon of August 11, 1965. Because the answers are significant to the conduct of Marquette Frye—who must be considered one of the catalysts, though certainly not the cause, of the Los Angeles riot—they deserve examination.

Marquette and Ronald each offered different estimates at different times about the amount of alcohol they had drunk. Each also supplied different versions of where and when they had consumed the spiked orange juice.

"Yeah, man, we was drunk," Marquette told a Los Angeles County deputy sheriff during the peak of the six-day riot.

Later, on August 20, Ronald Frye visited the Los Angeles City Hall office of Mayor Samuel W. Yorty, at the mayor's invitation, and said to the city's chief executive: "We had been drinking all afternoon."

Eleven days afterwards, on August 31, Ronald recalled for the benefit of D. Sterry Fagan, a deputy district attorney, that he had drunk only two screwdrivers and Marquette "about two." The same day Marquette told Fagan: "Oh, I'd say I had three or four screwdrivers—vodka and orange juice."

In later conversation with the authors, Marquette lowered his personal count to "just two." Both stepbrothers insisted their drinking had occurred in the family apartment about a block from where they and Mrs. Rena Frye—Marquette's mother and Ronald's stepmother—were arrested the evening of August 11. But another version had them enjoying the screwdrivers at the home of two young women to whom Marquette had introduced Ronald, a stranger to Los Angeles, the day before.

Fagan asked Ronald during their dialogue in the Los Angeles district attorney's office if they had drunk anything "at your own house" before leaving about 5 P.M., and Ronald replied: "No."

Yet in the same room, the same day, Marquette insisted, when asked by Fagan if he and Ronald had drunk anything at the home of the young women: "No. Because the girls weren't home."

He repeated this assertion to the authors several weeks later.

Amounts, times and places aside, it is enough to know that the two young Negro men, both inexperienced in the use of alcohol, had been drinking intoxicants during the afternoon of August 11—and perhaps into the early evening. And it is significant, considering what developed, that Marquette Frye in all probability was drunk. According to Joseph Lee Gabel, a salty-tongued tow-truck driver who had a chance to observe Marquette at close range shortly after 7 P.M.: "Well, let's put it this way: if he wasn't drunk, he was either crazy or doped."

At almost precisely 7 P.M., August 11, Marquette Frye sat behind the wheel of an aged gray Buick, traveling north on Avalon Boulevard. The 1955-model automobile was the property of Marquette Frye's mother, Rena, and his stepfather,

Wallace Frye, a genial, easygoing fifty-year-old parking lot attendant. Marquette's lone passenger was Ronald, whose even temperament was known to closely approximate that of his father, Wallace Frye.

The stepbrothers were returning from a crosstown visit to the home of two young women to whom Marquette the day before had introduced Ronald, fresh out of the Air Force and a newcomer to Los Angeles. As Marquette drove along El Segundo Boulevard in an area patrolled by the California Highway Patrol, his motoring attracted the attention of the driver of a pickup truck. The man, a Negro, slipped into anonymity after hailing and reporting his observation to Highway Patrolman Lee Minikus. Minikus acted quickly on the truck driver's report.

It still was light; darkness was not to close in for another hour at least.

"That's a reckless driver," the man in the pickup truck told Officer Minikus, and the Highway Patrolman recalls: "I pursued the car northbound on Avalon from approximately 122nd, where I started my clock. I clocked the defendant approximately 50 miles in a 35-miles-an-hour zone."

Between 119th and 120th Streets on Avalon Boulevard, Officer Lee Minikus decided he had observed enough. He turned on his motorcycle's flashing red light and sounded its siren.

By now both pursuer and pursued were within the territory of the City of Los Angeles which, as it wends its way southerly, jigsaws aimlessly in and out of county and suburban boundaries.

The two vehicles traveled past the National Motel, past Doyne's Medical Clinic, the A & J Market (liquors and groceries), a Rocket gasoline station and the Grace Temple Baptist Church. They went past Brice's Bookkeeping ("Income Tax Returns Prepared"), where Richard A. Brice, a young accountant, was preparing to close his business for the night, and past the building housing Bill's Cleaners, the Pink Lady Beauty Salon and Gaines' Barber Shop, where Joyce Ann Gaines, a tall young woman in a light blue smock, was preparing to accommodate a customer.

"There's a cop behind you," Ronald said to Marquette.

Marquette caught a glint of the flashing red light in his rear-view mirror and pulled almost immediately to a stop at a curb on the east side of Avalon between 116th Place and 116th Street, a short block to the north.

Officer Minikus stopped his cycle and got off it. Marquette stepped uncertainly from the car.

That, plus the earlier sound of the siren, attracted the neighborhood's curious, of which there were many.

"Let a siren blow on this street and in two minutes you'll have a hundred people around," Walter Crawford commented later as he sat in the neat living room of his home about 50 yards away. He resided in a complex of apartments which fronts on the 11600 block of Towne Street, the next west of Avalon, where the family of Wallace Frye also rented.

By the time Marquette Frye and Officer Lee Minikus were on the sidewalk, sparring verbally in a cautious yet friendly way, between twenty-five and thirty persons had streamed from nearby apartments and walkways and encircled the pair. All were Negroes, for this was a totally Negro neighborhood. Some, on this very hot evening, were sipping from beer cans. The onlookers were not unfriendly, but good-natured and rather amused, chiefly at what they considered the comedy supplied by Marquette Frye.

Walter Crawford was preparing to walk to the grocery when he saw the motorcycle and gray Buick stop directly opposite him. He decided to delay his errand. He remained apart, however, from those flocking into the street, electing to observe developments from the exterior steps of a two-story stucco apartment house on the west side of Avalon.

At almost the same time, Richard Brice completed "securing"

his business for the evening. He watched briefly from the front of his shop as the crowd surrounded the Highway Patrolman and a young man he recognized as a resident of the neighborhood. Then, because the growing crowd obscured his vision, Brice walked toward it "just to see what was going on."

Two and one-half blocks to the south of Brice's shop, Joyce Ann Gaines, twenty, light-skinned and red-haired, also watched and wondered. She had heard sirens as the brief pursuit passed her father's shop, where she and two older sisters were employed as barbers. Before joining the crowd four blocks to the north, Joyce exchanged a few quick comments with Mrs. Vergie Nash, proprietress of the adjacent Pink Lady Beauty Salon, who also had heard the "commotion . . . the sirens and what have you."

"Look—what's going on?" asked Mrs. Nash.

"Something's happened down the street," replied Joyce.

Something was indeed happening down the street. At that moment, it was quite innocent. But as Joyce and Mrs. Nash's twenty-two-year-old daughter Joan walked toward it, the happening was about to become deformed, and the innocence would give way to ugliness.

2

AFTER HAVING curbed Marquette, Officer Lee Minikus was the picture of police-textbook propriety—efficient, agreeable, authoritative. Swiftly, he went through the routine procedure of asking Marquette Frye for his driver's license. Marquette explained that he had lost it a few days earlier. Then Minikus, who "noticed an odor of alcohol," put Marquette through a routine "field sobriety test." This consisted of having him walk a straight line and touch his fingers to his nose. In Minikus' opinion, Marquette failed the test.

From across the street, Walter Crawford made the judgment that "the guy was drunk—he couldn't walk the line." Minikus, having formed the same impression from a much closer vantage point, informed Marquette that he "was under arrest for driving under the influence of intoxicating beverage." He also "advised him of his constitutional rights to remain silent, right to counsel and that anything he said might be held against him."

If anyone had suggested to Minikus at that moment that the commonplace drunk-driving arrest would deteriorate with stunning abruptness, the officer would have laughed in his face. Minikus, in fact, was smiling at that very second. For it appeared to him "there couldn't have been a better approach between officer and defendant at the time."

Marquette Frye was thinking the same thing. Later, he said: "The officer that stopped me was as polite as an officer of the law can be. I mean, the reason that most people started gathering around was because I was joking with the officer—I mean, we was getting along, getting along." As Walter Crawford observed from his perch across the street, "The crowd was laughing at the fellow and kidding with one another."

Minikus noted that, despite his announcement of the arrest, Marquette Frye remained a "very happy-go-lucky drunk." It struck the officer that Marquette, while thoroughly cooperative, "thought everything was a joke."

"Man, you ain't going to have to take me to jail," Marquette said, grinning engagingly.

When Minikus began to fill out an on-the-scene arrest slip, a witness in the crowd overheard this snatch of conversation between Minikus and Marquette:

Q—What color is your hair?

A—Black—see, I'm black all over.

To which Minikus replied: "You're a comedian."

Seconds later, in compliance with California Highway Patrol procedures, Minikus radioed for his back-up motorcycle officer and a transport car to carry Marquette to the Firestone Sheriff's Station, since it was his impression, and later that of other CHP officers, that the arrest had been made in county territory.

Robert Lewis, Minikus' back-up officer, and Larry Bennett, driver of the Highway Patrol transportation vehicle in the area, were nearby and responded quickly. Upon their arrival, Ronald Frye, who had remained in the Buick after Minikus stopped it, emerged from the car also, because: "A little crowd started gathering and they were joking and the crowd was laughing. So I got out to hear. You know—to laugh a little bit myself."

Two miles southeasterly in Compton, one of many suburban communities which borders on the southerly part of the City of Los Angeles and portions of Los Angeles County, a request was made to an establishment known as South East Tow: Pick up for impounding a 1955 gray Buick "near 116th and Avalon in the City of Los Angeles, involving an arrest by the California Highway Patrol."

Recalls Joseph Lee Gabel, one of two drivers on duty at the Compton tow station: "We got two calls at the same time, as a matter of fact. The other driver, he was first up. So he went out on the other call. I always have to be lucky—I was attached to this one. So I rolled out to 116th and Avalon. When I got there, the scene was just about like it usually was—but only this one was just a little bit different."

Many nasty face-offs between white policemen and Negro crowds had occurred in Los Angeles and satellite communities in the preceding few years. These had left a residue of ill feeling on both sides; among Negroes resentment ran deep. But little bloodshed had accompanied these confrontations and most had escaped public attention.

Most of Los Angeles simply didn't know how the vast and largely invisible Negro community felt about the white cop. But it was to learn soon enough. For, as Joe Gabel detected upon his arrival, what was developing at 116th and Avalon was indeed "just a little bit different" from past police-mob scenes in Los Angeles.

"When the lady came and got me, I was sitting there, about ten minutes after seven. I was cooking a rabbit, and she came and told me they had Marquette and Ronald around the corner and were taking them to jail."

Mrs. Rena Frye was forty-nine, a small woman, just five feet tall, with placid features and a slow manner of speech which she owes to her native Oklahoma. She was born there on a farm. She remained there until after her first marriage.

While languid in appearance, Mrs. Frye was capable of swift movement and decisive action. Her son Marquette always believed he inherited his own quick temper from his mother.

From Rena Frye's apartment to where her son and Officer

Lee Minikus then were occupied was less than a short block. To get there, one had only to pass through the courtyard of the building in which the Fryes lived, cross an alley and travel through the courtyard of the apartment building on the west side of Avalon where Walter Crawford watched from the steps. Mrs. Frye needed but seconds to make the trip.

Her loose-fitting dress flapping, she bustled through a crowd which, by now, had grown to more than one hundred—and still was multiplying. (Just how large the mob eventually got before the first missile was aimed at a police car must remain a matter of speculation. In the confusion, different observers arrived at different estimates, ranging from "maybe, one hundred and fifty to two hundred" to "oh, there were thousands.")

Joe Gabel, about to hitch the Frye Buick to his tow lines, glimpsed an indignant figure in a red-flowered smock, approaching him. It was Mrs. Frye.

"I wasn't hooked up to it yet, to be honest about it, when this little woman—lady—come running across the street and hollered at me it was her car," Gabel said. "So I told her I didn't have anything to do with it."

Gabel nodded toward the Highway Patrolmen, indicating to Mrs. Frye that they were the proper persons to consult with. Mrs. Frye approached Lewis. She told him the car belonged to her and asked him to release it so she could drive it to her nearby home. Since Minikus was the arresting officer, Lewis referred her to him.

"What are you going to do with my car?" asked Mrs. Frye, identifying herself as Marquette's mother.

"We are going to store it," Minikus replied.

"I'm the registered owner," Mrs. Frye informed him.

"Fine," said Minikus. "We'll release the car to you."

Minikus walked to Gabel, then patiently awaiting instructions. The officer told Gabel not to attach the tow to the Buick, but, instead, to release the car to Mrs. Frye and enter on his storage papers the disposition "no hold."

"Fine," said Gabel.

Seconds later Ronald Frye said to Gabel: "The police officer says it's all right if you unhook the car so I can take it home."

"All right," Gabel replied.

Then as the tow-truck driver remembers it: "I throwed the hooks back in the truck, started going into the cab, when I looked—I looked back and seen this whole thing going on."

What was "going on" was this:

Mrs. Frye and Marquette gravitated toward one another. To Walter Crawford it appeared "the mother was trying to get the boy to go along with the police." To others closer by, it was obvious that the mother had spoken sharply to her son. As nearly as is possible to reconstruct it, this was the mother-son dialogue:

Mrs. Frye: "Something's wrong with you. Are you drunk?"

Marquette, putting his arm around her shoulder: "Mama, I'm not drunk."

Mrs. Frye: "You've been drinking—I can smell it on your breath. You know you shouldn't drive when you've been drinking. You better go with the officers."

"But, Mama, I'm not drunk."

Mrs. Frye, shrugging Marquette's arm from her shoulder:

"You're not acting normal. You're not acting right. Get away from me."

Marquette reacted savagely. "To all appearances," said Minikus later, "this appeared to incite Marquette to refuse to submit to physical arrest." And, according to Transportation Officer Bennett: "This seemed to upset Marquette and he ran—or walked away fast—back to the sidewalk from the street."

Later a probation officer drew this conclusion regarding Marquette's sudden switch in mood after the brief conversation with his mother: a lingering "low feeling of self-worth in the racial area" suddenly "combined with apparent rejection by his mother no doubt caused him to act in irrational fashion."

"Irrational" probably is as apt a description as any of the way

Marquette began behaving. He whirled from his mother, screaming: "Those mother-fucking cops ain't going to take me to jail." He flattened his back against the building and, as Minikus advanced on him, yelled: "Don't touch me, you white mother-fucker. I'll kill you."

Recalls Officer Lewis: "He was about half crying, and screaming and jumping around like he had gone out of his mind."

Recalls Officer Minikus: "I attempted to take hold of the defendant's—I believe it was his left wrist. He yanked his arm away, pulling back, screaming obscenities, saying that he wasn't going to be taken to jail. At this time, he took a swing at me with his right hand and I blocked that blow with my arm and stepped back two or three paces. I told him that he was under arrest and why didn't he come peaceably."

But Marquette was unmoved by the entreaty. Minikus, joined by Bennett, renewed attempts to persuade the fuming youth to surrender.

Marquette snarled: "You're going to have to kill me to take me to jail."

Ronald, who had been preparing to drive the Buick away, suddenly reversed himself. Mrs. Frye, too, moved closer to the officers and her son. By now, spectators who had been laughing with and at Marquette seconds ago fell sullen.

A steady procession of arrivals continued to flock to the scene, but Richard Brice had seen enough. With the exception of an elderly acquaintance, he probably was the only person in the crowd who made the choice. The elderly man said forlornly as he and Brice departed: "I better get back to my house because I have a bad heart."

His decision was a wise one. For in the next few minutes, the boiling scene would be unsafe even for persons with reliable constitutions.

In an effort to quiet the ranting Marquette, Bennett turned to his stepbrother and urged: "You better talk to him. You better try to cool him down and get him to come with us."

Bennett recalls that Ronald "did say something, to the effect —to his brother—to cool it, or start behaving himself."

But by then it had become apparent to Minikus and Bennet that further conversation with Marquette was useless. Bennett said: "We're going to have to get him now because he's probably going to fight or struggle."

The transportation officer, whose job it is to drive prisoners to jail, took out his handcuffs and handed them to Minikus, and both officers converged on Marquette.

"We got within arm's distance of him," said Bennett. "We reached out to grab him and place the handcuffs on him. He eluded this and ran off—made a half-circle around and came back—well, firmly back on the sidewalk again . . . still we didn't have control of him."

By now the growing crowd was openly hostile. Officer Lewis sensed it, thinking "we were in a hazardous condition." He yelled at Minikus and Bennett "to back off and get out of there." Then he "grabbed my transmitter on the motorcyle and put out a call for '1199,' which means officer needs help."

The time was 7:19. Minikus and Lewis removed their riot batons from their cycles. Bennett got his shotgun from his car. Help gathered swiftly. When it arrived, about two minutes later, it arrived in considerable force. "Man, at one time I counted twenty-seven squad cars alone down there," said Walter Crawford.

But until reinforcements appeared, the three Highway Patrolmen experienced tense moments. Returning from his car with his shotgun at "port arms" and with no shell in the chamber, Bennett noticed children—"some as young as seven, eight, nine years"—run at the sight of the weapon. From the crowd, he heard a shout: "Get back—shotgun."

The sight of Bennett's weapon appeared to have a momentary sobering effect on Marquette Frye. But several adult onlookers, mainly young men, bristled. "They just stood their ground—just stood looking at you," noted Bennett.

Then Marquette erupted again. He screamed profanities and leaped toward Bennett who, at that moment, saw Ronald moving toward him. "Stay out of it now," Bennett warned Ronald. "You don't want to get into trouble too," added Officer Lewis.

"Go ahead and kill me," Marquette shouted as he lunged at Bennett. The officer chopped at Marquette with the butt of his gun, but no contact was made because Marquette backed off.

At that moment, the first of the reinforcements, two other Highway Patrolmen, arrived. First came Wayne N. Wilson. Sergeant Veale J. Fonville was seconds behind him.

Wilson rushed to assist his fellow patrolmen with Marquette. By the time Sergeant Fonville dismounted, the first physical contact had been made and Wilson had already joined the face-off with Marquette, as the latter moved once more toward his initial adversary, Officer Minikus.

A flurry followed. As is invariable in such frenzied circumstances, exactly what transpired it hazy. Each participant remembers such a sequence of events only as it applies to him—and those not too well.

But it appears that in going to Minikus' aid, Wilson jabbed the inflamed young man in the stomach with his riot baton, and Marquette flailed out at both Highway Patrolmen. Minikus remembers that Marquette "struck out at myself and also at Officer Wilson. As he tried to hit Officer Wilson, he also tried to grab Officer Wilson's baton and it appeared that Officer Wilson struck Marquette on the forehead."

Wilson did indeed strike Marquette. He moved toward Marquette, who again had retreated to the side of the apartment building and flattened his back against it. "I attempted to jab him in the stomach, and when I did this, he grabbed hold of the baton I had," Wilson said. But Wilson hung on, regained control of the baton—and swung. A lump appeared over Marquette's eye. Blood trickled from it. The wound was not serious, doctors concluded later, but rather a stunning injury which left Marquette, according to Minikus, in a sufficiently "weakened condition" to be overpowered.

Said Wilson: "As near as I can recall, he just stopped all the fighting, and by this time Officer Lewis [along with Minikus] had taken hold of him physically."

The blow fell with a crack that did not escape the crowd. From it rose shouts of protest. But the embattled officers had little time to consider them.

With Lewis helping him, Minikus wrestled Marquette to Bennett's transportation car. "I took him around the neck and brought him toward the patrol car and threw him across the front seat, face down and handcuffed him," he said.

As this was happening, Rena and Ronald Frye joined the struggle. Officer Lewis recalls that as he was helping Minikus tug Marquette toward the patrol car, "Ronald took a swing at me and I just shoved him aside. Then as we were putting Marquette in the vehicle, I noticed Ronald had hold of one of Minikus' arms and the mother jumped on his back. I went over there, and pulled Ronald aside, and, then, as I grabbed the mother by the arm, I noticed Minikus' shirt was torn and she went on the back of Officer Wilson." Minikus' blouse was ripped almost the length of the back to the belt line.

Officer Fonville saw the mother jump Wilson. "I grabbed her. I grabbed her by the arms from behind. Both arms . . . in the area of the elbow." Mrs. Frye fought back, he added, until he bent her over the fender of a patrol car. "She kept saying 'help me,' and a few of them [spectators] started up, started toward me. I ordered them—turned around and looked over my shoulder—and told them to get back on the sidewalk. They stopped and by this time a number of units were rolling in with red lights and sirens."

Together, Lewis and Fonville handcuffed Mrs. Frye and placed her in the back seat of the transportation car. Marquette already was in the front. Ronald soon joined them.

The swiftly growing band of officers subdued him, handcuffed him and placed him in the rear seat beside his stepmother. What apparently had spurred his outburst was the sight of Mrs. Frye's struggles. Ronald said in a statement later: "The police officers were pushing my mother against the car and I went over to one of the police officers that had hold of her and I touched his arm and said: 'Why don't you leave her alone? She isn't doing anything.' And the officer yelled: 'Get him.'

"By then, I don't know how many police cars had come up and two police officers grabbed me. One of them put my hands behind my back and another one started hitting me with a stick in the stomach and then they handcuffed me and they had handcuffed Mother.

"Marquette had come up off—off the car. He was sitting in the front seat of the police car and he had come up off the car when he saw the policeman beating me with the stick and one of the policemen hit him across the face with a nightstick and they started—just a whole lot confusing . . . Everybody was fighting. They was just fighting us. And they threw us in the car and we left."

Ronald's version jibes closely, but not entirely, with that of the officers, though they concede a few pokes into the stomach with a riot baton were required to subdue him. Those officers present, including members of the Los Angeles Police Department, insist, however, that the only force expended was that necessary to take custody of the three Fryes.*

When Ronald spoke of Marquette's "coming off the car," he referred to another development which sent new ripples of anger through the crowd and raised, for the first time that evening, the cry of "police brutality."

Many different versions of what happened exist. Apparently, again, the officer involved was innocent of using anything more than a restraining force. Nevertheless, the angle from which many persons saw the action—or thought they saw it—and their subsequent elaboration on it had ugly repercussions.

* After an exhaustive investigation, during which more than seventy officers and witnesses were interviewed, the district attorney's office reported in a 1,300-page file of testimony, facts and findings that it could find no evidence that excessive force was used on either the mother or the stepbrothers.

Marquette Frye tried to get out of the patrol car. California Highway Patrolman Harry Taylor, who had arrived just in time to see the Fryes subdued and placed in the car, was standing at the right rear of the vehicle when: "I saw the right front door opening and there were no officers on that side of the vehicle. Everybody that was involved was on the left side of the vehicle at this time, and, ah, the man in the front seat appeared to be trying to leave the vehicle."

When Taylor reached the open door, Marquette was partially out of the car. The officer shoved Marquette back onto the front seat by pushing against his shoulders with his hands. Then, Taylor said: "I used my knee to shove his legs back into the vehicle because I had my back to the people on the curb, approximately three feet behind me, and I wanted to get the door shut so I could turn around and not have my back to them."

Taylor and other officers who saw him place his leg against Marquette's described it as a pushing action. Taylor then slammed the car door.

To many in the crowd, it appeared—or they preferred to believe—that Taylor not only had kicked Marquette, but slammed the door on his feet.

One spectator who was certain that Marquette had been kicked was Mrs. Vergie Nash, who had driven the four blocks from where she had been talking to Joyce Gaines minutes earlier. "Why did you have to do that?" she called out. "That boy's already handcuffed and bleeding. You didn't have to do that."

Mrs. Nash, who had arrived with daughters Janet, twenty-four, and Justine, eleven, and grandson Lance, three, had remarked seconds before to a woman standing alongside her that she thought it "a shame" Americans were fighting in Vietnam "if this is the way they're going to treat people." Then she shouted: "Does it take all these people to arrest three people?"

Hers was an attitude that, by now, had become prevalent among large sectors of the crowd. The arrival of each new police unit brought a fresh outburst. What had been merely grumbling gave way to taunting. "White trash," came a cry from a clump of women.

"Where are the colored policemen?" a man jeered.*

Apparently encouraged by some of the more brazen spectators, Marquette Frye tried for a second time to emerge from the police car. Officer Wilson intercepted him, and to prevent a third attempt, the Highway Patrolman shackled Marquette's feet. Just after that, the transportation car, with Officer Bennett behind the wheel and Highway Patrolman Joseph Thompson in the rear with Ronald and his stepmother, bore the Fryes away.

But by then the mob was a roiling, wounded animal, spoiling for one more aggravation that would provide it with an excuse to unloose its pent-up rage. The Fryes, merely the instrument through which its distemper had been aroused, were gone from sight.

But there remained the old enemy, the old object of the bitterness which had festered so long beneath so many black and bronze skins in South Los Angeles: the white policeman, who represented, in most of the eyes there, the white establishment. And the white establishment represented repression.

Both the Highway Patrolmen and the Los Angeles city policemen at 116th and Avalon recognized that their continued presence was an open invitation to violence. Ranking officers, sergeants, of both the CHP and the LAPD knew a swift departure was the only answer. Yet a swift departure through the swollen mob was almost impossible. Still, the attempt was made and might have succeeded.

* At least one Negro officer was present. Ronald G. Farwell of the Los Angeles Police Department's 77th Street Division, like his fellow white officers, was having his trouble with the crowd. "You're a 'brother'—you know how they treat us," he heard one spectator yell.

"I got everybody out in the middle of the street," recalls Highway Patrol Sergeant Leonard F. DeGroff, Jr. "We were ready to go. I got on my motor, started up, looked back and everybody appeared to be moving."

But moving slowly, because, as Highway Patrolman Donald McGravie thought at the time: "I didn't know where the people were coming from—but they just kept coming. It seemed like they had a telegraph set or telephone party line in every house up and down the street. And these people just kept coming and coming. . . . I couldn't estimate the amount of people that was there because it just—just volumed up in such proportions so fast."

Somewhere in that crush of humanity was the young woman barber, Joyce Ann Gaines. The spark was about to be ignited.

3

IT SEEMS APPROPRIATE at this point to inquire more closely into the backgrounds of Mrs. Rena Frye and the stepbrothers, Ronald and Marquette. Particularly worth examining is Marquette Frye, born Marquette Price twenty-one years earlier in the tiny Oklahoma farm town of Lima (population 90) in Seminole County, southeast of Oklahoma City.

Marquette became a symbol of the 1965 riot in Los Angeles. But only those totally insensitive to the broad socio-economic influences which underlay the August violence would mistake Marquette as a cause, much less *the* cause, of the uprising.

However, because he happened to conduct himself in a certain manner in a certain place at a certain time, Marquette, in the terminology of the FBI, supplied a "kind of provocation" when "conditions were ripe" and "ingredients available." And while he was not the cause of the riot, and probably a weak symbol at best, he certainly was a symptom of the many causes behind it—long before August 11, 1965.

Ronald Frye—no. Rena Frye—no. Marquette Frye—yes.

Ronald's involvement in such a situation, at another time or another place, would have made little sense. He was a quiet, almost shy young man, gifted with at least average intelligence, perhaps above average.

A probation officer made this evaluation of Ronald shortly after the arrests: "It would seem that the behavior which caused his arrest could be considered out-of-character for him. He is a recent arrival in this city who appears to have been caught up in a situation which he knew little about and acted impulsively."

Rena Frye, of course, reacted like a mother—first angry over what she considered her son's misconduct; then, as almost any mother would be, furious at what, in her eyes, constituted physical abuse of her son.

Marquette was something else again. In him festered the frustrations, the resentments, the embitterment that fueled the midsummer insurrection. Marquette, with minor exceptions, closely followed the classic pattern of the angry young Negro male who that mid-August torched and looted and stoned in the streets of Los Angeles—though Marquette himself did none of these.

Marquette was a high school dropout, with a juvenile police record. His brushes with the law clearly left him rebellious, distrustful of authority and believing he was persecuted. It is impossible to say how justified he was for feeling as he did.

Marquette was the third of four children born to a man named C. L. Price and the former Rena Davis, daughter of an Oklahoma farmer. Six months after Marquette's birth, the Prices moved to Wyoming, to a hamlet called Hannah, then experiencing a postwar mining boom. Not long after, the Prices were divorced and Rena married easygoing Wallace Frye, who, like Rena, had four children by a previous marriage, one of them Ronald. Ronald's mother also remarried and lived with her new husband in Superior, Wyoming.

Wallace and Rena Frye remained in Wyoming until 1957—until the Hannah mining boomlet flattened out. Then they moved to California, taking with them Rena's four children.

On a coolish but sunny afternoon two and one half months after their arrests, Mrs. Frye and the stepbrothers talked to the authors about their remembrances of life in Wyoming. Wallace Frye joined in the reminiscences and so did Marquette's older natural brother, Charles, twenty-three, an Air Force jet plane mechanic, visibly unhappy because events in Vietnam had caused the military to extend his tour of duty just as he was about to be discharged.

Marquette and Charles contrasted their Wyoming days with the life they had come to know in California. In comparing their Wyoming education with what they received in California, both were emphatic in insisting that the schooling they received in Los Angeles was poorer and that community and school attitudes in the Southern California city were at the root of Marquette's educational and employment difficulties.

"People there [in Wyoming] were much better. The school curriculum was better. The kids' vocabularies were better. When I came to California, the kids here resented my speech, they resented my intelligence," Marquette said. "In Wyoming, a human being is a human being. There were only about eight Negroes in the school where we went and we were accepted by the whites. When we came to California, we got into an all-Negro school. It was all new to us. I'd never been to an all-Negro school before."

In 1961, said Marquette, a vice principal at Los Angeles' Fremont High School "gave me the choice of quitting or being expelled. I knew I could do the schoolwork if I'd had the chance; I made 'A's' and 'B's' back in Wyoming. But I kept getting suspended for fighting. It wasn't a racial thing—the whole school was Negro. It was a neighborhood thing. At school, if you lived where we did, you were considered 'Watts.' The other side was 'Slauson.' If you're Watts [actually Marquette did not live within what are considered the community boundaries of the Watts area of Los Angeles], then you run into trouble with the Slauson kids."

Mrs. Frye said: "The first day he got here, when he was thirteen, the kids at school began picking on him because he was new. His temper is short—like mine—so he don't take no pushing around."

Said Marquette: "You really don't go to Fremont to get knowledge—you go there to meet people who might be violent to you." While Marquette insisted that he left Fremont only because of the vice principal's ultimatum, his probation officer reported that Marquette had told him: "I got tired of school."

After leaving Fremont, Marquette found steady employment difficult to find. "I would answer an ad," he said, "fill out an application, then never hear from the people when they saw I was colored. I looked for work, but I just didn't get the jobs."

What work he did find, when he did find it, did little for his ego. He worked part-time as a service station attendant and full-time, for short periods, as an automobile pickup and delivery man. The longest job, in 1963, lasted five months. "His working experience," reported his probation officer, "consisted primarily of unskilled odd jobs. . . . The area of employment is one he did not make a good adjustment to."

Marquette's August 11, 1965, arrest was not his first, but it was his first arrest as an adult. On June 9, 1960, he was arrested for petty theft, counseled by juvenile officers and released. On May 18, 1961, he appeared in Juvenile Court on a charge that, on the previous March 26, he had entered a grocery and helped himself to an odd mix: wine, cigars and gum. While awaiting a final hearing on that, he was seized for an $18 November 23 robbery and wound up, for a time, in a juvenile forest camp.

When Marquette was asked by the authors about his juvenile record, he mentioned only one incident and that, he insisted, was a bum rap. "They accused me of taking some money from a person when I was sixteen," he said, glowering. "When they picked me up I was broke." Looking at the floor, he added: "If they would leave me alone [meaning policemen] . . . when you're pushed, for no reason, you're going to push back."

Marquette said that he had been "engaged for four years"—not to one of the girls whom he and Ronald had visited the afternoon before their arrests. "We haven't gotten married," said Marquette, "because I never felt I had security; I didn't feel I should get married until I got a better job."

According to the probation officer who interviewed him in

August: "He admits that he now has the girl friend pregnant and that he plans to marry her as soon as his court matters have been taken care of."*

The day the authors talked with the Frye family, they were not hostile, but they were suspicious. The Fryes' ground-floor apartment is in one of the many two-story apartment complexes abounding in the neighborhood. It was spotless but cluttered with knickknacks and old-fashioned overstuffed furniture which made the living room seem cramped. A gold-colored bust of the late President John F. Kennedy overlooked the room from atop a chest.

Wallace Frye appeared frankly puzzled over the issues raised during the conversation; he took little part in it. Marquette's older brother, Charles Price, appeared to take a great deal of pride in his handling of the language; he was articulate for a young man of twenty-three. Unlike Marquette, he had finished high school and appeared knowledgeable about what went on in the world. Both young men exuded a similar arrogant bitterness and an undisguised suspicion of the white man.

Charles, married and father of an infant daughter, said when he finally obtained his release from the military he hoped to continue his career as a jet airplane mechanic. "I'd like to work in one of the big aircraft plants down here—if they don't base employment on whether you're black or you're white."

* After their arrests, both Ronald and Marquette entered guilty pleas; Mrs. Frye pleaded innocent. Marquette pleaded guilty to misdemeanor drunk driving, malicious mischief and battery; his stepbrother to battery and interfering with officers. When they appeared for sentencing, they asked to be permitted to change their pleas to innocent. Ronald claimed he had pleaded guilty so Marquette could get immediate medical attention for the knot on his forehead; Marquette said he was groggy and uncertain of what he was doing. The judge denied their request, but the stepbrothers appealed. In March the appeal was denied. Mrs. Frye, meanwhile, received a jury trial, was found guilty of obstructing an officer and was fined $250, a sum she was to be permitted to pay at the rate of $10 a month by a judge who told her: "I have a reason for this. On the first of every month when you have to pay $10, you will be reminded of this case."

Marquette claimed that during the four years he had lived in the neighborhood, he had hardly seen a white face there. "The so-called Negro leaders don't know us either. If Caucasians would just come into this neighborhood and stand on the sidewalk and talk to us—if somehow they would just let us people here know they were interested in a better way of life for the colored people. In this neighborhood, there is nothing for a young man to do. So you just stand around. And when you stand around, the next thing you know there come the police to roust you."

After the Fryes were released on bail following their arrests, the family rarely ventured out of the house during the days and nights of rioting that followed. But they closely watched the fiery developments on television. Marquette recalls thinking: "They blamed that on us—but what happened was on the surface for a long time."

Mrs. Frye, Ronald, Marquette and Charles each believed the rioting would improve the lot of the Negro. They regretted the bloodshed, they said, but it was an eye-opener for the white community. This was a view echoed frequently throughout the torn neighborhood in the days that followed.

"Never again," said Marquette, "never again in this neighborhood will any young men, like my brother and me, stand by and take abuse from an officer."

Marquette, who had never joined the Congress of Racial Equality but had participated in demonstrations with friends who were members, embarked on a somewhat different enterprise the Sunday after his arrest and while rioters and police and Guardsmen still battled in the streets of Los Angeles. He spoke at a meeting of the Muslims, the black nationalist group. At the time, he denied affiliation with the Muslims, but he reportedly told the closed meeting in the Mosque on Los Angeles' South Side: "Your leader and teacher, Elijah Muhammad, has been teaching the doom of the white man for a long time and now we understand. . . . These troops don't understand. They haven't seen anything yet."

Marquette said two and a half months later in the family living room that he had gone to the Mosque to speak simply because he had been "invited." He had visited the Mosque once before, he said, because he was "curious." He said: "I had heard people talking about it and I went there just like you would go to any other church."

To the authors he gave a softer version of what he had said at the Mosque than reports had indicated. "I got up before them and told them I didn't know what to say. I said: 'Your leader and teacher, Elijah Muhammad, has been teaching you that the end is near not only for the white race but for all people if they don't learn to live together. He said while he considered the Muslims primarily a religious order, "In this day and age, as far as the Negro is concerned, a united stand is the only answer. The Muslims are the only ones doing that for the Negro. They're the one group looking for a better way of life for the Negro."

Marquette wore a spotless white shirt with a neat tab collar, a narrow black tie and tight black pants. He appeared the very image of young Muslims seen on streets of major American cities, selling the sect's newspaper, *Muhammad Speaks*. This moved an interviewer to ask: "Well, from what you say, would it be safe to say that if you aren't now a Muslim we can assume you will someday become one?"

"You can," Marquette replied solemnly.

Charles Price, who had been listening intently, then spoke of the course of future unrest in Negro neighborhoods, not just in Los Angeles but throughout the nation. He warned that a loosely knit but highly militant Negro organization capable of instant communication with its many parts had evolved in major American cities. Reprisal would be immediate and general throughout the nation if another flare-up such as the Los Angeles riot of 1965 were to develop. He likened the organization to the Ku Klux Klan, and said: "The next time the trouble won't be in the Negro neighborhoods, it'll be in the white man's neighborhoods. And the rich men and the politicians down at City Hall, they'll feel it. They'll even feel it in Washington. When it starts in one city, it will spread to all cities."

4

WHEN JOYCE ANN GAINES heard the motorcycle siren as Highway Patrolman Lee Minikus pursued the Frye Buick past her father's barber shop, she was preparing to cut a customer's hair.

Barbering males is an unusual profession for an attractive young woman of twenty. But, in Joyce's case, it ran in the family. Besides her father and Joyce, two older sisters and two of her brothers were barbers.

The father, graying and mild-mannered, probably could have trained his children himself, experienced as he was in the business. Instead, he sent each of the five to barber college, as required by state law. Eventually, the two brothers set up shops of their own; the three sisters worked for their father.

But on August 11, 1965, even though she had a customer waiting and even though she normally was not off until 8 P.M., Joyce's work for the evening was cut short soon after 7 P.M. The sound of other sirens drew her out of the shop. When she stepped onto the sidewalk, the entire neighborhood seemed to be flowing northward, toward 116th, four blocks from the Gaines Barber Shop at 11905 South Avalon Boulevard.

After her brief conversation with Mrs. Vergie Nash about the excitement, Joyce joined the flow. "I have a number of friends who live down that way," she explained later. "I heard the sirens and things, so I was walking down to see what had happened. I thought it was an accident or something." At the time, Joyce wore white capris, largely covered by a blue barber's smock. Her reddish hair was rolled in pink curlers.

It took Joyce and Joan Nash, Vergie Nash's twenty-two-year-old daughter, about five minutes to reach the point where the officers were occupied with the Fryes. Joyce knew none of them, although her father's barber shop stood less than a half mile from the Frye residence and in a busy commercial neighborhood where Marquette Frye was known to other store owners.

Joyce and Joan were joined by the latter's mother who with two other daughters and a grandson had driven from 119th Street in her car. Mrs. Vergie Nash was among those in the multiplying assemblage who was outraged by what she deemed mistreatment of the Fryes by police officers, an allegation not later borne out by an exhaustive investigation.

Nearby stood Mrs. Lacine Holland, who lived several miles north on 136th Street, but who had seen the human multitude around the officers and the Fryes while driving away from a visit to her mother's home at 116th Place and Stanford Avenue, a block east of Avalon. Mrs. Holland returned home and found her mother, Mrs. Bernice Hogan, and a neighbor woman in the yard. The older woman asked her daughter to drive her and the neighbor to the scene of the excitement. Mrs. Holland complied and soon found herself near Joyce and Mrs. Nash.

Mrs. Holland was the woman to whom Mrs. Nash complained when she thought she saw Officer Harry Taylor kick Marquette Frye and slam the door of the transportation car on his feet. Mrs. Holland overhead other spectators "talking about the way the man was kicked after he was handcuffed and pushed into the car."

Mrs. Holland, an employee of the Los Angeles County Health Department for seventeen years, thought she, too, observed a "kicking motion," like "someone shutting the door of a closet that's too full."

By the time Joyce Ann Gaines had positioned herself in the crowd, the Fryes not only were in custody but were being whisked to jail. Above strident roars of arriving motorcycles, she heard the angry babble of the crowd and she thought specific phrases that filtered through to her ears were harsh, the crowd "unhappy."

Joyce's description of the mob, in the opinion of policemen there, was far too mild. "I saw people with rocks, full bottles of pop and just empty bottles in their hands, all capable of being used as a weapon," recalls J. J. Fedrizzi, a Los Angeles policeman.

By the time Joyce had arrived, supervising officers of both the Highway Patrol and city police present—in this case sergeants—considered themselves and their subordinates endangered by the mob's hostility. Such was the assessment of Highway Patrol Sergeants Leonard DeGroff, Jr., and V. G. Nicholson and Los Angeles Police Sergeant Richard Rankin. Sergeants DeGroff and Nicholson agreed among themselves that violence best could be averted at this point by getting the policemen, most of them white, away from the neighborhood as quickly as possible. This was precisely what Sergeant Rankin of the city police was thinking, even though he had just arrived. Rankin conferred with one of the CHP sergeants and told him: "I think our problem here will end as soon as we get our units out of here."

The Highway Patrolman replied: "I will work with you anywhere you want, seeing it is in your city."

"Okay, fine," said Rankin. "I will try to get our units out of here."

"Swell," said the Highway Patrol sergeant. "I'll stand by until your units have left."

But it was not that simple. Pulling together the widely dispersed officers attempting to maintain a semblance of crowd control required time. It had been no easy job, as a matter of fact, for late-arriving police to thread through the crowd of onlookers and the parked law enforcement vehicles, even though normal traffic through the neighborhood had been sealed off at key intersections. Sergeant Rankin, traveling with

Officer Gary Bebee in a "mobile command post," a police station wagon, estimated it took "from five to ten minutes to track down" all the officers along the street and get them moving.

Police units streaming out of the neighborhood then told drivers of other emergency vehicles headed toward it to turn around: "Go back. Stay out of the area." As officers inched their way northward, they were followed by taunts: "Police brutality." . . . "This is just like Selma." . . . "We got no rights at all."

Among the last to join the sluggish northward movement were Officer Taylor, who had shoved Marquette Frye back into the transportation car, and Highway Patrolman James Vaughn, who gunned his vehicle upon hearing a voice he believed to be that of Sergeant DeGroff bark over the radio: "Let's go, CHP."

Both Vaughn and Taylor, who was slightly ahead of him, started their machines at the same time. Nearby, Highway Patrolman Gale Reed Gilbert also was heading into the procession of departing motorcycles, then traveling "more or less in a column of two's." He and Sergeant Nicholson were the last pair in the column, and according to Gilbert: "Just as we started leaving, there was a girl who hadn't said anything standing between these two large, foul-mouthed colored women, the most foul-mouthed that I noticed. The girl stepped forward and spat at the officers ahead of me."

The officers ahead of him were Taylor and Vaughn, who said: "I noticed this colored lady lean and spit in my direction. I thought I felt it strike my shirt. But I continued on."

Gilbert, who earlier had helped Officer Wilson cuff Marquette Frye's legs, jumped from his mount. "I got off my motor and ran over and grabbed ahold of her by the arm."

Almost simultaneously, Sergeant Nicholson, upon seeing spittle fleck the back of Vaughn's shirt, stopped his motorcycle and dismounted. He and Gilbert were alone in the crowd, as Taylor and Vaughn had traveled some distance up the street before swinging about and returning.

When Nicholson saw Gilbert disappear into the swarm of people, he snatched up his radio transmitter "to get the other fellows back before I actually even got into the crowd."

Up the street, Sergeant DeGroff heard: "DeGroff. DeGroff. Come back."

Sergeant Nicholson elbowed his way toward Gilbert and Joyce Gaines. "The people just jostled. They wouldn't move," he said.

When Nicholson reached his fellow motorcycle officer and the young woman, some in the crowd had taken hold of her. Joyce remembers what followed as a "tug of war."

Nicholson saw a "large male Negro" clinging to Joyce with his right hand. "With his left arm, he was waving in the direction of the crowd and saying: 'Come on, let's get them.' " Nicholson pulled the man away from the young woman barber. "I kept pushing him and talking to him and pushing him and managed to get him out into the street, almost out of the center of the crowd. Then the crowd came back around us again, out in the center of the street, but I managed to keep him occupied until the other units got back."

Again, as was the case with preceding events, no one version of this occurrence jibes precisely with another; some are at great variance.

Officer Gilbert, for instance, remembers that after leaping from his motorcycle and reaching Joyce: "She got back into the crowd and there were three or four people standing beside her. I grabbed ahold of her arm and just held on because there were several hundred coloreds trying to pull her away.* I just held on until several other CHP and LAPD came over and broke

* Gilbert denies using provocative force in the engagement, a contention supported by fellow officers. But large segments of the mob thought otherwise. Those close by the action, who thought Gilbert's treatment of Miss Gaines abusive, were quick to broadcast their view of the encounter to those in less advantageous positions. Many of these persons relayed more fanciful versions to neighbors still farther removed. Thus, rumor began working overtime.

the crowd away from her and I took her out in the street and someone assisted me—I don't know who."

The "someone" was Negro policeman Farwell's partner, Lee Castruita of the city's 77th Police Division. Castruita, who led a police lunge through the crowd toward Gilbert, Nicholson and Joyce Ann Gaines, recalls: "She was flinging her arms back and forth, trying to break away from them [Gilbert and Sergeant Nicholson]. I ran immediately to their assistance."

Nearby, Los Angeles Policeman Harvey L. Eubank stepped from his patrol car and saw the two Highway Patrolmen struggling with the young woman and Castruita pressing toward them. "I observed her break away from the two CHP officers and try to get back into the crowd which was on the east side of the street," said Eubank. "One of the CHP officers grabbed the lady around the neck to restrain her and pull her off balance and away from the crowd."

A few feet away, Farwell, the Negro officer, was busy trying to press the crowd back from the principals. It appeared to him, from that vantage point, that Gilbert had a "bar-strangle type hold on her but did not appear to be choking her, more or less restraining her movements."

Eubank, who, like Farwell, considered Gilbert's response reasonable, made the observation at that point that Joyce was "cursing and trying to break away." He claims to have heard her snarl: "Take your hands off me, you white mother-fucker. You no-good son-of-a-bitch white cop—turn me loose. I haven't done anything. Take your hands off me." Instead of relaxing his hold, Eubank said, Gilbert continued "gently walking her backwards. She was walking. He was not dragging her. He merely had her unbalanced."

At this point, Castruita shouted to Gilbert: "Let's get her handcuffed and out of here." Castruita recalls: "I removed my cuffs. I handcuffed her and started walking toward my vehicle. But by this time, I was unable to get through—as other police units had completely blocked my vehicle in. So I continued walking with Gaines in a northbound direction. I yelled for someone to give me a hand."

Eubank heard Castruita's call. "So I immediately went and helped Castruita walk the young lady to the police cars," Eubank said.

It was not a pleasure hike; Joyce protested vigorously each step that her arrest was unjustified.

Such, basically, is the police version of Joyce Ann Gaines' seizure.

Joyce herself, Mrs. Nash and Mrs. Holland saw it in a totally different light. So did large numbers of the inflamed mob; they looked on Joyce's being led away as one more humiliation of the Negro by the white policeman and, as it turned out, a final insult they were not prepared to accept without retaliating.

Many of those on the sidelines embroidered on what they had seen—or thought they had seen. Distorted versions of the Gaines arrest spread through the neighborhood—and rapidly leapfrogged far beyond it. The particular nature of the Frye and Gaines encounters with white policemen was an open invitation to the circulation of near-truth, half-truth, partial-truth and, finally, uncontrolled rumor that provoked the outrage soon to follow.

5

THE RECOLLECTIONS of Joyce Ann Gaines, Mrs. Vergie Nash and Mrs. Lacine Holland contrast sharply with those of police, regarding the seizure of the young woman barber.

Joyce's own remembrance is of listening to persons around her expressing their bitterness over the arrest of the Fryes. As the police prepared to move in their two-by-two motorcycle column north on Avalon, she may have heard an officer say, as some in the crowd claim to have: "Let's get the hell out of here."

Mrs. Nash insists she overheard such a remark and responded: "That's what you should do. What you should have done in the beginning. You're causing too much disturbing." But Joyce recalls being in a different frame of mind from Mrs. Nash, a completely unembittered one. She remembers "talking a lot" and "giggling," then deciding she had better return at once because "I had a customer waiting."

"So," she said, "when I turned to walk away—we were going to ride back with Janet, Mrs. Nash's other daughter—when I turned around, before I knew it, the police officer had grabbed me. And then there was two—first it was one Highway Patrolman, then there was another one, then there was a Los Angeles policeman grabbed me. I had got just a few steps, maybe, on the asphalt from the sidewalk. As a matter of fact, I was still smiling, until they all grabbed me and was pulling me out in the street, I mean, just dragging me. He never told me I was under arrest or anything. He was just manhandling me." Joyce insists she did not resist, but recalls her hair curlers shaking out of her hair and falling to the pavement, and then: "A number of people were pulling me and the officers were pulling me. So—they had a tug-of-war going with me. He [Gilbert] had me by the neck—he was practically choking me to death. And the other ones were grabbing at me too and they were grabbing me until I didn't know what was going on."

When Gilbert grabbed for Joyce, Mrs. Nash recalls she, too, was preparing to leave and had turned her back on the scene. But she spun about when she heard eleven-year-old Justine cry: "Mommy. They got Joyce. They got Joyce."

Mrs. Nash's three-year-old grandson Lance echoed Justine's cry and began to whimper. After attempting to calm him, Mrs. Nash, already resentful of what had gone on before and admittedly outspoken, charged to Joyce's aid, but her daughters restrained her. "In fact," she said during an interview later with investigators, "I have a scar where the kids tried to pull me back to keep me from getting out there." She bared her shoulder to show a mark on it to interviewers.

Mrs. Holland took only a slightly less passionate view of the occurrence. She shouted her disapproval so vigorously that her mother, Mrs. Hogan, felt constrained to reprove her and urge her to return home. "Lacine, you should go home," said Mrs. Hogan. "Don't get upset like this."

Mrs. Holland remembers the episode and her reaction to it this way: "All of a sudden I looked up and this Highway Patrolman was running toward the girl and he was trying to grab her, and she was backing off and off, and, I guess—I don't know why—maybe she didn't know what he was after. The girl was laughing at first. She was trying to get away. But all of a sudden he got her around the neck. And then this look of fear came over her face—after he had grabbed her, you know, and shook her, and her curlers fell out of her hair. And he drug her into the street. I became frightened, because—gee—all the people started crowding around, you know, and I said—well, gee—maybe I'd better get out of here. I could see the look on—especially the men's faces—when they saw the Highway Patrolman grab the girl around the neck. This is when the crowd became angry. They resented this; they resented the kicking. But they went along with the arrest of the prisoner [Marquette Frye], which, as I say, I didn't see from the beginning. It seemed the crowd accepted the man being arrested. But what really started it was, as I say, when the Highway Patrolman grabbed the girl."

Because many in the crowd did not know Joyce Ann Gaines, the billowing appearance of her blue barber smock led to a general belief that she wore a maternity dress. Mrs. Frye's flowing shift earlier had created a similar impression.

As Joyce Ann Gaines was subdued and led off,* Officer Farwell heard harsh protests, all in the same vein: "Look how they're treating a pregnant woman." . . . "They're misusing a pregnant woman." . . . "They don't have to be rough with a pregnant woman."

While he himself thought his fellow officers could have handled Joyce in "just no other way," he understood the crowd reaction. "She was wearing a barber smock and many people thought she was pregnant."

There was no opportunity to correct the spreading misapprehension. By now, the throng was past the point of reason.

"I repeatedly gave orders to the crowd to disperse, but they paid no heed," said Highway Patrolman Leonard W. Moore. To his dispersal order, the mob replied with profanity and shouts of: "Let's get them cops." . . . "Bogulusa—this is the end for you, white man."

The surging horde took up the chant of defiance and pressed in upon officers attempting to push it back onto the sidewalk with their plastic batons and nightsticks held level with both hands. "It took a considerable amount of force to hold them

* Three days before Miss Gaines was to appear for trial on battery charges in November, her case was dismissed.

back with nightsticks held at horizontal position," said Los Angeles Policeman Joseph P. Scanlon, one of the beleaguered officers. "It was necessary to physically shove some back. When we did have them contained in a group—myself, I had my nightstick squarely against one male's chest, and, to show the temper of the crowd at this time, although my face and his were only about eight inches away, he said: 'You white motherfucker, you won this one. But the next time, it won't go your way.'

"You can talk all you want," snapped Scanlon, "but the next time you use those words, you're all going to jail, because there's women and children around here." Scanlon turned to an officer beside him in exasperation and said: "If he uses that language again, I'm going into the crowd after him."

Officer Farwell walked into the crowd, faced Scanlon's antagonist, talked to him and, as Scanlon recalls: "This male returned to his original position, but he never swore or said another word." Beyond the man's shoulders, however, Scanlon could see that, by now, many in the throng had picked up "rocks and bottles—full bottles and empty bottles."

Los Angeles Policeman J. J. Fedrizzi, facing down another belligerent man, shrugged off his curses and threats, thinking: "You just hear them all the time down here. Hear them and forget them." But Fedrizzi sensed that the present was quite unlike past clashes between police officers and aggrieved Negro groups. He recalls: "They wanted—they wanted to hang some policemen real quicklike, if they had a chance—right there. But there were too many of them [officers] to do anything. If there were only, say, one or two policemen, they probably would have. We would have been one or two police short right now."

That reflects the appraisal of the moment of Fedrizzi's superior, Sergeant Rankin, and the two ranking Highway Patrol officers, Sergeants Nicholson and DeGroff. But the three sergeants were less certain than Fedrizzi appears to have been that their manpower was sufficient to contain the mob. Like Fedrizzi, they believed that if they were to move, they had to move out in strength, leaving no stragglers to face the rage of the wrathful assemblage.

Though not liking "the way they treated that girl," Walter Crawford, by this time, had become apprehensive over the growing menace. He headed back toward his apartment when he heard this exchange between two young men:

"Ain't no white man got any business down here."

"No nigger either—if he's too light."

Crawford said: "I couldn't cut along with that kind of stuff. Beside, I was getting scared myself."

Officer Gary C. Bebee watched Sergeant Rankin conferring with a Highway Patrolman, and remembers: "Sergeant Rankin and the CHP motor sergeant got together and agreed we would move out of the location, hoping the people would disperse and go back into their homes with our departure." Then Sergeant Rankin turned to Policeman Edward W. Ryan and said: "Let's get out of the area; see if they'll quiet down and go about their business."

Sergeant Nicholson remembers "giving the signal to leave" after he, DeGroff and city officers "concluded that the best thing we could do was get organized and leave the scene at the same time. I think it would have been too dangerous to have left two or three officers there. We got organized. We proceeded to leave the scene."

Sergeant DeGroff recalls the departure this way: "As soon as we could, we got all the units together . . . and everybody left in one group. This time we [the Highway Patrol contingent] went down to Imperial [Imperial Highway, two blocks north of 116th Street] and Central Avenue [five blocks east of Avalon]."

And Sergeant Rankin: "We again had the same problem [moving out] the second time we had the first time, with units having poured into the area and officers having gotten out of their cars, leaving them parked helter-skelter because of the emergency of the situation . . . so that when we got ready to leave the scene the second time, it took a long time. Or it seemed like a long time to me."

The police station wagon occupied by Rankin and Officer Bebee was the last unit to leave the scene and it could not penetrate the thick, howling mass of humanity. Ryan, whose car was the next-to-the-last police unit to depart, pulled to a stop at 115th to wait for Rankin's "mobile command post." This is what he saw behind him: "The crowd was complete across Avalon and as he [Rankin] couldn't go forward—or he would drive right through them—he backed up."

Ryan watched helplessly as portions of the mob broke off from the main body and pursued the station wagon in its backward flight. Many, who at the outset of the incident had been swigging casually at beer cans and beer bottles and soda pop bottles, now gestured menacingly with the containers.

Ryan may have experienced a sense of relief when he saw Rankin wheel the station wagon through a quick backward U-turn, point the vehicle's nose northward and pick up forward momentum. If he did, he was premature. For Officer Ryan had not heard what Walter Crawford had as he stole away from the angry horde: "A sound like something heavy hitting tin." Nor had Ryan heard Lacine Holland call fearfully to Mrs. Hogan: "Mother, it looks like there is going to be a riot." Nor had Ryan seen, as had Sergeant Rankin and Officer Bebee, the first projectiles hurtling toward the station wagon in which they were traveling, a dread-inspiring sight.

Said Rankin: "My car was stoned and bottles hurled at it. One or two of the stones struck the car, but the bottles fell short and shattered in the street around us."

Bebee, in those confused seconds, thought the aim more accurate than did Rankin. Said Bebee: "The people ran into the street, started running after us—yelling, screaming. They began throwing anything they could get their hands on. Bottles and rocks were bouncing off the back of the station wagon."

The hot, humid evening exploded. Above the frenzied shouting rose the manic and defiant voice of a wide-eyed young man. The three staccato words he unloosed struck a responsive chord. Other young men and teenagers picked up the phrase, already familiar to them. Soon bitter, rebellious adults would adopt it.

The battle chant of the insurrection was born when the perspiring, goggle-eyed young male shrieked:

"Burn, baby, burn!"

The spark was ignited. The conflagration would rage for six days and Los Angeles never again would be the same.

6

FOR DAYS NOW, a relentless heat wave had staggered the city. Nowhere was the chafing heat felt more keenly than along the populous black corridor which cuts southward from the core of Los Angeles.

Wednesday, August 11, marked the third day of 90-plus weather following a series of warm, humid days and nights. On Monday, the 9th, when the temperature peaked at 98, the Los Angeles Water and Power Department reported a record power drain: 2,198,900 kilowatts at the time of high load. That same day newspapers told of Negro voter registration successes in Selma, Alabama, and in the Louisiana delta country's marshy segregationist strongholds.

Normally, no matter how hot the day, Southern California sundowns bring a cooling off, one of the natural blessings of the region. But such was not the case this mid-August. Nighttime readings remained in the 70s, and it was sticky as well as hot. Before temperatures and passions cooled, both would rise again. On Thursday, the thermometer fell to 92 from Wednesday's high of 94. But on the infamous Friday that followed, it climbed once more to 94 and reached that figure again on Saturday. On Sunday, when the high was 89, a tapering off began. The normal high for that time of year was 84.

Following the mid-August strife there was speculation concerning the influence of the unusually hot weather on the emotions of a frustrated people. Two men qualified to speak on the subject, a professor of police administration and a university psychiatrist, agreed publicly that, while not a cause of lawlessness, hot weather is a contributing factor. The observation was rather elementary and certainly not new. Every rookie policeman quickly shares the antipathy of veteran officers toward sultry nights. This police sentiment has a genuine basis in fact. Even the most haphazard bookkeeping on crime shows that prolonged heat brings out the worst in men and women.

This, then, was the climate as the last of the Highway Patrol and Los Angeles police units streamed north from 116th and Avalon about 7:45 P.M., Wednesday, August 11, amid a shower of stone, glass, concrete and wood plank. Any object that could be lifted and thrown flew after them. But the officers resolutely continued northward. Their superiors believed, with considerable reason, that for police to remain at the scene of the Frye and Gaines arrests would only aggravate the friction. They felt the crowd would simmer down after their departure and that its members would return to their homes.

But this was not to be. The mob, by now estimated at one thousand, broke into angry clusters. Men, women and children surged along the street and over the sidewalks; they did not go home. They enlarged on the Frye and Gaines incidents, weaving a tapestry of rumor which spread past the immediate neighborhood, east across Central Avenue, chief artery of Los Angeles' black corridor, and into a part of the city called Watts.

From wherever the half-truths and the rumors were repeated, bands of Negroes advanced on Avalon Boulevard to join the surge of humanity already there. Or they congregated in and along the streets of their own neighborhood, trading ugly reports about police abuse of "pregnant women." Most groups were comprised chiefly of idle young men or aimless teenagers.

Sergeant Richard W. Rankin, who drove the last police unit north on Avalon under a barrage of stones and bottles, had requested that LAPD officers in the procession assemble at 108th Street and Clovis Avenue. This was about eight blocks north and five east of 116th and Avalon. Highway Patrolmen rendezvoused farther east to await a possible call for assistance from Los Angeles police, within whose jurisdiction the matter now fell. After about 45 minutes, according to Patrol Sergeant V. G. Nicholson's estimate, the state officers had received no request for assistance. So they returned to their normal duty.

The first reports of mob retaliation Wednesday night reached the Los Angeles police assembled at 108th and Clovis. Sergeant Rankin had just begun telephoning his watch commander at the 77th Street Police Station to report the stoning of his car and what had developed at 116th and Avalon.

"While he was making his phone call," recalls Gary C. Bebee, Rankin's partner, "there was a bus containing passengers stopped. They complained that they had been rocked when they drove through this area. There were big dents in the side of the bus and windows knocked out. Approximately, oh, five to ten more cars stopped. Windows had been knocked out, people had been hit with bricks, and they had the same complaint. Same location. Heard calls coming out on the radio that there were cars out on Central and Imperial that also had been victim of the stoning."

The driver of a car traveling out of the trouble zone onto Imperial Boulevard, two blocks north of 116th but to the east of the arrest scene, yelled to Highway Patrolman Robert J. Wallin: "You better get some help back down there—they have a white man trapped in a car and are trying to turn it over."

Another car passed. Its windows had been smashed. Then Wallin received a radio report about a damaged car which had halted in a county area within his jurisdiction.

"I went to El Segundo and Avalon," Wallin said. "In a gas station on the northwest corner there was a Mexican family. I believe they were from New Mexico visiting. And the wife, or woman, who was in the right front side had been struck with a brick or stone in the right side of the face and had a broken nose and bad lacerations on her eye. Her son [a thirteen-year-old] was in the rear seat and had been cut by a stone. There was another man, a Mexican fellow by himself in a station wagon, and he had all his windows smashed out and demanded we run back up and arrest everybody. We again called Los Angeles several times and I believe at this point our radio—our dispatcher—broadcast back that LAPD requested all uniform personnel to stay out of the area, and, shortly after, I went off duty and wasn't involved in no more of anything."

But if that ended, for the night, anyway, the involvement of Wallin and his fellow Highway Patrolmen, it was merely the beginning for Los Angeles policemen, many of whom had been active at the scene of the Frye-Gaines arrests. For it had become obvious that the police retreat at 7:45 P.M. from 116th and Avalon, designed to encourage the mob's dispersal and to dampen the threat of violence, had misfired. Avalon Boulevard for innocent motorists, Negroes as well as whites, became a nightmare alley of flying missiles—whiskey and beer bottles, hunks of asphalt and slabs of cement. Anyone or anything strange, particularly in vehicles, was the target.

The mob was not content with battering automobiles, busses and returning police units. The more brazen elements, after stopping vehicles, snatched their terrified occupants from them, beat passengers and drivers and overturned the cars.

"A friend and I were driving near the intersection of Avalon and Imperial in an open Volkswagen," said one motorist who happened to pass through the storm center. "Those crazy people started coming out into the street, throwing bottles and four-foot planks. I got about ten marks on my car. I made a U-turn and got out of there. If I'd had a gun when one maniac came up and threw a board at my windshield, I would have used it."

Others were less fortunate; they did not escape the mob wrath without teeth knocked out, bones broken.

Most of that first night's predators were young men and teenage males. But few of the adults watching acted to stop them. Many, perhaps, were afraid to try. An untold number, sickened by what they saw, hurried home, wondering where it would end. One such was Mrs. M. J. Ellis, a religious worker and resident of the neighborhood, who said the next day: "I came home from church and there were these hundreds of teenagers in the street. It was pitiful. Glass was all over the street. Those teenagers threw rocks at everybody driving through the area. I saw a rock crashing through a white man's car. My husband and I prayed all night. I was scared. My knees were wobbling. I'm praying that God protects those policemen. I am asking God to help the police fight their battle."

As complaints about ambushed motorists set police switchboards crackling, officers now were aware that they did indeed have a battle ahead of them. The mob not only had not dispersed of its own accord, but was growing and reacting like a wounded animal. Realizing this, Los Angeles police who had moved out of the area an hour before returned. They assembled at 118th and Avalon, with some reinforcement. The sergeant in command sought to seal off a five-block-long, four-block-wide zone, bounded by Imperial on the north, 118th on the south, San Pedro on the west and Stanford on the east. But the following notation on a summary of the Police Department's log for the evening attests to his relative lack of success: "Personnel available was insufficient to prevent potential victims from entering the area."

Considerable criticism fell upon police for not immediately mobilizing officers from other divisions to meet the threat, and on the Highway Patrol for departing the scene of the Frye-Gaines arrests in the face of mounting mob hostility. Los Angeles Police Chief William H. Parker, who considered the original outbreak part of a nationwide pattern of civil disobedience, answered the next day: "You cannot second-guess this type of situation, and you must protect the rest of the citizens of this community of four hundred and fifty-seven square miles. You cannot take every officer and rush them to a hot spot."

Parker, often critical in the past of civil rights zealots, went on to say: "You cannot tell people to disobey the law and not expect them to have a disrespect for the law. You cannot keep telling them that they are being abused and mistreated without expecting them to react." Parker was inclined Thursday to minimize the fury of the night before. He said he believed the violence at an end, adding: "The magnitude of this affair is not as great as some prepare to make it—you should watch the misreporting done on TV from New York."

Tough, dedicated Bill Parker may have had some justification for his remarks about television coverage then and on succeeding days, but he proved a poor prophet.

By 9:36 P.M. Wednesday, police had established a field command post at the intersection of Imperial and Avalon where 82 officers attempted to control a mob now numbering about 1,500, most of whose members were in their late teens or early twenties. By then, newspapermen, television crews and radio broadcasters were descending in force. By then, too, police sensed the time had come to move against the mob. Yet again, as the police summary notes, there was at that time "insufficient manpower for a sweep of the area." At 10 P.M., however, it records this development: "Two ten-men teams were sent to disperse crowds and six squads held in reserve and 28 officers were held at perimeter intersections."

The police strategy was to use the two teams to seal off about two blocks of Avalon, where the mob was thickest, by cutting off entry and exit from cross streets, and "let 'em," as one officer phrased it, "simmer in there for a while." This was done. However, the officers stationed at the side streets remained within sight of the command post.

Meanwhile, motorcycle officers threading through the thick of the mob to take its temperature and to try to apprehend the eagerest missile-slingers caught the brunt of the retaliation. "Motorcycle officers," the police summary noted, "became the prime targets and had to dismount." One who poked his cycle into the crowd at 20 miles an hour found it necessary to retreat "going at least 60."

As motor officers penetrated the crowd, youths pelted them with rocks and other objects, then ducked into doorways or lost themselves amid clumps of men and women. Police who sought to isolate and seize them discovered the neighborhood afforded ample cover for such hit-and-run tactics. It was a mixture of long, two-story, barracks-like apartment buildings and small, neat homes. The little frame houses were well maintained and set back from the street. The apartment buildings abutted the sidewalk. Though built in recent years, they rapidly were going to seed, either from shoddy construction or from neglect and overcrowding. In what came to be known as the "curfew area," many who took aim at the motorcycle officers probably found refuge beyond the doorways of the warren-like dwellings.

Taunts of "Get out, Whitey" and "You mother-fucking white cops" met the officers cycling into the throng. The policemen were not wholly unsuccessful in combating their rock-wielding tormentors, so that new waves of resentment were whipped up by what many spectators judged to be unduly harsh police reprisal.

Sixteen-year-old David Cole, watching from the Oasis Shoe Parlor on Avalon near Imperial where young men of the neighborhood gathered frequently, observed a piece of this action. As he appraised it: "They was throwing bricks at the police as they were passing, and they [the police] stopped. . . . The police was chasing kids, ah, up and down the street, and he hit a young man in the head with his club."

Another habitué of the Oasis Shoe Parlor, who chose to be identified only as "Joe," offered a more severe judgment on the police reaction. Joe, even more than Marquette Frye, was the stereotype of the disadvantaged young male who stoned, looted and burned during the rioting. Twenty and Los Angeles born, he was fatherless, jobless and a police suspect at the time violence flared. Unlike Marquette Frye, he was an active participant in the uprising. This is his memory of Wednesday, August 11:

"I was nearby that first night when it started. I was hanging around a shoeshine stand at Imperial and Avalon, north of where the patrol stopped the car of the boy they said had been drinking. A lot of people gathered. They told me the police had been trying to give the boy a ticket and when the boy drew back, they jumped him. They told me the boy's mother came there then and she was pregnant, but the police hit or kicked her anyway. That's what they told me. I don't know if it was true.

"I stood around. Everybody was talking. But I thought it was all over. Then the police started telling everybody to 'make it'—to leave. As far as I was concerned, I had nothing to do with it, so I stayed. Then people began throwing rocks. There seemed to be two groups doing it, and the cops kept going from one group to another but couldn't control them.

"I was getting ready to get out of there. I've never been to jail and I figured now wasn't the time to start. Then I saw the cops grab a boy I knew down the street, grab him and search him and hit him. But I went home.

"Then some little kids came to the house and said: 'They are fighting out there.' I said: 'Still fighting?' And I went back out to see. . . . When I got back out there, a cop said if I didn't leave he was going to run me in.

" 'Why do I have to leave when everybody else is out here?' I said. He grabbed me and said if I didn't leave, he'd run me in. When he drove away, I was mad. I threw my first rock. Two of them. I broke a wing window in the cop car. He didn't have to grab me like he did, that cop. Eventually, I was mad at all police.

"After I threw, everybody started again. The smaller kids were using the words 'burn, baby, burn.' It's a swing slogan that had been going through the neighborhood. After that night everybody was saying it. . . ."

Later, as Joe reconstructed it: "I heard the cop yell: 'Nigger.' Then the people went after him. I ran with them. But the others caught him first. They beat him. Bad. I chased that cop. But the others got him first. They beat him bad. Bad."

Joe, as he talked, studied his black fingers as if pondering what they might have done had he reached the white policeman first. The fingers were strong, strong enough to claw out chunks of rubble and hurl them at countless other white faces. He spoke again: "The first night, Wednesday, I was running with the crowds. Every time the cops ran one bunch, another came back. The cops couldn't handle them, but they just kept hitting at them. They never took time to stand and talk. They were hitting everyone. Girls and little kids. The cops drove up to the clusters of people and got out and started swinging their billy-clubs. The little kids were there and they got hit just like everyone else. And when I say little kids, I mean real little kids. Ten. Nine. Eight. Anyone. It didn't matter.

"That's what got the people mad. There probably wouldn't have been another night after that, if it hadn't been for them hitting the little kids. . . .

"I went out there the first night because it was my neighborhood and I wanted to see what was happening to my neighborhood. In my neighborhood, the people know one another. A person can't let other people come in and brutalize his neighbors, and that's what those cops were doing."

As Joe said, the officers did attempt to scatter the clusters of men, women and children, though whether they used force against the latter is questionable. But it was like pushing against a taut strip of elastic; an officer or officers made a portion of the mob give ground, only to have it snap back when he or they moved against another.

In time, the tactic was abandoned and officers ceased their penetrations of the crowd. For a while, the physical conflict ebbed. A kind of standoff prevailed for about an hour and a half. During this period, the mob inched steadily northward and eventually spread over all four corners of the Imperial and

Avalon intersection, encircling the mobile command post there, a police station wagon.

Private vehicles no longer moved along Avalon, the traffic flow having been halted much earlier when police returned to the neighborhood in force. During the period of the standoff, the mob found sufficient outlet for its energy taunting the police and clowning for and howling at television cameras. As the cameras zeroed in, their sound tracks registered a persistent chant: "Police brutality, police brutality."

The television crews themselves also provided a new source of antagonism. Sergeant Rankin, because he figured in the original stoning, was seized upon immediately by telecasters for interviewing. He and other officers gave their versions of what had happened and was happening. Their pronouncements were easily audible to the crowd—and many in it disliked what they heard. From the mob came shouts: "What about our side of it?" . . . "How about our story?" Several Negroes pressed toward interviewers and asked to be allowed to speak to the viewing public. Their requests were turned aside, and the rejection rankled. "Fuck you, I'm not interested in your story," witnesses claim to have heard one television reporter say.

A group of Negro ministers appeared at the intersection. Their spokesman, the Reverend Frank J. Higgins, pastor of the True Baptist Church which was about two miles northeast of the intersection, approached Police Lieutenant Frank Beeson, in command at the time. Mr. Higgins asked permission to pass the police lines into the crowd. He said he and his fellow ministers, nine in all, believed they could calm the people and persuade them to return home.

Mr. Higgins said it was the ministerial delegation's belief that "a group of teenagers is in control" of the mob, and that the howls of "police brutality" indicated to him the "police relationship" with the crowd was "not good." The minister turned to a newsman and said: "It is my personal feeling that the police are not going about this the right way."

Lieutenant Beeson, a harried officer trying to keep his eye on dozens of brushfires of crowd emotion, denied the ministers permission to circulate among the mob. When Police Inspector Karl Lee arrived a short while later, he observed to a newspaper reporter that it was "too hazardous" for officers to attempt further entry into the crowd.

Deputy Police Chief Roger Murdock, who the next day made the observation that Wednesday "was just a night to throw rocks at policemen," also appeared at the mobile command post. Not long after came a switch in the police strategy of containment. It hardly was noticeable at the outset.

7

TO PHILIP FRADKIN of the *Los Angeles Times,* first newspaper reporter on the riot scene Wednesday, police handling of the mob throughout the whole of the opening night appeared "indecisive." As a result, officers, to a large degree, allowed the mob to dictate the pattern of police response. Because they numbered less than 100, ranged against as many as 1,500 antagonists, the police may have had no choice but to try to contain the demonstrators within the neighborhood. Which they did—until shortly before midnight.

Then came the major decisive move of the night: a repetition of the earlier tactic of withdrawal, a stratagem that had been markedly unsuccessful almost four hours before. This time, however, the leavetaking followed a different course. Instead of departing en masse, as had been the case earlier, officers left almost unnoticed in twos and threes until, according to Fradkin's estimate, "only about a dozen were left."

"We're the only attraction here. If we go away, they won't have anything to yell out and they'll probably go away," a police lieutenant explained to Pulitzer Prize-winning Jack Gaunt, one of five *Times*men by now covering the developments.

"I told our crew that we'd better get out of there since the police were going to leave. There was Joe Kennedy and Don Cormier [photographers] and Phil and Bob Jackson [another *Times* reporter]," Gaunt recalls.

At that moment came a new eruption, exceeding anything that had gone before, and which, in newsman Fradkin's estimate, set the pattern for the bloody days and night ahead. The fresh outburst left the tall, athletic-looking, thirty-year-old writer among the fallen.

"For some reason," Fradkin said, "the police took after a group of troublemakers on one of the four corners. Then the whole scene seemed to disintegrate—with people running in all directions. It was a visual thing, almost impossible to describe. That was when the real riot began. Until then, the people had directed their venom specifically at the police. But just before midnight, the pattern of the next few days of senseless, brutal, non-discriminatory attacks emerged. The people began attacking, not just the white policemen, but anyone who was white. After that, I'm not really sure what happened. I got hit."

This is the way Gaunt later described the sudden, manic flare-up: "Bottles and rocks were thrown at us. The police formed a wedge and rushed the crowd. But they ran past a lot of the crowd. And those they bypassed fell on the newsmen and the few officers who remained at the command post. I saw a woman fall down. Rocks and bottles were flying through the air like a hailstorm. Automatically, I ran out into the intersection to take a picture.

"I heard a rock smash into my car, which was behind me. I turned to fall back and I heard Phil shout: 'Help. Get me out of here. I'm hit.' I could see Fradkin leaning over the car, holding his shoulder. One of the reporters had been using the radio [to the *Times* city desk] in my car and had locked the door. I fumbled in my pocket for the key as shouting Negroes ran in every direction. I found the key and got into the car with Fradkin climbing in beside me. I turned on the switch. There was just a slow grinding sound, as the motor lugged. The battery was nearly dead. Finally, the ignition fired. I breathed a sigh of relief.

"People were screaming at us and more rocks struck the car. I drove off, heading east on Imperial up to Century, then turned in the direction of the Harbor Freeway. Fradkin was in pain. I took him to Central Receiving Hospital [about ten miles to the north] and he was treated for a contusion on the right collarbone. I thought that his collarbone was broken for sure. Blood was soaking through his shirt. It turned out the bone wasn't broken, but I guess even if it had been, he'd have been lucky. Because one of the rioters had tried to bash in his head with a brick. Phil must have ducked and caught the blow on his shoulder.

"Central Receiving was chaos, there were so many injured people being brought in. I saw one police officer who had been stabbed in the leg by a woman when he tried to arrest her. Later I took Phil Fradkin home."

Gaunt's fellow photographer Don Cormier also retains vivid memories of the eruption. At the time of the police withdrawal, he was impressed by the fact that all four corners of the Imperial-Avalon intersection "were just jammed with people.

"A lot of them," he said, "didn't know what was going on. They'd ask me what was happening. A bottle cracked against my car, close to my head. I ducked. I decided to make a picture of the mob. I was raising my camera, pointing it at them. I was pretty close to a crowd of people. A Negro ran up to me. He said, 'You're not going to take that picture.' I thought to myself: 'Here we go. If I shoot the picture, who knows what they'll do.' "

Don Cormier, being a good newspaperman and photographer, "tripped the shutter and the strobe light lit up the scene." Then, he said: "The mob yelled: 'Get him.' I had told the guy before I pressed the button: 'Yeah, I'm going to take it.' When I did, he said to me: 'You're a fool.' Then I realized what he meant. It was what the crowd wanted me to do. They wanted the publicity.

"There were two lines of police cars in the middle of the street. I got back between them. One thing that impressed me was that these Negroes who were hurling stones were throwing them right into their own people. That's why I believe this didn't start out to be a race riot. These were just young hoodlums working off their frustrations. They were out to do destruction. They just wanted to hurt anybody, black or white.

"Suddenly, I heard another cry of: 'Get him, get him.' I looked around and saw a running figure do a somersault in the air and then crash against a car. The figure disappeared from view and I knew he had hit hard. I could see several Negroes clustering around whoever was down. I trained my camera on them, and they saw me. They ran off. They didn't want to be photographed. It scared them away."

Cormier's photographic instinct may have saved Philip Fradkin's life, kept him from being the first to die in the Los Angeles riots of 1965. "The man who had been knocked down," said Cormier, "slowly got to his feet. It was Phil Fradkin. He was shaken and bleeding and said to me: 'Let's get out of here.' I got into my car with Bob Jackson. Fradkin got into the car with Jack Gaunt. We left."

As the *Times* photographers and reporters departed, so, too, did other members of the press and the last of the policemen on the scene. But in those few electric seconds before the white retreat from the intersection was complete, at least one other reporter was mauled and bloodied.

Nicholas Beck of United Press International was telephoning a report to his downtown office from a booth on a gasoline station lot on the northwest corner. Stones began raining against the glass panels. Beck realized he was in trouble. "I hung up and left, only to be confronted by a tall, young Negro blocking my way," he said. "I braced, but his right fist caught me in the face, smashing my glasses. Others joined him and under repeated blows, I sank to my knees and buckled up on the ground. I don't know how long the beating lasted—fifteen seconds or a minute—or if they used fists, feet or weapons. I was told later my back had been slashed."

Then he felt his tormentors being pulled off him. He looked up to see a calm young Negro man, holding a clipboard. His rescuer turned out to be Robert Hall, a dedicated civil rights worker. On that and subsequent nights, Hall, a member of the Non-Violent Action Committee, worked tirelessly to try to pacify rioters.

The crew of KNXT-TV, the Columbia Broadcasting System affiliate in Los Angeles, barely escaped a fate similar to that of Beck and Fradkin. Though trapped in the neighborhood after police left, they slipped out unharmed—but their $10,000 cruiser was reduced by arsonists to a white-hot skeleton of steel. The two were soundman Pierre Adidge and cameraman Jack Leppert.

Adidge recalls that just before Beck and Fradkin were struck and the final police retreat was begun, "a guy, I think he was a free-lance television cameraman, backed his car into part of that huge crowd gathered on the gasoline station lot. That really got them mad, really got them riotous. Four or five policemen tried to stand up to the crowd. Then someone threw a piece of glass. They threw more glass. The police withdrew—and then everybody began running in all directions and throwing chunks of glass.

"Jack ducked behind a house on the opposite corner, and I followed him. We stayed there just a short time. Things seemed to be getting worse, and people in one of the homes started pitching rocks at us. I ran across Imperial when I saw a car coming through. The fellow in the car was just going to work the swing shift. As Jack and I got in his car, a pop bottle hit it. But he got us out of there. Our cruiser was still parked in the gasoline station lot. But the rioters were between us and it. As we passed by, leaving, it already was on fire. Work shifts in plants and factories were just changing at that time. I think a lot of cars passing on Imperial were fellows going to or from their nighttime jobs. Nobody was traveling down Avalon."

With the police now gone, motorists moving along Imperial

and unaware of what had developed, drove into the teeth of a yowling beast. What the drivers experienced, traveling unsuspectingly through the violated neighborhood, followed a pattern:

"My wife, Pat, my daughter Erin [six] and I were driving in our convertible about midnight near Imperial and Avalon. The car was hit four or five times. I don't know what they were throwing. They cut a hole through the cloth top and damaged the windshield and a side panel. I'm surprised someone wasn't killed. The man behind us got a rock through his windshield—it missed him and struck the dash," said Darrel Hirsch, a thirty-two-year-old engineer living in the seaside suburb of Redondo Beach.

"My sister and I were in the car with her three children and my two," said Mrs. Lena Markus, a Fresno housewife visiting relatives in Los Angeles. "We stopped for a light at Imperial and Avalon. Several youths approached the car with bricks tied to two-by-four boards and began beating it. They knocked out every window. They dented the fenders and scared all of us half to death. It was awful."

"My husband Henry and our sixteen-year-old daughter and I were driving on Main Street near 116th, where we saw about one hundred Negroes on each side of the street," said Mrs. Winnifred Ghigo, a forty-nine-year-old housewife living in South Gate, southeast of the scene. She recalls hearing a cry: "There's some more whites. Let's get them!" Then, she said: "Bricks and bottles started flying at us from both sides of the street. My daughter had just rolled up the window in time to avoid a brick which could have killed her. It shattered the window. Slivers of glass flew everywhere. A half-inch piece cut a vein in my daughter's forearm. My husband thought it was just some kids on the street at first. But when the big barrage started, we knew they weren't playing around. A big dirt clod hit my husband in the back of the head. We couldn't get out because the traffic was moving slowly and had us locked in."

The mob did not discriminate as to color as its rage mounted. Said Bobby Bennett, a thirty-six-year-old Negro employee of an automobile firm: "I stopped at Avalon and Imperial about 1:30 A.M. A man ran up to the car and struck me through the windshield with a two-by-four and ran."

The faces of hate were many that night. But as darkness edged toward morning light, weariness and primitive satisfaction with the destruction they had wrought overtook the rioters.

Some store windows remained to be broken, some fires to be set, some few more cars to be stoned. Few white citizens and almost none of the Los Angeles' political leaders recognized that Wednesday night was little more than a rumble of the volcano soon to erupt.

Gradually, a kind of cooling in the temperature did come in Thursday's pre-dawn hours, and, with it, a diminution in the mob's passion. Slowly, the horde disassembled. Segments sloughed off and drifted homeward. By 1 A.M., an ebb in the angry tide was noticeable. By 2 A.M., only stragglers roamed in the stricken Avalon-Imperial neighborhood. Police, however, continued to receive reports of sporadic outbursts until dawn, not only from there, but from Watts to the east, and from Lynwood, a Los Angeles suburb easterly and southerly of Watts.

But by dawn, it appeared done. Deputy Police Chief Murdock's "night for throwing rocks at policemen" appeared to have been an ample cathartic for what ailed one Negro neighborhood.

Sunup came, hot and cloudless. When it did, it seemed, to all appearances, merely a time to assess the statistics of the long, violent night and inscribe them in police records. The statistics were disturbing, but no one suspected at the time how fractional they would become.

The first night's toll: 19 policemen and 16 civilians injured, 34 persons arrested, 50 vehicles damaged or burned, two of them fire trucks.

At dawn, a soot-smudged Negro youth skipped erratically along an Avalon Boulevard sidewalk. He looked exhausted yet strangely exhilarated. He waved his hands wildly. "Burn, baby, burn," he yelled.

8

"BURN, BABY, BURN."

Morning after morning for six months, the slight man with the resonant voice had boomed the expression into Radio Station KGFJ microphones. Throughout Negro neighborhoods, Magnificent Montague's audience responded enthusiastically, particularly the teenagers. With listeners, it was:

"Ya-ah—burn, baby, burn."

By mid-August, Montague had been in Los Angeles just half a year as disc jockey for the city's most widely listened-to Negro radio station. But already he had made his flip trademark a catchword among youngsters who were "with it."

The catchy expression was not at all new to Montague, a nifty dresser with a pencil-line mustache and a nonstop, staccato patter that had won him an instant Los Angeles audience. He'd used it before in New York and Chicago before taking it west. But it never had caught on in the two biggest cities the way it did in the third largest.

In Los Angeles, the glib thirty-seven-year-old went by no other name than Magnificent Montague, and his lively rock-'n'-roll 7 to 10 A.M. program, five days a week, reached an estimated 100,000 listeners daily. "It's got a rapid tempo with little 'air' between it," said Arnold Schoor, KGFJ's general manager, in the language of the industry.

As Montague explained it, "Burn, baby, burn" was just his

way of getting listeners in the hip, receptive mood required to best appreciate the vernacular of the records he played. "It's like saying: 'Cool it,' 'What's happening?' 'Dig it,' 'Get yourself together,' " he said.

Not once during the rioting did Montague mention the violence on his three-hour program, and he immediately ceased using the expression. His station's news reports covered developments closely, as a public service, and one of its mobile units was stoned. But unintentionally, Magnificent Montague had given the rioters a rallying cry. The first night a few teenagers shouted it in jest, then defiantly, and, finally, with fire in their eyes and rocks in their fists. Young adults seized on it later. Then so did their elders.

As mobs shrieked "burn, baby, burn," large parts of Los Angeles would do just that. What novelist James Baldwin had called "the fire next time" would become the fire now, to the rebel screech of: "Burn, baby, burn."

9

SOUTHERN CALIFORNIA sunrises are wondrous to behold, and this one, that of Thursday, August 12, was no exception—even though it warmed the air too soon and promised that the day and night would be long and hot.

In most Los Angeles neighborhoods, the August 12 dawn was little different from any other, more sultry perhaps, but still invigoratingly beautiful for those who rose early enough to enjoy it. Along a portion of Avalon Boulevard, however, this sunup was quite unlike any the neighborhood ever had known. Broken glass, chipped stone and charred remains of automobiles were strewn along the scarred boulevard. It was an unsettling sight.

But business went on as usual. Stores opened. Men went to work. Women did too, more of them probably than males because of the character of that complexly disadvantaged neighborhood. Other women went to market, a vast percentage carrying the receipts from welfare checks.

Little suspicion of what impended existed at high levels, but public agencies, as is their nature, stirred. Police Chief William H. Parker made his defense of his department's conduct during the previous night. Almost alone among public officials in the upper stratum, he sensed that the early morning quiet might be deceptive. He remarked on this later, saying he thought it "unusual" the way the rioting had stopped, "because usually the pattern has been for rioting to continue until the fury has been spent." He said he was "not blind to the possibility" that rioters were merely "resting" and that the trouble might resume that night. Mayor Samuel W. Yorty kept a speaking engagement in San Diego. From that city, he appealed to Los Angeles residents to stay out of the trouble area and to keep their children home.

It is unfair, perhaps, to say that Chief Parker almost alone among public officers recognized the possibility of a new outburst. For, as a study commission appointed by Governor Edmund G. Brown would note later, commendable efforts were made by "Negro leaders, social workers, probation officers, churchmen, teachers, educators and businessmen . . . to persuade people to desist from their illegal activities, to stay in their homes and to restore order."

But, in the past, civic leaders and public officials generally had shrugged off the possibility of trouble in Los Angeles' Negro communities with a smug "it-can't-happen-here" attitude. So while public agencies and some well-meaning individuals did bestir themselves Thursday, a sense of urgency and a sense of appreciation of what lay behind Wednesday night's disorder appeared lacking.

The Los Angeles County Human Relations Commission called a 2 P.M. meeting in Athens Park, about a half mile southwest of the scene of the previous night's trouble. Its express purpose was to lower the fever of the community.* Through no fault of the well-intentioned commission, the Athens Park meeting not only proved an utter failure but actually aggravated matters.

* Efforts to establish a city human relations commission, similar to the county's, had been rebuffed in the past. City officials took the view it was unnecessary in a city that considered its race relations exemplary or they expressed the opinion it would only duplicate county commission functions. But five months after the riot, the City Council voted to create such a commission. This only precipitated a squabble between Mayor Yorty and councilmen, however, which the mayor won when the council capitulated to his demands for changes which gave him almost complete control of the new city body.

As organized, it seemed ideally suited to its purpose, for it brought together representatives of all neighborhood groups and men purported to be the Negro leaders of the city. (Later, when rioting resumed, one commission member observed that he and others who had worn the mantle of leadership had been talking in the past "to the wrong people—to the middle-class Negro, not the thousands with deep-seated grievances." As it turned out, the latter bitterly resented much of the so-called Negro leadership, considering it a symbol of "Uncle Tom-ism.")

Also attending the Athens Park meeting as observers were representatives of elected officials, the sheriff's office, the district attorney's office, and police, plus the various news media.

About 250 persons assembled in a concrete block building in the small park. Most were teenagers. Among the speakers urging that residents remain in their homes that night was Mrs. Rena Frye, bailed out by then, who said: "Help me and others calm this situation down so that we will not have a riot to-night."

According to Chief Parker, the meeting had been called without consulting the Police Department, and when Parker learned of it, he had misgivings. As it developed, his misgivings were realized. For the meeting deteriorated from an attempt to restore law and order into a forum for those with grievances against police and those wanting to air other Negro vexations.

Mrs. Frye gave her version of her arrest, which hardly helped matters. Then teenagers took over the microphone. They sought to justify the previous night's violence. It was, they cried, the result of "police brutality," "persecution." A sixteen-year-old boy, his face contorted, stepped to the platform. His inflammatory language echoed that night, not only from television sets throughout the city, but throughout the nation.

Rioting would resume that night, he warned, "whether you like it or not." The violence, he said, would spread to white neighborhoods. "We're not gonna fight down here no more," he shouted. "We're gonna do it in the white man's neighborhoods tonight."

Those chilling remarks undoubtedly triggered the first rush by white homeowners in the city and suburbs on stores selling guns. Before the rioting ended, this became an unprecedented stampede. Chief Parker defended gun purchases by fearful citizens; Governor Brown denounced them.

The Athens Park audience, meanwhile, responded enthusiastically to the militant teenagers. When the youths tired of speaking, most of the assemblage left.

At the close of the meeting, John Buggs, head of the Human Relations Commission, asked for a show of hands from the 50 or so persons remaining. How many would work to prevent a new outbreak? Only about a dozen persons raised their hands. Nevertheless, Buggs, a tireless, sensitive public servant, termed the meeting a success. The teenagers, he explained, had been given a chance to "let off steam."

Following the breakup of that meeting, some adult Negro leaders—including Buggs and the Reverend H. H. Brookins, long considered by the white community as a spokesman for the Los Angeles Negro—adjourned to hold an informal discussion with young men representing neighborhood gangs.

"What would pacify the community?" was the question asked. These proposals were made and the adult leaders were empowered to submit them to police:

1—Withdraw uniformed officers from the troubled neighborhood and allow selected community leaders to undertake the responsibility for law and order.

2—If police found the first proposal unacceptable, substitute for white officers Negro officers in civilian clothes and unmarked cars.

The adult leaders took the proposals about 7 P.M. to Deputy Police Chief Roger Murdock at the 77th Street Police Station, where what developed had far-reaching repercussions.

Earlier Thursday, another gathering was held in another

neighborhood park. This assemblage was strictly informal. Nobody was invited. But throngs of murmuring Negroes, again mostly teenagers and young adults, showed up.

Will Rogers Memorial Park, about two miles northeast of Athens Park and often the site in the past of civil rights meetings and demonstrations, long had been a popular gathering place for the restless, idle young. What happened there Thursday is significant in the light of later speculation as to whether the riot was wholly spontaneous or organized incendiarism.

No few persons, including some associated with law enforcement (but not Chief Parker), saw the violence as Communist or Muslim inspired. Others viewed it as gang incited and directed. Some considered it a combination of all these, or, at least, an opportune circumstance seized upon by Communists, Muslims and organized gangs to promote their own ends. Most responsible judgment held, however, that the riot began spontaneously; that looting, sniping and arson, for the most part, were spontaneous, but that some loosely organized individuals were responsible for some of the riotous acts.

The governor's study commission on the riot, known as the McCone Commission after its chairman, John A. McCone, former Central Intelligence Agency director, made this assessment four months after the uprising: "After a thorough examination, the Commission has concluded that there is no reliable evidence of outside leadership or pre-established plans for the rioting. The testimony of law enforcement agencies and their respective intelligence officers supports this conclusion. The Attorney General, the District Attorney and the Los Angeles police have all reached the conclusion that there is no evidence of a pre-plan or a pre-established central direction of the rioting activities. This finding was submitted to the Grand Jury by the District Attorney.

"This is not to say that there was no agitation or promotion of the rioting by local groups or gangs which exist in pockets throughout the south central area. The sudden appearance of Molotov cocktails in quantity and the unexplained movement of men in cars through the areas of great destruction support the conclusion that there was organization and planning after the riots commenced. In addition, on that tense Thursday, inflammatory handbills suddenly appeared in Watts. But this cannot be identified as a master plan by one group; rather it appears to have been the work of several gangs, with membership of young men ranging in age from fourteen to thirty-five years. All these activities intensified the rioting and caused it to spread with increased violence from one district to another in the curfew areas."

One of the young men who drifted to Will Rogers Park that Thursday was Joe, the jobless, fatherless twenty-year-old who had been caught up in the mob fury the night before. He had this to say of what the McCone Commission called "pre-established plans" and "pre-established central direction": "They say it wasn't organized—but it was. Not in the regular sense. But the people met in the park and talked about what had happened and what they planned to do that night. A friend of mine plays the drums. I play the flute. We go to the park practically every day and play and drink a couple of beers. We did Thursday and people came and listened and I heard them talking.

" 'Man, did you hear about last night?' one fella asked.

" 'Yeah, they put my brother in jail. I'm going back tonight.'

" 'Me to. Yeah, man, they hit my sister on the head.'

" 'See you up there later on.' "

Elsewhere, young Negroes clustered on street corners or elbowed into neighborhood hangouts. They engaged in similar conversation. "Anyone with any sense will stay out of here tonight," threatened one teenage boy. "We're really going to show those cops." And in out-of-the-way niches of the neighborhood, and beyond it, other young males—and perhaps some of their elders—prepared for sundown, assembling and stockpiling Molotov cocktails, a simple but explosively effective arrangement of bottle, rag and inflammable liquid.

Sundown came all too soon for police. Officers still hadn't fired a shot; now they were being armed with long-range tear-gas guns that they were instructed not to use until so ordered. As Chief Parker explained later, officers, because of the brutality charges to which they were subjected, reluctantly fired for the first time only when they decided they had no other choice.

The 7 P.M. meeting at the 77th Street Police Station between Negro leaders, armed with their suggestions of ending the tension, and Deputy Chief Murdock achieved nothing. Instead, it produced ill-feeling on both sides. Murdock rejected the proposals. The manner in which he did so was a particular affront to Buggs, a reasonable man who, at one point, interpreted a remark made by the deputy chief as a reflection on Negro policemen.

Buggs claimed Murdock turned aside the suggestion for the use of Negro plainclothesmen by saying: "Negro police officers are all right because they don't make a conspicuous target at night."

Murdock charged that Buggs "took my words out of context," and contended: "Buggs was saying that we should withdraw white officers and replace them with as many Negro officers as possible. He said the use of Negro police officers would make police less of a target. I said, if he meant at nighttime, I would agree with him. It was a facetious remark. I just meant that black men are harder to see at night than white men. Of course, I was joking. I don't want any of my policemen to be targets."

Murdock said later he regretted the remark. But he said it came when "tension was kind of rough. We were losing the battle. I didn't have time to stand there and engage in a long sociological battle."

Later, the McCone Commission upheld the deputy chief's rejection of the proposals, saying of them: "They envisaged a new and untested method of handling a serious situation that was rapidly developing. Furthermore, the proposal to use only Negro officers ran counter to the policy of the Police Department, adopted over a period of time at the urging of Negro leaders, to deploy Negro officers throughout the city and not concentrate them in the Negro area. Indeed, when the proposal came, the police had no immediate means of determining where the Negro officers on the force were stationed. At this time rioting was breaking out again, and the police felt that their established procedures were the only way to handle what was developing as another night of rioting. Following those procedures, the police decided to set up a perimeter around the key twenty-block center of the trouble and keep all the crowd activity within that area."

Chief Parker said afterward: "We had complaints about ghettoizing the Negroes in the Police Department. So we accommodated this request to the point where we overdid it. Of the 200 Negro policemen, only seven were at 77th Street. Now we're criticized for not having enough Negroes there."

Reverend Brookins left the meeting at the 77th Street Station feeling as if Deputy Chief Murdock had "taken the attitude of a Jim Clark" (Sheriff James Clark of Alabama's Dallas County, scene of the Selma civil rights clashes). To Mr. Brookins, Murdock's rejection of the Negro proposals was "like lighting a fuse." When he and Buggs reported back to the seething community, they were met with contempt. "We were told," said Mr. Brookins, "your leadership does not amount to much—let us do it our way."

The explosion came near dusk, just as it had the day before. It came like the thundering confluence of many raging streams —cataracts, in this case, of frustration, bitterness and strangling self-denigration.

As early as 4:30 P.M., Mrs. Lacine Holland—who the night before had said to her mother after the Gaines arrest, "there's going to be a riot"—sensed the impending outburst. "I had been hearing on the radio all day that they expected a riot because of the heat and humidity," she said. Because of this, she decided to check on her mother who lived near the scene of the previous night's trouble. "And so I went to my mother's," she remembers, "and there were police all in the neighborhood."

Avalon Boulevard also was clogged with roving bands of young men, talking in angry, arrogant voices. "Mother said policemen had been going up and down the street all day," said Mrs. Holland. "When I got there, there were four carloads over by the [Grace Temple Baptist] church, and . . . it took me five minutes to get out onto Avalon because of the police cars. A policeman was going very slow. He'd stop and stare at the people. I thought, 'Well, gee, what are they expecting? Why are they here? . . .' To me it was a great mistake for them to be in this area."

Mrs. Holland's eyes may have deceived her as to the number of officers patrolling Avalon. Police recognized that unusual numbers of officers in the neighborhood would only aggravate residents further. "We endeavored to stay out of this area, so we wouldn't be an irritant. We utilized only five cars here, in an 18-block square area. We emphasized that officers stay on the perimeter," said Chief Parker.

About the time Mrs. Holland reached her mother's, Chief Parker came to a decision that must have been difficult for him considering his personal pride in the capability of his department. At 4:52 P.M. he telephoned the commander of the California National Guard in Sacramento. The Los Angeles police chief told Lieutenant General Roderic Hill that Los Angeles policemen might need help from the citizen-soldiers.

Parker's telephone call was in line with a procedure Governor Brown had suggested a year earlier. The governor and the Los Angeles police chief had discussed what to do in the case of a riot of any kind. On July 27, 1964, Parker had received a long-distance call from Sacramento.

Governor Brown was on the other end of the line, and, as Parker recalls: "He read me a statement to the effect that the military should be used in the event of riots." Procedures then were agreed upon by the governor and police chief, and, with his call to General Hill, Parker merely activated the first step in that program; the call to Hill simply alerted the general that the Guard might be needed in Los Angeles.

As a result, Hill sent his aide, Colonel Robert Quick, to Los Angeles to serve as a liaison with local law enforcement. He also advised Lieutenant Governor Anderson of the deteriorating situation. In the absence of Governor Brown, vacationing in Greece, Lieutenant Governor Anderson would have to act on the formal request when and if it did come. Hill also alerted commanders of the Southern California-based 40th Armored Division.

As the crowd in the tense Negro neighborhood continued to grow late Thursday afternoon and early evening, Chief Parker took another decisive step: he opened a specially outfitted Emergency Control Center at Police Headquarters in Los Angeles' modernistic Civic Center. This long, rectangular building, a many-windowed structure, is referred to as the "Glass House" by those from Negro communities who have visited it under less than pleasurable circumstances.

Police were as ready as they could be for what was to come. And when it did come, police—despite preparations—couldn't cope with it.

The pattern of the night before was repeated—with some savage refinements. The lawlessness began as it had Wednesday with stoning and overturning of cars and the beating and terrorizing of motorists. Again automobiles were set afire.

Firemen, about 7 P.M., during the initial moment of the riot's renewal, went into the neighborhood to answer alarms about torched autos. They were bombarded with rocks—and shot at. In the days and nights that followed, firemen had to retreat from many such situations simply because they were unprotected. In some instances, they could not even come near raging fires. In others, they fought blazes under sniper gunfire. A major task of Guardsmen and other law enforcement officers later was to protect firemen from being shot at.

But fiery autos, stoned and beaten white men and women were not enough this Thursday night to satisfy the mob lust. Not long after the riot resumed, the first fire was set in a commercial establishment, a store only a block from the scene of the Frye-Gaines arrests. Looting began on a wholesale scale. When the mobs could find no policemen on which to vent their rage, officers were lured into reach with decoy calls to police switchboards.

Cries of "get Whitey" pierced the early night air. And as each new car or business establishment shuddered from the force of an exploding Molotov cocktail, then was engulfed by flame, onlookers chortled raucously: "Burn, baby, burn."

Police strategy again was aimed at containing the violence within a limited arena. But this proved impossible. The cordon of officers, many now from police districts other than the 77th, gave ground. As the evening wore on, rock-throwing looters ranged for the first time outside the perimeter police sought to hold.

On Imperial Highway, Los Angeles County deputy sheriffs who went to the assistance of police that night, along with Highway Patrolmen, fought off a mob which had overturned a Volkswagen driven by a pretty young woman. The deputies involved remember that particular incident because the young woman was French and newly arrived in this country. "They'd already pulled her from the little car and struck her. God knows what would have happened if we hadn't been able to force them back," said one young sheriff's officer.

The deputies remember the mauling of the young French woman with outrage, and also with sadness, because one fellow officer associated with her rescue, Ronald Ludlow, would not be alive that time the next night.

There was little reason the mob should have spared the young Frenchwoman. No car bearing a white motorist was spared. Whenever one entered the neighborhood, word spread like wildfire: "Here comes Whitey—get him." While their elders watched in the background, urging them on, young men and women rushed the cars.

"Kill! Kill!" bystanders chanted. It was a miracle no one died that night. Some were saved by the intercession of ministers and other responsible Negroes circulating among the horde, trying to pacify it.

In one instance when a mob jumped two white men and felled them, several ministers rushed to the beaten Caucasians. One had an eyeball hanging from its socket. The ministers carried both white men into a nearby apartment building and called an ambulance: The mob cursed the ministers, spat on them and howled: "Hypocrites."

Another Negro clergyman, Methodist Bishop R. J. Morris, standing later on another street corner, saw a mob set upon a car occupied by a terrified teenage couple. "I was at Imperial Highway and Central Avenue when the young couple stopped for a traffic light," said Mr. Morris. "The crowd threw bricks through the car's windows. They dragged the young man into the street and began beating him. They threw bricks and stones at the girl. I ran over and told them to stop. 'Go back to church and pray,' they said. 'If you fool around here, we'll blow up your car.' I told them I had to help those youngsters.

"Suddenly, they changed their minds. I got my car and some of them helped me put the kids into it. The boy was really hurt. Then they said: 'Now get out of here, because we're going to blow their car up, and we might blow you up too.' I took the boy and girl to the hospital."

Light-skinned Negroes often fared no better than whites. Frequently they found themselves imperiled, until recognized by a friend in the mob or until one of their attackers yelled: "Lay off—he's 'blood.' "

Negro storekeepers stuck hastily scrawled signs in their windows: "Blood Brother" or "This is a Negro Business." Often these did no good: mobs looted and burned the shops anyway.

"Once the looting started, everybody started drinking, even little kids eight or nine years old. The rioters knew they had the upper hand. They seemed to sense neither the police nor anyone else could stop them," Robert Richardson, a Negro newspaperman, wrote of that Thursday night in the *Los Angeles Times.*

10

INTO THIS VENOM-CHARGED atmosphere rode the one representative of news media who came closest to losing his life during the six-day uprising—Ray Fahrenkopf, a stocky, gray-haired, soft-spoken ABC-TV soundman.

Fahrenkopf was not a man to panic at what he heard and saw that night. During preceding weeks he had covered bloody civil rights demonstrations in Bogalusa and just six months earlier had returned from the battlefronts of Vietnam.

He, ABC cameraman Ralph Mayer and correspondent-announcer Piers Anderton had stopped first Thursday night at the 77th Street Police Station for a briefing. Chief Parker thought television crews should stay out of the riot area. He believed cameras attracted exhibitionists and that, once crowds gathered, violence inevitably followed. Police had advised television station personnel that their presence could be harmful.

But, rightly or wrongly, television station officials believed they were obliged to cover the developments as a public service. Some scenes shown viewing audiences, it was later believed, provoked lawlessness by their inflammatory nature. Be that as it may, as Chief Parker said, "They went ahead—as was their privilege."

Fahrenkopf, Mayer and Anderton arrived in the heart of the most violent area at one of Thursday night's most violent times. They reached Imperial and Avalon about 9 P.M, about the time police found it necessary to request assistance from deputy sheriffs and Highway Patrolmen.

The television crew parked its sedan, identified in clear lettering as an ABC news car. The three men unloaded their equipment. After that, said Fahrenkopf, "We walked up the block and the first thing we witnessed was police putting a couple of Negroes in their car. I was trying to pick up the sound. The cameraman was shooting footage. One of the rioters was jumping up and down, angry because he didn't think we were shooting film of the policemen pushing one of the suspects into the car. He was yelling that it was police brutality.

"Mayer asked me to go back to the car and pick up another hand camera. I started walking back. The street was dark and missiles were flying all over the place. I made it safely to the car and opened the door to get the camera. I discovered that the car had been badly damaged by flying rocks. I locked the door and began walking to rejoin my crew. But they were gone. And so were the officers.

"I could see a car burning up the street farther ahead and figured that they were there. Suddenly, some men—I don't know how many—came up behind me and struck me on the left shoulder with a heavy object.

"It broke my shoulder open. I dropped the camera. Someone shoved me from behind and I fell. My glasses flew off, together with the hard hat that I'd been wearing for protection against the flying stones. They started kicking me in the chin and on the face. Others beat me over the head with their fists. I could hear two colored women who were standing there beside me, pleading for those hoodlums to leave me alone. Then they went away.

"I managed to get to my feet and pick up my equipment. I thought I was free, I could still see that car burning up the street and I thought that was where my guys were. I decided to cross the street and head up in that direction. Maybe it would be safer. I began to walk. I was dizzy from the beating. When I got out into the middle of the street, I saw a new group coming toward me. I knew they were going to attack me.

"I hollered 'Police!' as loudly as I could several times. They crowded around me. One guy crashed a fist in my face. Then another. They were beating me savagely. I went down. While I was lying on my face, one of them must have leaped into the air and come down on top of my back with all his weight. Someone must have smashed me over the head with a club, for it took a number of stitches to close a deep gash behind my ear. I remember they kept kicking me in the face while I lay there. Then I fainted."

Fahrenkopf lay bleeding in the street, clothed only in shredded trousers which had been new that morning. His gums were bloodied, teeth missing. The soundman's assailants ripped off his shirt and undershirt in a frenzied search for valuables. They took his wallet containing $200 and identification cards, the camera and a tape recorder he had been carrying, and his wristwatch. His eyeglasses and a dental bridge presumably were ground to dust in the stampede around his fallen figure. Next day, his eyes were so swollen from the beating, it was feared, for a time, he had been blinded. He required medical treatment for weeks.

Fahrenkopf has no memory of lying in the street and being stripped. "The next thing I remember," he said, "is that I was in a car on the way to the hospital. Two white men were in it, one driving. But I never did find out who they were. The strange thing about all this is that the hospital has a record of admitting me at 9:37 P.M. That means from the time we arrived on the scene until the time I arrived at the hospital, only 37 minutes had elapsed. It's a half hour I'll not forget."

About the time Fahrenkopf was beaten, California Highway Patrolmen received their first request for assistance from Los Angeles police. A contingent of about 35 CHP officers in about 15 squad cars, which had been waiting for just such an appeal, responded. The Patrolmen went to Central Avenue and Imperial Highway, about a half mile from where Fahrenkopf was attacked. A second call from city police summoned the CHP officers to Avalon Boulevard after the Fahrenkopf beating.

Even before arriving at Central and Imperial, however, Highway Patrolmen Leonard W. Moore had a foretaste of what he and his fellow officers were headed for. He recalls that a city policeman stopped him on his way to the Imperial-Central intersection and "told me one of the LAPD boys had been stabbed."

Moore, along with many of the other officers in the CHP contingent, had responded the night before when his colleague Lee Minikus issued his call for help. He was able to look about him Thursday night and recognize Sergeant V. G. Nicholson, who had directed the withdrawal from the Frye-Gaines arrest scene, and Officers Bob Wallin, Dennis Hamilton and Keith Albers, all of whom had been present Wednesday night.

On arriving at Imperial and Central, the CHP officers watched car after car come away from the heart of the Avalon Boulevard violence with evidence of damage. Almost without exception, the vehicles' windows had been smashed. One carried the victim of a heart attack. "The people were running wild," said Moore, twenty-eight, a Patrolman for just two years, who, despite his inexperience, would prove himself a cool operator under fire. "Negroes driving by kept the inside lights of their cars on—so the people could see who they were and leave them alone. Some whites came into the area out of curiosity. They were stoned," the young officer said.

On Avalon Boulevard, amid the rampaging mob to which the Highway Patrolmen were soon asked to direct their attention, Joe, the twenty-year-old habitué of the Oasis Shoe Parlor, stoned and snarled along with other rioters. He commented later about white curiosity seekers: "After the rioting started, more and more other whites just seemed to keep coming into Watts. They kept coming in—even though they'd been warned not to. They came to see us put on a show. I wasn't particularly interested in giving them a show. I wanted revenge. I'd seen my friends beaten and hurt. After a while, every white face looked the same to me. . . .

"You hear people say it wasn't a race riot. Let them. The average person out there in the streets knew what it was and he considered it a war. A civil revolt. That's what it was—a civil revolt. At first it was against the white police. Then—not just the police, but all whites. I saw only two Negro cops all the time I was in the streets. And I was in the streets all the time. I hardly ever slept those days and nights. They should have known better. Why did they send in so many white police? Especially into an all-Negro neighborhood? It was almost like they wanted to start something—so they could hit. . . .

"The second night, I got more involved. More and more of my friends got beaten. I got hit in the head with a billyclub. I was there when a car got burned up after the white driver got out and ran. They didn't kill him. But they beat him up real bad. I ran after him to hit him, too. But I couldn't catch up. A Negro man came out and got the man and took him into his apartment and called an ambulance."

Just before 10 P.M., Highway Patrolmen received the Los Angeles police request which sent them racing from Imperial and Central to 111th and Avalon, scene then of the fiercest rioting. The Patrol cars traveled in single file westbound on Imperial. "Almost from the moment we left," said one officer, "we were under a heavy bombardment of rock, bricks, fire bombs and anything else that people could throw. Along the way, I saw five cars on fire."

Drivers of the CHP vehicles had to prod them into the swarm on Avalon. Rioters responded with a salvo of bricks, stones and wooden planks. Cars were burning around the Patrolmen as they parked and leaped into the mob. The CHP officers went to the assistance of Los Angeles policemen who were being shoved, kicked and struck. It appeared to the Highway Patrolmen that less than ten city officers were engulfed by the mob of more than one thousand.

"There was a dryness in my mouth as I got out of the car, not knowing what to expect," recalls Sergeant Nicholson. "We were walking targets in the middle of the street. We couldn't see them in the darkness, but they could see us [street lights had been shot out]. Then a rock hit my helmet, another grazed my side. Every officer showed remarkable restraint in not shooting. I know what it is to feel in a situation like that."

Patrolman Moore remembers that besides the small force of Los Angeles policemen trapped in the crowd, several other white persons also had been encircled. They apparently were motorists who had been yanked from their cars. "They were being stoned," Moore said. "We formed a perimeter to save these people. The people elected to remain there all night. We were busy bandaging people who had been hit by hurled objects. There was one woman who had an apparent heart attack and we were administering to her. It was during this period that we refrained from shooting, on more than one occasion, at cars who tried to run a roadblock we later set up."

CHP Officer Philip Angell recalls that the moment Patrolmen stepped from their vehicles they were met by a rain of rocks and bottles, thrown by "Negro youths, male and female."

"I saw several officers get hit by debris," said Officer M. G. Stapleton.

Both Angell and Stapleton wrote later in their reports that the fact that about half the Highway Patrolmen, unlike city police, carried shotguns appeared to give them a distinct advantage in combating the mob. Noted Stapleton: "CHP officers spread out around the scene and when the rioters saw the shotguns, they pulled back immediately. This gave officers a chance to start forming a plan of action. At this time we were holding about two blocks on Avalon—110th and 111th Streets. Any man by himself who would have gotten ten feet off Avalon on either side would have been a dead man."

Observed Angell: "LAPD officers expressed appreciation at the presence of the CHP, and, in particular, the shotguns, which seemed to give an advantage to the officers, as the rock-throwing became less and those responsible for it retreated to 112th and Avalon."

Stapleton said, from that time on in that particular area, city police "did not make a move without several CHP officers with shotguns. . . . Every group that went anywhere had CHP officers out in front. . . ." Then Stapleton observed: "It is this officer's opinion that having the shotguns made all the difference in winning and losing. A Los Angeles police inspector came over and told us that we had just saved their butts, that before our arrival they were getting ready to pull out—that they could not have held the two blocks without the CHP and their shotguns."

As the officers regained control of the two-block area, the mob turned its attention from them to passing motorists again.

"At this time," said Stapleton, "there was a large group north from us on Avalon at about 110th Place. I observed them stone many vehicles that tried to get by them. They hit a man southbound on Avalon and knocked him out with rocks. They pulled him out of his car and threw him into the street and set fire to his new car and burned it."

In time, the officers lost patience with merely protecting their two-block perimeter and trying to aid innocent passers-by, many of whom required first aid. "It was decided," said Stapleton, "that a sortie of about 15 men [including him and Angell and Dennis Hamilton] would go north one block and clean out this nest of rioters. We went by way of an alley approximately one-half block west of Avalon. The alley came out behind the rioters."

The manuever worked. Or, as Stapleton noted: "The attack was successful and another block was secured. During this attack officers were fired upon by an unknown person. He, however, missed the officers and hit another rioter in the leg."

From the intersection, people "fled in all directions," said Angell, and, "from that time on, I and approximately four other officers remained at that location to secure the intersection and prevent further damage. Other groups of officers were doing the same at other points along Avalon."

Stapleton, Hamilton and other officers continued northward. When they had advanced about two blocks, recalls Stapleton: "A vehicle came southbound on Avalon toward the officers. The LAPD officers ordered the vehicle to stop. The vehicle picked up speed and headed toward the officers. The LAPD officers opened fire on the vehicle. The vehicle got past them. This put it among other officers. LAPD officers kept firing. Their bullets were now flying among other officers. This officer had two rounds go by his head about ten feet away, between him and another CHP officer. One of the glancing bullets hit a CHP officer in the right thigh, wounding him slightly. Not one CHP officer fired a round, because to have fired any way but due north would have been shooting into other officers. The vehicle was stopped and its occupants taken into custody."

Hamilton was the other Highway Patrolman nearly hit by the shots. He said: "We hit the pavement prone and the shooting continued. I heard someone yell and looked to my right to see a CHP officer from the East Los Angeles Station grab his leg and fall. He was about 20 feet away. The shooting subsided. Several people were arrested and removed."

"When some semblance of order was restored in the area we were controlling," Keith Albers reported later, "we found the area was in a shambles. Store windows were broken, a liquor store had been looted and several vehicles had been completely consumed by fire in the middle of the street. The streets were littered with broken bricks and broken glass. Several CHP vehicles were damaged and many officers had been struck by flying missiles."

As Albers walked back south on the west side of Avalon toward Imperial, his eyes were caught by white scraps among the rubble. He may have been the first law enforcement officer during the riot to sight what the McCone Commission described later as an "inflammatory handbill."

The sidewalk beneath Albers' feet was "littered with hundreds of leaflets" bearing a picture of Chief Parker and above it the legend: "This Man Says: YOU Commit More Crime and Violence Than Anyone Else." To the young officer, it was clear that the leaflets "were distributed among the crowd of Negroes early in the evening." The name "Watts Action Committee" appeared on them.

Later, between 1 and 2 A.M., a man was seized while distributing another piece of provocative literature. Officer Wallin, who participated in the arrest, saw the man, a Negro, "walking on the sidewalk by a cluster of people who had been slowly working their way back to the alley blockade point west of Avalon on 110th Street. . . . We flashed our lights on him and ordered him to come across the alley toward us."

The man complied, and officers confiscated from him single sheets of Muslim hate literature entitled *Muhammad Speaks.* The man who had been their distributor and five others identified by CHP officers as Muslims were taken into custody and turned over to city police, who later released them. "We were told there was no ordinance against handing out leaflets in LA city," Wallin noted. The leaflets proclaimed in large letters: "Stop Police Brutality." Smaller type advertised a 2 P.M. meeting at the Muslim Mosque scheduled for the coming Sunday—the day Marquette Frye spoke there.

Rioters and looters stormed through a vastly expanded area Thursday night and early Friday morning. Still Chief Parker held off putting in a formal request for the Guard, because:

"A problem came up which still is of some concern to me. We had some Negro officers in the crowd as undercover agents and one insisted that they were dealing with not more than 200 people in the area. This presented a dilemma. I couldn't justify calling out the Guard if only 200 people were involved.

But by 3:30 A.M. Friday, at least 75 stores had been burned and countless officers and innocent whites injured.

New incidents of rioting were erupting throughout broad areas of South Los Angeles. The Fire Department had received 2,500 calls from the area and had been forced to begin operating on an emergency basis.

These statistics are quoted only because Chief Parker estimated this particular time marked "the actual beginning of the proliferation of the riot which eventually took in a 46-mile curfew area."

More meaningful is what happened to individual human beings during this time—to those who looted and burned, to those who fought to control the looters and burners, to all the others who were swept up in the wild race of events. They are the true story of the riot.

11

HENRY M. KNAWLS was born in Texas and reared in Portland, Oregon. By the summer of 1965 he had lived in Los Angeles for three years and had been a paid employee of the Neighborhood Youth Corps, an arm of the Economic and Youth Opportunities Agency, since the previous March. He was twenty-five, unmarried and a well-educated and totally dedicated young man. He particularly liked his job specialty: working with high school dropouts in poverty areas and high school graduates experiencing a bitter time while looking for employment.

An ex-serviceman and former student in Northwestern University's school of commerce, Knawls, a Negro, was perplexed at what news media were reporting. Until recently he himself had been a resident of the riot area, and, he recalls: "I didn't believe what I was hearing and seeing on television and reading. I couldn't go along with it."

If it were true, he told himself, he could not condone the rioting. "But I knew their feelings, their frustrations. I've had experiences myself with police. I could see where these people might react violently against policemen," Knawls said.

He still had friends living in the riot area, and he was concerned about them, if what he had been hearing and reading were true. But more important was his growing curiosity about the riot. Shortly after sundown Thursday he got into his car and drove south. "I had to get the pulse of these people whose involvement was so total," he remembers thinking.

He arrived in the riot area about 9 P.M., or close to the time of the attack on Ray Fahrenkopf, the television soundman. He left shortly before dawn. So moved was this young Negro man by what he saw and heard and felt, he switched on his tape recorder immediately upon reaching home and dictated this account of his experiences and the observations he made as a result of them:

As I was making a right turn on the street where the action was centered, several Negro youths ran up to my car. They said, "Turn your inside lights on, Blood, so we can see who it is." This I did unquestioningly. I proceeded very slowly up the street, trying to avoid the various sorts of debris, glass, bricks, sticks, by weaving back and forth across the thoroughfare.

Large numbers of men, women and children were gathered on both sides of the street with bricks and other objects in their hands. Just up the street was a car which had been upturned and set afire. From their comments, "We gon' mess over some devils," "Don't let no gray boys get through here," and "Paddies better stay out of here tonight," one could assume that they were anxiously waiting any car with white occupants to come driving down the street.

After driving back down the street and parking my car, I mingled with the crowd. At just about this time a car came roaring down the street. The crowd yelled: "Whitey! Get him!"

Bricks, stone and pipes, hurled from both sides of the street, dented both sides of the car. The front windshield was smashed. The car speeded up and kept going until it was out of the area. People screamed: "Don't let no more get away." And: "Dammit, they got through." They were disappointed that they had not been able to stop this car and inflict more damage upon it and its driver.

Down the street was heard: "We got him, we got one." I ran up the street with several people and saw a Caucasian man being pulled from his car. One group began pummeling the man, and others proceeded to overturn his car and put a torch to it. The man was allowed to run away after he had been thoroughly beaten; he could run only with a stumbling gait and both hands were covering his bloody face.

Several police cars came driving down this street and were stoned with missiles from both sides of the street. The police did not stop, but made U-turns and headed back the way they had come. I proceeded up the street for two or three blocks, and across the street, at a gas station, approximately nine or ten police cars were forming a semicircle in front of the station. The policemen were crouched down behind their cars with their pistols and rifles drawn and aimed at the crowd facing them. The police made no attempts to disperse the crowd, which was continually taunting the officers to shoot, and calling them names.

After about fifteen minutes, all of these policemen got into their cars and left, with red lights flashing and sirens screaming. They went down the street toward the area where the riot supposedly started. They were bombarded with missiles as they sped down the street.

Another car with a Caucasian driver came cruising down the street, much slower than the first one. The people rushed into the street in front of the car, forcing it to stop. The driver jumped out of the car before he could be pulled out. In his hand was a .45-caliber automatic pistol.

He did not fire the gun, but, instead, started running down the street. The crowd pursued and finally caught him, took the gun away and began beating him. His car also was turned over and set afire.

The people around, watching the man being beaten,

kept yelling: "Beat that —— ——. Teach him to keep his ass out of Watts."

A brick came out of nowhere and smashed through the window of a hot dog stand across the street.

Someone yelled: "That's Whitey's, tear it down." A number of people from both sides of the street converged on the stand and began breaking all the windows. Several men climbed into this stand and began passing out Cokes and other beverages to the people outside.

After they had completely depleted the stock of wieners, Cokes and everything else of value that could be carried out, they evacuated the stand and began walking down the street toward a couple of stores. They did not set fire to this stand.

As they passed a small gas station, several people wanted to set it afire. One of the people standing nearby the station told them: "Let it stand. Blood owns it."

A liquor store and grocery store were the next targets. First, the windows were knocked in. Then the people poured into the stores—men, women, children. They rushed back and forth, in and out, carrying as much as they could: groceries, liquor and cigarettes.

Two police cars came roaring down the street and pulled up in front of the store. The people inside came rushing out and ran right by the policemen who made no attempt to stop or apprehend them. The police got out of their cars and set up a temporary blockade in front of the store with their rifles pointed toward the crowd across the street. They remained there for approximately fifteen minutes and left. Before they had gotten a half a block away, the looting resumed.

Next door to the liquor store was a meat market. These windows also were smashed and people in cars drove up and began loading meat into the trunks of their cars. Two young boys (they looked to be nine or ten years old) came running out of the store and across the street carrying a side of beef. The crowd roared its approval and greeted the boys with laughter and cheers.

Several men came walking toward me laden down with liquor. One of them paused in front of me and asked: "What do you drink, brother?" He and the other stopped right there on the street to have a drink. My reply was: "Whiskey."

They opened a bottle of whiskey and handed it to me. I drank a large swallow and handed it back. Twice around and the bottle was empty. We laughed and they continued down the street. Looking back the way I had come, there was another burning car which had been turned over.

A cry went up the street: "One-Oh-Three. Hit the Third!" It referred to 103rd Street, the business center of Watts (a mile to the east and the north). The people piled into cars and headed for 103rd Street. Others followed on foot. As I was getting back into my car to drive to "One-Oh-Three," several men jumped into my car and said: "Let's make it, baby."

After parking the car approximately a half-block off 103rd on a side street, we all piled out and separated when we reached the main street (Central Avenue). A few hundred people had already arrived.*

The iron gratings in front of the stores and businesses were forced first. Then the windows broke. Dozens of people climbed in and out of the stores with armloads of clothing, appliances, guns and liquor.

There were three squad cars that went back and forth on 103rd. The policemen made no attempt to get out of them and stop the looting. However, the people would run out

* This incident appears to have been the first major eruption in Watts, the community which was to be best identified with the August, 1965, riots in Los Angeles. The nomenclature for the uprising often is simplified to "the Watts riots," "the Watts rioting," or "the Watts riot."

Marquette Frye, *right,* whose arrest touched off riot, attends a State Senate fact-finding committee hearing into the case with his brother, Ronald, and mother, Rena, who also were arrested. In rear are attorneys Stanley R. Malone, *left,* and A. L. Wirin.—John Malmin, *Los Angeles Times*

An exuberant, jeering crowd shouts at photographer early Thursday morning, August 12, as police officers attempt to hold them in check. Mob violence soon followed. —Don Cormier, *Los Angeles Times*

Two buildings on Avalon Blvd., the left one at 107th St. and the right one at 108th St., go up in flames in this picture from a helicopter.—George R. Fry, Jr., *Los Angeles Times*

Friday, August 13. A drugstore at 107th St. and Avalon Blvd., put to the torch by rioters, is completely engulfed by flames.—George R. Fry, Jr., *Los Angeles Times*

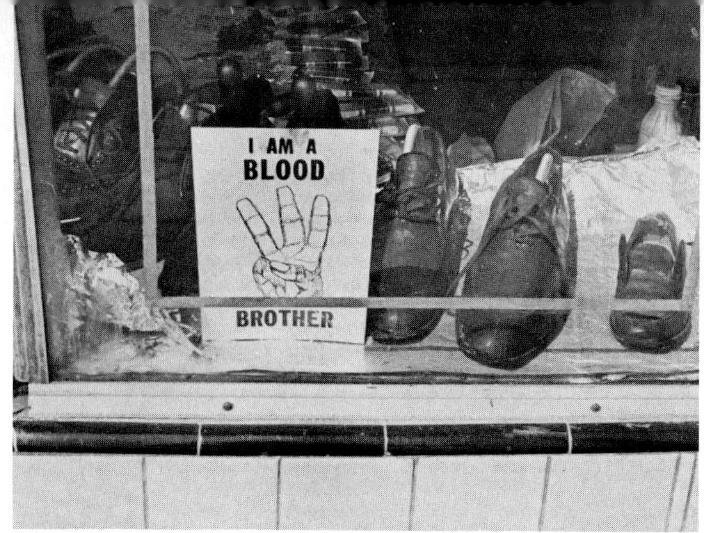

Signs such as this appeared in the windows of stores owned by Negroes to protect them from looters and arsonists. In some cases, they were disregarded. —William S. Murphy, *Los Angeles Times*

103rd St., looking west from Wilmington Ave. A building burns in the background, while looters prowl both sides of the street searching for stores to ransack.—Larry Sharkey, *Los Angeles Times*

Mute testimony to the intensity of the fires that raged uncontrolled in Watts. The metal on this street parking meter melted from the heat.—John Malmin, *Los Angeles Times*

Saturday, August 14—103rd St. in the heart of the Watts business district, showing a row of destroyed store buildings. Order was slowly being restored as troops of the California National Guard arrived on the scene. —Ray Graham, *Los Angeles Times*

As members of the Los Angeles County Fire Department work to extinguish flames in a blazing furniture store, a National Guardsman stands vigilant to protect them. Sniper fire was still prevalent along Imperial Ave. in the Watts area when this picture was taken early Saturday morning, August 14. Many firemen were shot at and injured by hurled bricks and other objects as they fought to control the conflagration.—Ray Graham, *Los Angeles Times*

of the stores just as the police cars approached the business area and hide in the alleys or behind the stores.

As soon as the cars had passed the looting would continue. Walking back and forth on both sides of the street, I paused at a pawnshop and observed several people coming out with portable TVs, record players, sewing machines and clothes.

One man came out with a stereo console on his back.

A youth who looked to be about thirteen or fourteen years old came running out with four or five rifles in his arms.

Suddenly, someone yelled: "The fuzz." A Negro woman came rushing out with two portable TV sets. She was unable to move freely with both sets, and as she was coming out, she asked me: "You want one of these?"

I replied: "I ain't got no place to put it, baby."

She dropped one of the sets on the sidewalk and ran off into the night.

The police cars slowly passed the pawnshop and kept going. I walked back up the street and stopped in front of a large department store.

The metal grating had been pulled up from the street and a large window had been smashed. People were rushing in and out with armloads of clothing. A yell went out that the police were coming back.

Some of the looting crowd ran out and behind the store, but just as many simply crouched behind the counters in the store. One police car swerved around the corner by this store.

A very young Negro boy was picking up a case of cuff links someone had dropped. A policeman roared: "Put that down."

The boy quickly dropped the case and walked away. The squad car pulled around and continued down 103rd. A crowd converged on the store as soon as the police left.

No buildings were set afire. Every burglar alarm on this street was ringing, however. I walked across the street and stood in front of a laundromat. Four of the police cars parked about fifty feet away and the policemen got out and started walking toward me. There were four city policemen and four county (deputy sheriffs) or state (Highway Patrol) policemen. They came up to me and asked, not too courteously: "What the hell are you doing on the street?"

Before I could answer, a heavyset Negro woman who had been in the laundromat answered: "He's washing, —— ——. Is that all right?"

The officer replied: "Well, get off the street and stay off the street."

The woman stood very defiantly in front of them and made no move to go back inside the laundromat. The policemen looked menacingly at her and then at me. They turned and walked back to their cars.

Turning around, I saw approximately fourteen Negro people who had been inside the laundromat now standing in the doorway.

Had the policemen made any attempt to take into custody the Negro woman or me, I feel reasonably sure that there would have been an incident.

The Negro woman who had come to my defense then cautioned me: "Listen, baby, don't put your hands in your pocket like that when they're talkin' to you. They'll burn you in a minute."

I thanked her and walked into the laundromat with her and talked for several minutes. She expressed concern over the people who had been, and were going to be, hurt in this thing. But she felt that maybe this would make them, the police, stop treating the people like dogs because now people would stand up to them.

While walking back to my car, I saw someone throw a brick through the rear window of my car. I ran up to the car and the young men around me asked if it was mine. I said it was.

They told me I should have parked farther down the street and that they didn't know it belonged to a "Blood." They helped me clear away the glass and I drove off.

Driving back up 103rd Street, I watched a car pull up in front of a store. I recognized two of the men as residents of an area far removed from Watts. In fact, they lived in what is regarded as a middle-income Negro area.

Then, I was stopped by a police roadblock as I was leaving the area, told to get out of the car, searched and allowed to proceed.

As I drove through the predominantly Negro-inhabited central section of Los Angeles, I saw only one other incident, a car with white occupants speeding through a barrage of rocks and sticks.

The car was approximately a block and a half in front of me. After it had passed the crowd, the people turned toward my car. I turned my inside lights on, slowed down, honked my horn and yelled out the window: "Burn, baby, burn."

Some of these people echoed my words. And I was allowed to pass by unmolested. From 103rd Street down to Adams Boulevard (approximately 26th Street) there were large numbers of Negroes congregated on porches, in parked cars and just standing along the curb, even at this early hour of the morning.

It was then about 2 A.M. Most of these people had nothing in their hands. But it seemed to me they were just waiting. Three observations remained keen in my mind:

One—The involvement of the community: those not actually throwing stones or looting appeared to be in favor of those who were. Both older men and women, and young boys and girls, were committing overt acts of hostility.

Two—The widespread hatred throughout the rioting

Negro community of Chief Parker; at one period several groups were chanting: "Send Parker out here."

Three—No community leaders were apparent, making attempts to calm or halt the mobs. It is my opinion that this would have been an ineffectual gesture anyway. The mobs throughout the area seemed to be of one mind in striking out against the police, and Caucasians in general.

I did not feel like an outsider at any time during the night. While my involvement was passive, and some of the sights I witnessed appalling and saddening, I felt a strong bond with these people.

12

DICK GREGORY, a most successful Negro comedian, had grown to manhood in a squalid, tenement-lined ghetto of St. Louis. In appearance, it was not at all like that of the Los Angeles riot area, whose pastel-colored homes and apartment buildings and broad palm-graced boulevards projected a misleading façade of cheeriness. Behind the false front, the people in the sun-spangled Los Angeles ghetto lived the same lives of desperation, shared the same deprivations and frustrations that the comic had known as a boy, had put behind him—but had not forgotten.

Gregory, the man, commanded huge sums of money for nightclub and television appearances. His engaging, incisive wit was known across the nation. But the adult Dick Gregory had another side, only slightly less well known.

In recent years, he had advanced to the forefront of the civil rights movement. He had demonstrated in Southern cities at the risk of his life; he had been arrested in the South; he had begged riotous Negroes in Cleveland, Philadelphia and Cambridge, Maryland, to give up their arms, and he had done so in the face of clear personal peril. But it was not until mid-August, 1965, in Los Angeles that he was shot.

When the rioting broke out, Dick Gregory was performing in a night club in Ontario, a bustling city in nearby San Bernardino County. What was going on in Los Angeles streets, he believed, could only set back the cause of the Negro, his cause.

Ironically, however, only two weeks earlier in a television interview in Washington, he had predicted precisely what now was happening. He said that while a Negro breakthrough appeared imminent in the South, the Northern cities of Los Angeles, New York and Chicago, where he lived, would "go up in smoke" before the Negro struggle for equality ended.

After finishing his night-club stint Thursday in Ontario, Gregory traveled to Los Angeles, about 25 miles by way of the San Bernardino Freeway. He met Cleveland Wallace and Don Smith, members of the Congress of Racial Equality, and Robert Hall, the young representative of the Non-Violent Action Committee who had saved the United Press International reporter on Wednesday night. Wallace, Smith and Hall had been circulating among rioters, trying to calm them.

Gregory walked into the 77th Street Police Station just before midnight. He wore the CORE "uniform" that had been popularized in the South—overalls and a three-quarter-length dark denim jacket. He asked police for permission to enter the riot area. He was given that permission, plus a bullhorn with which to talk to rioters. He also had a note from the 77th Street commander, which would identify him to policemen in the trouble zone, who, by now, were fighting a guerrilla war.

A police car transported Gregory and other civil rights workers to a "hot spot" at Imperial Highway and Central Avenue. He got out of the police car with the others and walked along Imperial, a broad thoroughfare lined by what are the tenements of Los Angeles—row after row of low-cost housing projects.

The street was aglow with the blaze of torched commercial buildings. Swarms of Negro apartment dwellers stood behind fences along the sidewalk, jeering at policemen engaged in an often losing struggle to keep them off the street. Most of the apartment residents didn't recognize Gregory, but they learned quickly who he was.

"Don't come here from downtown and lie to us," yelled a young apartment dweller.

"We don't want Martin Luther King down here either," said another. The throng roared its agreement. The catcalls intensified.

But when Gregory spoke through the bullhorn, people listened.

"Get your wives and kids off the street," the comedian implored.

Cleveland Wallace thought this tactic a smart one. "Apparently," Wallace said, "this wasn't what they were expecting to hear. It caught them up short. He was concentrating on the men, trying to call their attention to the danger to the women and children, figuring if the women left, surely the men would. So they listened while he spoke. They were hostile but quiet."

Still, when Gregory put down the bullhorn, the taunts resumed and the crowd stayed where it was.

Gregory tried again: "I didn't come out here to tell you what to do," he said. "What to do and what not to do. I came here to tell you the only thing to do is to get the women and kids off the streets. If anything happens, they'll be the first to get hit."

Again the crowd was quiet as the cool, eloquent entertainer spoke. But when he paused for breath, the jeers and boos resumed. For two hours, at least, Gregory walked for blocks, up and down Imperial, exhorting the throng to return to its apartments.

"Where you playing tonight, baby?" sneered a voice from the crowd.

West Indies-born Assemblyman Mervyn Dymally, a Negro legislator, also was trying his persuasiveness nearby, but with no greater success.

A boy moved out of the crowd onto the street near the assemblyman. "Who you with?" he demanded.

"I'm with you, man," Dymally answered, in an effort to calm the boy.

"Then here's a rock, baby—throw it."

Gregory continued to move along the crowd, as gunfire

crackled and rocks and bottles flew. Police made a renewed effort to push the crowd back from the sidewalk. Gunshots greeted them.

"I'm hit," Gregory shouted, as a bullet bit at his thigh, grazing it. "I've been hit."

Then he, Wallace and Smith dashed into the doorway of a restaurant near the fiery intersection. They took cover there briefly. Then Gregory, crouching down, ran back to the policemen, ducking behind their cars.

"Stay down, stay down," officers urged Gregory.

But, Wallace recalls: "He got up and headed straight for the crowd behind the fences. He said he was afraid someone was going to get killed. He found the man who shot him. The man apologized. I saw Dick Gregory motion toward the crowd with his hands. He told them: 'Go home, get in, before somebody gets killed.' The crowd broke up."

The thirty-two-year-old entertainer recalls walking "out past the barricade to a man standing there with a rifle in his hands. I told him, 'You shot me once. Now get off the street.' "

Don Smith thought it "the greatest display of courage I've ever seen."

Police took the comedian to Central Receiving Hospital where he was treated for a wound in the fleshy part of the thigh. Those who saw him there recall that he was anxious to return to the riot area. He did. By then it was dawn.

He returned the bullhorn to the police station, then, for a time, walked among the milling crowds. He appeared satisfied that some tension had eased, and he decided to leave.

As he did so, he could hear a shout from the throng: "We're going to burn again tonight."

"Five hundred police officers, deputy sheriffs and highway patrolmen used various techniques, including fender-to-fender sweeps by police cars, seeking to disperse the mob," the McCone Commissioners reported in describing Friday's pre-dawn action.

By 4 A.M. Friday, they noted, "the police department felt that the situation was at least for the moment under control." However, mobs still roved the streets, looters still were active and fires still sprang up. Nevertheless, the violent incidents were largely isolated. By 5:09 A.M., police officials felt sufficiently secure to withdraw officers from so-called "perimeter emergency control."

At 6:45 A.M., one of Lieutenant Governor Anderson's staff telephoned the Emergency Control Center at Police Headquarters. He was told by Sergeant John Eberhardt, an intelligence officer on duty, that "the situation was rather well in hand." This information was relayed to the lieutenant governor at his suburban Los Angeles home. Anderson, after instructing his staff member to keep in touch with him, left Los Angeles at 7:30 A.M. for a meeting of the Finance Committee of the University of California's Board of Regents in Berkeley.

But the subsidence was only a surface calm. The sight of wrecked and burned stores, or unguarded merchandise lying in the open, stoked the smoldering fires. Mobs regrouped again on Avalon Boulevard, now a mass of wreckage, and at "One-Oh-Three," 103rd and Central, and 103rd and Compton, in the heart of the Watts business district. They appeared in force along all the major commercial thoroughfares lacing the sprawling Negro neighborhoods, and, for the first time, they spread into the region just south of Watts in the county's Willowbrook area.

The night before, deputy sheriffs had gone to the aid of police on Avalon. Now the mob buildup invaded their own jurisdiction, that of the Sheriff's Firestone Station on Compton Avenue, just south of the county's boundary line with Watts.

The Firestone Station commander, Captain J. M. Arruda, was vacationing in the High Sierra at the time. In his absence, the acting commander was Lieutenant Isom J. Dargan, fifty-one, a suave, handsome veteran of nineteen years with the sheriff's department. Lieutenant Dargan is a Negro.

But in the hectic days that followed, according to Lieutenant Don Torbert, the No. Two in command, "Nobody working out of here even gave it a thought what color of skin our boss had." Nor did Dargan, who is a peace officer, first, last and always.

Dargan's day began with a furious flood of rumors, reports of the looting and violence. The manager of a large discount store telephoned to say that he had learned mobs planned to set fire that night to both his establishment and the Firestone Station. What he had heard was half true. Friday night, arsonists burned the store to the ground.

By noon, even a man as composed as Isom Dargan needed help.

He telephoned Torbert at his home in suburban La Mirada, though he was reluctant to disturb him. Torbert had gone off duty only three hours before—at 9 A.M. Most of the previous night he had spent at 120th Street, holding off a southerly movement by the mob on Avalon. Later he and other sheriff's officers had joined in a northerly "head-to-head" sweep along Avalon to 103rd, clearing rioters from the street.

"Hey. Get the hell down here—the phones are ringing off the hook," Dargan told Torbert, who was to have reported that night to a relatively relaxed beach area duty, as acting captain of the Sheriff's Malibu Station.

Torbert, tall, dark-haired, with movie-idol good looks, drove the 16 miles from his home to the station. A single thought crossed his mind upon his arrival: "This place has come unglued."

This was a better than adequate description of what was happening at that time throughout South Central Los Angeles. By mid-morning, 3,000 persons already had massed at 103rd and Compton in the Watts commercial district. Mobs also were rampaging through other Negro-area business districts. The police radio crackled crazily: "Manchester and Broadway, a mob of one thousand . . . 51st and Avalon, a mob of one thousand . . . Vernon and Central, looting . . . 88th and

Broadway, gun battle . . . 84th and Vermont, juvenile dispensing guns . . . 48th and Avalon, fire, units can't reach. . . ."

The rioting had broken out far to the north of the original flare-ups, within five miles of the Civic Center, the heart of Los Angeles, and in the very shadow of the Memorial Coliseum, one of the great shrines of sports.

Blocks of businesses owned by "Whitey" were afire—drugstores, markets, liquor stores, laundries and pawnshops. Before the mobs burned the latter, these shops provided the rioters with their arsenal. More than 3,000 weapons were stolen from pawnshops and sporting goods stores during the rioting, less than a third of which were later recovered. Sniper fire soon became widespread, but still no deaths were reported.

Police and news helicopters flying above the plundered neighborhoods were fired upon from below. None was hit. At 111th and Avalon, an intersection that was by now a complete shambles, 40 white employees of a business there were besieged, and finally rescued by police.

Arsonists raced through the streets, flinging Molotov cocktails into business after business, chanting, "Burn, baby, burn." Speeding cars crisscrossed rubble-crusted streets. Occupants exchanged finger salutes—gestures which were gang devices for identification purposes. One finger meant a Watts man, two a Compton man, three a Willowbrook man, according to Robert Richardson, who wrote of the manic scene in next day's *Times:* "The rioters were burning their city now, as the insane sometimes mutilate themselves. A great section of Los Angeles was burning, and anyone who didn't return the crazy password was in danger."

"Burn, baby, burn. Burn it down—it's Whitey's," screamed a Negro man as smoke spiraled from a large surplus store on Avalon, where mobs blocked the street as fire trucks sought to reach the blazing building, looted hours earlier.

Rioters stoned the trucks and their crews with bricks, bottles and jagged fragments of concrete. The firemen retreated as their tormentors yelled after them, "That's for Bogalusa." . . . "That's for Selma."

An hour later, two police cars led a dozen fire trucks back into the area from a station six blocks away. Three other stores and an apartment building now were afire there. This time the mob parted, its members standing grimly aside with arms folded as the equipment passed. But it was too late for the firefighters to do more than prevent flames from spreading to scores of nearby Negro homes and Negro-owned stores.

A shoe-shop owner, Rene Jackson, twenty-six, stared across the street at the flaming buildings and said: "I can't understand why they're doing this. Sure they think they're getting revenge against the whites by burning down white-owned buildings. But Negroes work in these places. Negroes don't have jobs as it is."

A handful of newsmen who had been trying to enter the blazing neighborhood followed the fire trucks in as the throngs watched in ugly silence. A dozen police cars arrived and, on this occasion, officers were able to keep firemen from being molested. But the rioters jeered them, and as firemen began controlling the blazes, they became more brazen. "White devils, what are you doing here," they chanted. A teenage girl shrilled: "White man, you started all this the day you brought the first slave to this country." Another called: "You created this monster and it's gonna consume you. White man, you got a tiger by the tail. You can't hold it. You can't let go of it. The next time you see us, we'll be carrying guns. It's too late, Whitey. You had your chance."

Behind a burning drugstore, one of the buildings which had been set on fire, one of the last remaining white residents of the neighborhood played a garden hose on his small frame home, trying to keep it from catching fire. "Thank God, I saved my house," said sixty-five-year-old Frank T. Rose, who, with his wife, had lived on 107th Street for twenty-six years. His face was ribboned with cuts and scratches. He and his wife, Musette, had returned home the night before from a trip in their camper and had run into a nightmare on their front doorstep.

"As we drove in," said Rose, "people by the hundreds ran into our yard. They jumped on my wife and me. They beat and kicked us. Finally, one of our Negro neighbors standing outside our fence spotted us and yelled to the mob: 'Let them go. Not them. Not them.' They left our yard. We didn't sleep all night. It was frightening. We just sat inside our house not knowing what to do. All we could do was sit and listen to the shouting mob outside."

Rose's wife said: "We like our neighbors and hope they like us. But these weren't our neighbors. These were hoodlums who took over. My husband just sat there with his shotgun beside him last night, and I prayed like I never did."

When Rose put down his fire hose and it appeared to firemen close by that they had checked the flames in the burned-out structures on Avalon, a dozen stores a mile away exploded in flames. The firemen raced toward the new conflagration on 103rd Street. Only a few policemen were there when they arrived, but surly crowds permitted the firemen to pass. New blazes erupted along the block, set under their very eyes.

"That's the hate that hate has produced," cried the Negro owner of a service station. "This ain't hurtin' us none. We have nothing to lose. Negroes don't own the buildings. You never did a decent thing in your life for us, white man."

Another onlooker shouted, joyously: "This is a grass roots thing, white devil. Negro leaders can't stop this. The U.S. Army can't stop this. It just has to run its course."

But soon a reserve arm of the U.S. Army—the California National Guard—would be mobilized to try to stop it. And in time—the bloodiest time, still ahead—it would succeed where nothing else could.

13

SHORTLY AFTER 9 A.M. Friday, Chief Parker and Mayor Samuel W. Yorty talked by telephone. They agreed that the darkening developments and police inability to cope with them left no choice: the time had come to call for the Guard. "The situation is completely out of control," other ranking police officers were reporting at the time.

After his telephone conversation with the chief, Mayor Yorty headed toward Los Angeles International Airport to catch a plane for San Francisco. He had spoken in San Diego the day before, and was scheduled to speak Friday noon in the Bay area metropolis. He was widely criticized later for keeping his commitment.

The McCone Commission made no comment on Yorty's decision to go ahead with the talk before the Commonwealth Club in San Francisco, but noted in its report that Yorty had told the governor's commissioners that "by about 10 or so, I have to decide whether I am going to disappoint an audience in San Francisco and maybe make my city look rather ridiculous if the rioting doesn't start again, and the mayor has disappointed that crowd."

The mayor returned to Los Angeles about 3:30 P.M. But while he was gone, Chief Parker was busy at home.

Half an hour after talking with Yorty Friday morning, the police chief met with members of his top echelon and Colonel Quick, the National Guard liaison, who even earlier had advised General Hill in Sacramento of intensifying pressure on police resources. In its report, the McCone Commission reviews subsequent developments:

"At 10 A.M., according to Colonel Quick, Chief Parker said, 'It looks like we are going to have to call the troops. We will need a thousand men.'* Colonel Quick has said that Chief Parker did not specifically ask him to get the National Guard. On the other hand, Chief Parker has stated that he told Colonel Quick that he wanted the National Guard and that Quick indicated he would handle the request.

"In any event, at 10:15 A.M., Colonel Quick informed General Hill by telephone that Chief Parker would probably request one thousand National Guardsmen. General Hill advised Colonel Quick to have Chief Parker call the governor's office in Sacramento. At 10:50 A.M., Parker made the formal request for the National Guard to Winslow Christian, Governor Brown's executive secretary, who was then in Sacramento, and Christian accepted the request. . . . By the time the formal request for the Guard was made, ambulance drivers and firemen refused to go into the riot area without an escort.

"At approximately 11 A.M., Christian reached Lieutenant Governor Anderson by telephone in Berkeley and relayed Chief Parker's request.

"Lieutenant Governor Anderson did not act on the request at that time. We believe that this request from the chief law enforcement officer of the stricken city for the National Guard should have been honored without delay. If the lieutenant governor was in doubt about conditions in Los Angeles, he should, in our view, have confirmed Chief Parker's estimate by telephoning National Guard officers in Los Angeles. Although we are mindful that it was natural and prudent for the lieutenant governor to be cautious in acting in the absence of

* More than ten times that many Guardsmen were called in before the riot was put down.

Governor Brown, we feel that, in this instance, he hesitated when he should have acted."

Anderson was the only individual singled out for criticism by the McCone Commission in the lengthy report it issued following a hundred-day study by the eight-member body into the causes underlying the uprising. Some commissioners, it is understood, also believed Chief Parker deserved an oblique reproach for failing to develop a plan for using the Guardsmen, once they were mobilized.

But in its report, the commission only suggests "that law enforcement agencies and the National Guard should develop contingency plans so that in future situations of emergency, there will be a better method at hand to assure the early commitment of the National Guard and the rapid deployment of troops." The report makes the suggestion after noting that "neither the Los Angeles Police Department nor officers of the Guard deployed any of the troops until shortly after 10 P.M. [Friday]."

Lieutenant Governor Anderson, wanting to consider Parker's request further, returned to Los Angeles by way of Sacramento in a National Guard plane and reached McClellan Air Force Base near the state capital at 1 P.M. As the McCone Commission reports:

> Anderson met with National Guard officers and civilian staff members and received various suggestions, ranging from advice from Guard officers that he commit the Guard immediately to counsel from some civilian staff members that he examine the situation in Los Angeles and meet with Chief Parker before acting.
>
> Although Anderson did not reach a decision to commit the Guard, he agreed with Guard officers that the troops should be assembled in the armories at 5 P.M., which he had been told by General Hill was the earliest hour that it

was feasible to do so. Hill then ordered two thousand men to be at the armories at that hour.

Anderson's plane left Sacramento for Los Angeles at 1:35 P.M. and arrived at 3:25 P.M. At the time Lieutenant Governor Anderson and General Hill were talking in Sacramento, approximately eight hundred and fifty-six Guardsmen in the Third Brigade were in the Long Beach area, twelve miles to the south [of Los Angeles], while en route from San Diego, outfitted with weapons, to summer camp at Camp Roberts.

We feel it reasonable to conclude, especially since this unit was subsequently used in the curfew area, that further escalation of the riots might have been averted if these Guardsmen had been diverted promptly and deployed on station throughout the riot area by early or mid-afternoon Friday.*

Early Friday afternoon, rioters jammed the streets, began systematically to burn two blocks on 103rd Street in Watts, and drove off firemen by sniper fire and throwing missiles. By late afternoon, gang activity began to spread the disturbances as far as fifty to sixty blocks north.

Lieutenant Governor Anderson arrived at Van Nuys Air National Guard Base [in the San Fernando Valley] about twenty miles from downtown Los Angeles at 3:25 P.M. After talking with Hale Champion [state finance director], who urged him to call the Guard, Anderson ordered General Hill to commit the troops. At 4 P.M., he announced this decision to the press. At 5 P.M., in the governor's office downtown, he signed the proclamation, officially calling the Guard. By 6 P.M., one thousand three hundred thirty-six National Guard Troops were assembled in the armories.

* Governor Brown, meanwhile, had received a briefing in Greece on the insurgency. He said he thought the Guard should be mobilized, the possibility of a curfew examined; he said he would return home immediately.

These troops were en route to two staging areas in the riot area by 7 P.M. . . .

In San Francisco, reporters covering the absent Mayor Yorty's Commonwealth Club speech thought he appeared "obviously in an emotional state."

The mayor spoke off the cuff. Despite his indignation over the rioting in his city, he insisted it "did not represent the feelings of the Negro community." He said: "Most Negroes deplore the violence. The sparkplugs have been young people roaming the streets in frustration, without jobs, without education. We are in a situation of anarchy. We have had to call in the Guard because we can't let innocent persons be injured." The mayor went on to blame recent liberal court interpretations, especially U.S. Supreme Court decisions, for the kind of trouble Los Angeles was at that moment experiencing. "How do you expect a young police officer on the spur of the moment to decide these questions? How do you expect him to be an expert constitutional lawyer?" the mayor demanded, in apparent reference to court rulings affecting search and seizure and the arrest, detention and questioning of suspects. "The front line in our defense of our constitutional rights is the policeman. American people had better wake up to that fact."

Back in Los Angeles, an awakening of another kind had occurred. The city suddenly realized that what it had taken for Negro leadership was a sham. The rioters simply wouldn't listen to those men who in the past either had assumed the post of Negro leaders or had been cast in that guise by whites all too eager to believe they were communicating with responsible representatives of Negro Los Angeles.

As Woodrow Coleman, a leader of the Non-Violent Action Committee, said despairingly Friday: "What's happening out there is out of the Negro leaders' hands."

As for Chief Parker, he flatly turned down a request Friday to meet with civil rights spokesmen on the grounds that no effective Negro leaders existed in Los Angeles. He said: "I am not going to sit down in any kind of mediation and meet with any leaders. These rioters do not have any leaders. I see no reason for a big meeting on this thing."

Coleman, speaking at a press conference with Assemblyman Dymally and entertainer Dick Gregory in the Ambassador Hotel, said that, to him, the rioting was "a direct result of the failure of the non-violent movement to make gains. This is the forerunner of organized trouble on a big scale. . . . I saw looters . . . guys who were hungry, saying: 'Maybe this will get us some jobs.' "

Dymally blamed the press for creating a false image of Negro leadership in Los Angeles. Everyone who called a press conference to make a statement, he said, "gets identified as a 'leader' until you have more Negro leaders than you have sand on the beach."

Hall, the young man who had saved a reporter's life Wednesday and been with comedian Gregory early Friday morning, said rioters were expressing the dilemma in their own terms by saying: "We don't want you to come down there with Dick Gregory or Martin Luther King if you're only going to laugh at us. Baby, if you're going to be one of us, here's a bottle—throw it."

But while the speechmaking went on and the formalities of mobilizing the National Guard were being observed, lacerated South Los Angeles was being abraded by new whipsaws of malevolence.

A Negro minister watched a white couple beaten on the street by a gang of young men. He protested: "What you're doing is not right."

One of the boys replied mockingly: "Look, reverend, you preach on Sunday—we're preaching today."

No longer were Negro businessmen who had posted "Blood Brother" signs in their windows immune to sacking. One, Felix Bell, a policeman who owned a dress store, simply hadn't identified his establishment quick enough. It was looted before he could put up a sign.

As youngsters headed toward the store of a white businessman who had a reputation for gouging his Negro customers, a shop about to be stripped and burned, one boy hooted: "Hey, man we ain't got old —— ——'s place yet; let's go get him."

Busses normally operating through the area were rerouted.

"At South Broadway and Santa Barbara Avenue, I saw dozens of people facing walks up to four miles to reach home when the bus driver said he had orders to go no further south," complained one man.*

Not far from the inactive bus-stop stood a market operated by a Japanese-American, well liked by his Negro customers. But it did not escape when a mob, apparently comprised of residents of another neighborhood, descended upon it.

"Fire trucks answered the alarm," said a witness. "But as soon as they came up the street, the mob stoned them and drove them away. Twenty-five or thirty people ran into the market and stripped it of everything—sides of beef, food, anything they could carry. I heard one teenager laugh and say: 'If we could have taken the light bulbs from the ceiling we would have.' "

"Crackers," "Okies," "blue-eyed devils," cried the rioters as police began evacuating many neighborhoods of all whites who had no business there. Those who chose to stay were warned by officers they were doing so at their own risk.

"This is just what the police wanted—always messin' with niggers. We'll show 'em. I'm ready to die if I have to," a Negro youth told two newsmen just before he seized a rock and smashed a passing white man over the head.

A hearse, traveling along a rubble-choked street, was set upon

* The McCone Commission, reporting the inadequacy of bus service through the riot area, especially crosstown, concluded: "This lack of adequate transportation handicaps them [residents] in seeking and holding jobs, attending schools, shopping and in fulfilling other needs . . . it creates a sense of isolation among the residents of south-central Los Angeles."

by a gang of young men. It was bombed with bricks and stones. Its leatherette top was ripped to pieces. The driver, Newlyn Bruton, escaped by gunning the hearse through a bonfire that had been set in the street.

Twice the Watts postoffice was smashed into. Looters swarmed through supermarkets like ants over rotting fruit. "Safeway's open!" one of them shrieked as a mob tore away big sheets of plywood that had been hammered over the plate glass windows of the supermarket. Throngs swept through it, stripping it of groceries by the caseloads.

The looters came in all sizes and ages. A small boy sobbed inconsolably on a pawnshop shelf. Each time he carried out a radio, he complained, someone bigger grabbed it from him. A fifteen-year-old boy walked along a street humming. He had stolen two dresses and was taking them to his girl. A grandmother and three of her grandchildren prowled through a market, grabbing everything they could lay their hands on. A little boy saw looters carrying boxes of produce and canned goods from another grocery; the child was selective—he took only boxes of chewing gum.

At one intersection, a mob methodically plundered an entire row of shops, stripping them of radios, TV sets, air-conditioners, rugs, musical instruments. "Man, I got clothes for days. I'm gonna be clean," gloated a bare-chested youth.

As soon as most stores were bare of merchandise, they were set afire, to calls like: "We're paying Whitey back." A youth, weighted down with loot, shouted: "That don't look like stealing to me. That's just picking up what you need and going."

Once police were able to make wholesale arrests of looters, as they were unable to at this time, such rationalizations, particularly among juveniles, were common. A brief catalogue would include: "Everybody else was taking stuff, so I decided to take some too." . . . "Everyone was taking things, the police weren't stopping them, so I thought it was all right." . . . "The stuff was just lying there in the street." . . . "People were taking things from inside the store and these things just seemed to have been tossed in the alley for anyone who wanted them."

Police could do little to halt the looting. Time after time, officers were seen standing bewildered as mobs swarmed through stores "shopping" for plunder.

Later Lieutenant Isom Dargan explained: "It got to this: the primary function of law enforcement is to protect lives and property—when you have to decide which to give up, property can be replaced. This function concerned us most at this moment. We knew any other action we might take would result in injury or loss of life. We didn't start making arrests [for looting] until late Saturday morning. It was more important to keep getting sufficient manpower in. The only thing to do was to stop wholesale slaughter."

Lieutenant Don Torbert said: "If we had concentrated on looters at this time, Florence Avenue would not be here today."

City police eventually arrested about six times as many adults as juveniles for burglary and theft before the riot ended, a ratio which surprised some persons who stressed misdeeds done by young hoodlum gangs. Of course the percentage of arrests may be misleading. As one officer observed: "If a high percentage of those arrested were adults, it is because nearly everybody joined the looting after a store was broken into—and teenagers run faster."

Three and a half months later, the Los Angeles County Probation department issued a report entitled, "Riot Participant Study, Juvenile Offenders." From this severely clinical document, based on studies of and interviews with about four-fifths of the more than 500 minors processed by Juvenile Court, emerged a clear profile of the typical youngster arrested during the August riot.

He was a seventeen-year-old Nego male with little or no previous contact with police. He was not a gang member and was not involved in a crime of violence, such as rock-throwing or sniping, at the time of his arrest. Rather, he was seized for looting and was within one mile of his home. He had been a Los Angeles County resident for more than five years and was a native of California.*

He came from a broken home, however, and a household from which the father was absent. The total family income was about $300 a month, primarily from welfare or wages earned by the household's head—in most cases the mother.

He usually was arrested with companions, tended to deny responsibility for his wrongdoing and claimed his involvement in the riot was incidental to legitimate business or sight-seeing. He attended school, but was not doing well. He lived in a rented home or apartment and had shown little interest in community-sponsored youth organizations and had had little to do with any church.

The composite was obtained by feeding data to computers at UCLA. The study was supported in part by a United States Public Health Service grant.

About a fourth of the youths surveyed had their cases dismissed. Most of the others were placed on probation; about three dozen were committed.

The report noted that while the typical juvenile arrested during the rioting was still a school student, the composite was misleading in this respect. Of the youngsters surveyed, 14.8 per cent already had dropped out of school.

"This dropout figure," the report said, "is quite high, not only because of the relatively young ages of these boys and girls but also because more than 50 per cent still are in the ninth grade or below. Thus, they still have to pass through the tenth and eleventh grades, which has been found to be the point at which most dropouts occur."

* Not true of the adults arrested, a large percentage of whom came originally from Southern states and at least 75 percent of whom had prior criminal records.

But it is unfair to blame the six days of violence totally on the educationally disadvantaged, adult or juvenile.

A college graduate, trundling cases of vodka from a liquor store, looked jubilantly at a supermarket blazing nearby and said with delight: "Oh, man, ain't that wonderful? Isn't it pretty? Oh, man, just look at that. I'm a fanatic for riots. I just love them. I've participated in two in Detroit, but they were far, far better than this one. In Detroit, blood flowed in the streets."

He spoke too soon. By the time the Los Angeles riot ended, it would be "far, far better" than Detroit's.

In retrospect, it must be regarded as some sort of miracle that no one died during the first two days, or at least up to sundown Friday, the third day. But even miracles must end.

14

RONALD ERNEST LUDLOW was the kind of young man of whom a police chief, sheriff or even an FBI bureau head was likely to say, at one time or another: "Damn, if only I had a few more like him."

At twenty-six, Ronald Ludlow had the physical equipment, the intelligence and the ambition for the job he chose, deputy sheriff. He stood six foot one, weighed 190 pounds and was a natural athlete. At Los Angeles' George Washington High School—where his grades were good and he was a member of the honor club—he had been a varsity basketball player and head cheerleader. "I always thought it fantastic," said his brother Robert, a year Ronald's junior, "that he broke the Washington High 50-yard record running in tennis shoes and using a man's foot as a starting block. The basketball coaches were making the team run sprints, and two of them timed him."

As an adult, Ronald played tennis twice a week. "He was a tremendous player. He always was athletic; it came easy to him. Sports were effortless for him," said Robert.

After leaving high school, Ronald attended Pepperdine, El Camino and Long Beach State Colleges. He met his wife while at El Camino, a junior college. Later he got a degree in history from Long Beach State, where he also took a heavy load of psychology courses.

"Ronnie worked full-time for the County Park system while he was in college," said Robert. "Much of that time he spent at

South Los Angeles playgrounds, devoting his time to Negro youngsters. Ronnie was an extremely liberal person. He used to argue with others over the rights of Negroes," said Robert Ludlow.

Even after joining the sheriff's department, while still attending Long Beach State, Ronald continued to work with underprivileged youngsters. At the same time he was raising a family of his own. "I also always thought it fantastic," said Robert, "that while Ronnie still was going to school, carrying a heavy study load and working on the side, he was able to buy a house, first in Lakewood and then a larger one in Walnut [both Los Angeles suburbs] where the kids would have a chance to roam."

In mid-August, 1965, Ronald Ludlow and his family lived in a five-bedroom, two-story home. He and his wife, Janet Rae, had two small children, Laurie, one and a half, and David Ronald, four and a half, and were expecting another.

"Ronnie was devoted to his family," said Robert. "That's a major reason he chose law enforcement for a career—he thought it would give him time to spend with the kids. But he also wanted to make that his career."

When Robert Ludlow drove to work Friday, August 13, he passed his brother's home and noticed that Ronald's car was not there. Concerned, he called the home of Janet Rae's parents, where she and the children were visiting. Robert learned that Ronald was there, too.

Ronald had gotten off work at 6 A.M. Friday, and because he was understandably weary, he had decided not to drive to his own home in suburban Walnut, but to spend the day sleeping at his in-laws', much closer to the Firestone Sheriff's Station. Ronald had been one of the deputy sheriffs from that station who had helped city police during the second day's uprising. Besides, he had been working long hours before that.

"For two weeks, since the Harvey Aluminum strike broke out, we had been working 12-hour shifts," said Lieutenant Don Torbert, one of Ronald Ludlow's superiors. "There had been violence at the plant and we were two-platooning for more manpower. All told, we used 150 at the command post there at 190th and Normandy." (About six miles south of Thursday's savagery.) It was from this command post that Torbert, Ludlow and other deputies rolled Thursday night when they got a police request for assistance.

Later, Lieutenant Jack Casserely, head of the sheriff's industrial relations staff, met with strike leaders, told them of the problems deputies faced with the rioting and the strike leaders agreed, as Torbert said, "to cooperate fully." After receiving those assurances, deputies were able to turn the command post at 190th and Normandy into a staging area for combating rioters to the north.

When Robert Ludlow first called the home of his brother's in-laws Friday, Ronald was asleep. "The second time, Ronnie was awake," said Robert. "We talked about the riots. He mentioned his concern about what was happening. He said he had been shot at the night before."

Ronald Ludlow, dark-eyed and with crew-cut black hair, had become a deputy sheriff on September 16, 1961. William B. Lauer, twenty-seven, a husky, boyish-looking six-footer with curly, close-cropped blond hair, had joined the department six months later.

Both were the kind of raw material peace-keeping agencies seek to attract. And by mid-August, 1965, both had had remarkably parallel careers, were almost equally esteemed by their superiors and had become friends.

Like Ronald Ludlow, Bill Lauer was an athlete. At California High School in Whittier, just east of Los Angeles, he had played football. Later, to help pay his expenses at Fullerton Junior College, he spent two summers digging ditches. He wanted to be a chemist. But he quit college just before graduating; he married and found he could not attend college and support a wife. He obtained decent jobs, first in an aircraft plant, then in an electrical plant. But he didn't find the work satisfying; he knew he wasn't doing what he wanted to.

"My wife was the one who suggested law enforcement as a career, and I agreed. Because I'd lived all my life in the Whittier area, and the sheriff's patrol worked my neighborhood, I was familiar with it. So I joined the sheriff's office, rather than LAPD," he said.

Ronald Ludlow was transferred to the Firestone Station a few weeks after Bill Lauer had been moved there. They'd met before. "We'd both been custodial officers at the County Jail at the same time," said Lauer. "That means doing mainly jailer's work, like taking prisoners to and from court. We first met at the jail where I spent two and a half years before going to Firestone. I'd never known him before. He was a guy who was easy to like. We didn't socialize outside, but we saw one another at work every day and got to be friendly.

"He was a guy who liked to laugh and joke. We never were partners in the same car. But we were in the sense that we were among the about 20 men who worked cars in the Willowbrook area."

Ronald Ludlow had good reason to be weary when he and his partner, Robert H. Cartwright, finally left Sheriff's Car 15 at the Firestone Station at 6 A.M. Friday.

The night had been the longest and most anxious he had spent as a deputy sheriff. His log showed it, even though he and many other deputies during the previous 12 hours often had been so busy they were unable to jot down notes on their complete activities.

But his worksheet showed that shortly after reporting for duty at 6 P.M. Thursday, he had halted a gun battle between two men over a girl. Five minutes later, at 6:37 P.M., he investigated "cold plates on a hot car" (a new set of license plates being switched to a car reported stolen).

Then:

7:15—felonious assault on 120th.

7:48—juveniles fighting at Carver Park, 1400 East 118th. Gone before arrival.

8:29—Rosecrans Avenue, husband-wife beef.

9:13—two kids, seven and nine missing, East 126th. They wandered home. Advised parents to supervise more closely.

At 9:45 P.M., the worksheet noted:

Imperial and Success. Shots fired, woman assaulted. (That was the incident in which the young Frenchwoman driving the Volkswagen was beaten. Lauer also responded. He remembers: "Her car had been turned over. Ludlow and I and other deputies helped pull her out. She'd stopped when her windshield had been broken. People charged into the street and beat the hell out of her. We had to force our way into the crowd under a shower of bricks and bottles to get to her." That was the first rioting action in which Ludlow and Lauer were involved.)

Ludlow's worksheet from then on deals strictly with incidents attendant to the riot:

11:07—Lax Pharmacy, 2265 El Segundo. Silent alarm. Looters.

11:25—Lynwood (a surburban city just east and south of the Los Angeles neighborhood of Watts) P.D. (Police Department) unit pinned down at Mona and Imperial. (Ludlow and other deputies went to the rescue of the Lynwood officers, apparently trapped by sniper fire at the intersection.

11:44—Silent alarm, Willowbrook Feed and Grain Company, 12907 South Willowbrook, windows smashed.

12:02 A.M. (Friday)—Looters in liquor store, Imperial and Compton Avenue.

1:39—Ambulance crew at Alameda and Imperial. Gunshot victim. Escort ambulance to Bon Aire Hospital, 120 and Broadway (where Ray Fahrenkopf, the television soundman, had been given emergency treatment three hours earlier).

3:22—136th and McKinley. Traffic accident, originally reported as a fire.

4:21—Riot spilling over Watts. Fire in lumber yard at Imperial and Parmalee. Four units. Actually a grass, not lumber, fire. Purposely set.

Ronald Ludlow left duty at 6 A.M. When he returned Friday night at 6 P.M., he and Deputy Cartwright got almost immediately in Car 15. He made only two entries on his worksheet after that:

6:13 P.M.—Looter call at Enterprise Park, 13055 Clovis. Supposedly breaking into park office. No one there when crew arrives.

7:59—County Fire Department requests crowd control from snipers at 1744 East Imperial.

Bill Lauer, in a brief pause just before dusk, kidded his friend about keeping up with his "paperwork." Ludlow laughed aloud, then quipped: "This is going to be the shortest log I ever wrote. I won't have to do much writing because the way it's going tonight, the log's going to be a very short one."

The story becomes Deputy Bill Lauer's:

"We began the evening by traveling in a southerly direction from the station, assisting Deputies Ludlow and Cartwright, rolling on rioter calls. We got to Imperial and began trying to shut off traffic to and from the project areas. The people living there were causing much of the trouble."

After Lauer's joking with Ludlow about his paperwork, the Lauer and Ludlow teams separated.

"Not long after, we got a call for any unit that could get there to assist Car 15 at Mona and Imperial. 'Looters in a liquor store,' the radio said.

"Apparently Ludlow and Cartwright had observed some looters in a liquor store that later was burned. When I got there, the looters were carrying off cases of liquor. We chased them a short distance and they ran into one of the housing projects.

"We couldn't drive into it. It was too dangerous then for us to go in on foot. The mobs on Imperial made it impossible at that time to drive further along the street.

"Scared? Damn right, I was scared.

"We went back to Mona and Imperial, then on to a command post. The looters were gone now. Ludlow and his partner went the other way, west toward Wilmington Avenue. That's when they apparently saw the Clock Liquor Store on fire."

The Clock Liquor Store on the southeast corner was the hub of a nondescript business district at Imperial Highway and Wilmington Avenue. Directly across Wilmington was a Mobil Oil Station and south of it, a grocery and another liquor store, S & M Liquors. Above the latter, a sign identified the second floor of the building as Gibson's Hotel. Most of the buildings close to the intersection were two-story structures.

South of Clock Liquor was a short-order restaurant known to residents of the neighborhood as "the hot spot." It never was hotter than it was that Friday night, with flames from the burning Clock Liquor Store whipping the early night air.

"It looked like the inside of an eggshell, an eggshell with its walls all pink," thought Deputy Sheriff Robert O'Sullivan as he responded to the same summons which took Lauer and Ludlow to the intersection. A block away a Safeway market also was aflame.

The time was 9 P.M.

"As soon as we arrived, there was shooting at us from several directions," Lauer said. "Some seemed to be coming from a small frame building. It sounded like a small caliber hand gun. Several cars, which had driven up near the fire, then left. Fires were illuminating the whole area. Then three men drove up in a 1956 Ford. They were westbound. They stopped on Imperial, oh maybe about 50 feet east of the intersection.

" 'Get out,' several deputies ordered. The three men just sat there.

"I left the cover of the radio car and went toward their car with a twelve-gauge shotgun. As I approached I could hear them talking."

Also walking toward the stopped automobile, just to the left and the rear of his friend Lauer, was Deputy Ronald Ludlow, moving in to assist Lauer.

"As I got alongside the car, the driver reached out and grabbed my shotgun. I was startled. But I was determined nobody was going to take that shotgun—it was a deadly weapon. As I yanked back, the gun went off. I looked back and saw that Deputy Ludlow had fallen.

"I walked over to him and asked: 'Are you hurt?' Then I saw the wound.

" 'Yeah, I'm hurt bad,' he said. Then he fell unconscious right away.

"The firemen never did arrive there after we called them. And an ambulance couldn't roll into the area because of sniper fire.

"The other deputies put Ludlow in a radio car. I guess I was just in a daze. They tried to make me sit down. I kept walking back to try to help Ludlow. One officer was trying mouth-to-mouth resuscitation. It was my duty to try to work. But they wouldn't let me get back in the car. I worked in the station the rest of the night. But I was back in the car Saturday and Sunday."

When Deputy O'Sullivan reached the intersection, he saw Lauer leaning against a patrol car. Recalls O'Sullivan: "He was emotionally upset—I couldn't say whether he was crying or not. Other deputies were holding the suspects at 'leaning rest.' "

"What happened?" O'Sullivan asked Lauer.

"Ludlow's been shot," Lauer replied.

"Did they do it?" O'Sullivan inquired, pointing at the suspects.

"I'm all confused," Lauer stammered.

Then O'Sullivan became aware of the circumstances and asked Lauer which of the three men had tried to wrest the shotgun away. "Tell me which one—while it's fresh in your mind," O'Sullivan urged.

Lauer pointed to a young man later identified as Phillip Bentley Brooks, twenty-two, and said: "That's him. I'm positive."

Brooks, the driver of the car, Joseph Lavine, twenty-three, who had been beside him in the front seat, and Harold G. Potts, twenty-two, a rear-seat passenger, were handcuffed as Ludlow lay nearby dying.

Two and a half miles to the north, Lieutenant Don Torbert heard a call over his radio that one of his men had been shot at Imperial and Wilmington. He had gone into the field about an hour earlier, leading a seven-car caravan of 27 men. "We were hitting and moving people," Torbert said. The sweeps by officers moving in strength were proving effective and later, when sufficient manpower was mustered, the technique would be employed by all agencies throughout the riot area, often with four officers to a car.

When Torbert heard the call about Ludlow, he led his caravan southward, sirens screaming. "I knew no ambulance would roll—and none did," he said. "But it would have made no difference."

The shotgun blast, at close range, had ripped into Ronald Ludlow's lower abdomen, fatally wounding him. But it was almost a half hour before he could be transported to a hospital, where he was pronounced dead. He was taken to the hospital in one of the squad cars, after Torbert's procession arrived and officers finally succeeded in breaking out from the sniper fire.

"I saw all kinds of people all over the place when we moved in there," said the lieutenant. "I told my men to wind their sirens wide open. This makes a lot of noise. I imagine it must have sounded to them like an army. People began to take off. They really moved in all directions."

To O'Sullivan, pinned down with the other deputies behind their cars by renewed sniper fire, the arriving caravan "looked like a line of boats coming out of a heavy fog. It made an impressive sight and sound, with the red lights flashing and the sirens screaming. The people in the neighborhood did scoot." Lieutenant Torbert said: 'Let's get those guys [the three suspects] in a car and get the hell out of here.' We left the suspects' car standing in the middle of the street—and that's what we did: get the hell out of there.

"We formed a line, moving north and driving back the people who had already run. We put Ludlow in the first car and it took him to the hospital. As we left, I could see where sniper bullets had dug holes in the pavement. As we pulled away, we got word that Florence Avenue had been hit—so back we went."

Two weeks after Ronald Ludlow's death, Brooks, Lavine and Potts were indicted for murder and held without bail. Three months later an appeals court threw out the cases against Lavine and Potts. Brooks also appealed.

On September 25, Janet Rae Ludlow gave birth to an eight-pound, one-ounce baby girl. She named the infant Janine.

Upon its return to Florence Avenue, Lieutenant Don Torbert's quick-striking team found looters running wild. "They were racing right through fire to get at the shelves. In one shoestore window, I saw a young mother of about twenty-five with her three small children. She was methodically fitting each one for shoes."

About that time a mile away, a sniper raised his gun from amid a throng of Negroes and fired at a squad of police cars. Officers returned the fire. A bystander named George Adams fell. The sniper fled.

15

UNTIL GEORGE ADAMS left to join the army in 1939 when he was nineteen, he had never been far from the Louisiana cotton farm near Shreveport where he was brought up by an aunt and uncle, Willie and George Bell. He was the fifth of his parents' eight children. The father was a poor cotton farmer and the Bells had no children, so it was convenient for George to live with them and help on their little farm.

George spent four and a half years in the army. He traveled a lot and came to realize there was more to the world than Northern Louisiana and more to do in it than cotton-farm. When he was stationed in Arizona in 1942, he visited California for the first time, traveling to Los Angeles where his sister, Ethel Hutson, worked as a cook.

George always liked a good joke. When he walked in on her, he caught Mrs. Hutson by surprise. "Watch out now, sister—stick 'em up." When Mrs. Hutson turned, there stood George, a huge grin on his handsome face.

Though she lived with her parents and George lived with the Bells, Mrs. Hutson and he were extremely close as children. She was overjoyed to see him and gave him a big party to which she invited many of her friends. The guests arrived bearing gifts for George. She urged him then to "come to California when you get out of the army." She said, "You can make good money out here. You're a good cook, too."

George, who had received a sixth-grade education, spent most of his military career as a cook. Once he was promoted to sergeant, but later was "busted." When he left the army as a private first class, he did, as his sister had suggested, "come to California." It looked good to him.

But like many another Southern Negro who moved to the West Coast in the post-World War II years, Los Angeles proved less than the paradise it had seemed from a distance. George found work first as a janitor, then as a cook. But steady jobs were hard to come by.

By mid-August, 1965, he was reduced mainly to picking up odd appliance repair jobs. Two of his friends, Richard Crowder, a housepainter, and Eddie Taylor, a carpenter, threw him what work they could.

"We both helped George as much as we could," said Crowder. "I tried to show him how to paint. George drank too much, but he always acted like he wanted to learn. Eddie had him working too. George liked to make jokes with us, play a few cards. But he was always broke."

What George Adams really would have liked, said Mrs. Hutson, "would have been to organize a little choir with his kids and maybe sing for churches. He had a beautiful voice. But he said he could never get the money together for the kind of clothes he and the kids would need."

At forty-five, tall, good-looking George Adams was literally surrounded by children, 15 in all, including two sets of twins. In 1947 he married a young woman of nineteen, whose previous husband had been killed in a motorcycling accident, leaving her with four small children.

George's young wife, too, had arrived in California from a small Louisiana farm. George fathered eight girls and three boys. The last born was Darlene, who arrived February 12, 1963. By mid-August of 1965 her parents were receiving welfare aid and living in a crowded frame house for which they paid $95 a month rent. Darlene's oldest sister and brother were school dropouts.

During the day of Friday the 13th, George had gone with his friends Richard Crowder, twenty-eight, and Eddie Taylor, fort, eight, to the Watts business district to "do a little sight-seeing

"Me and Eddie, with a girl Eddie knew who lived next doc to George, picked up him about four to go to Watts to see wha was going on," said Crowder, a sharp-eyed, self-confident littl man, whom his friends often called "Shorty" because of hi slight stature and boyish appearance.

Crowder was industrious and proud of the painting business he had built up. Married once, but divorced, he had arrived in Los Angeles about six years earlier from St. Louis and was living with his parents. In Independence, Missouri, where he was born he used to mow Harry Truman's lawn as a child.

"I was a little bitty thing then," he said. "I used to work with my uncle when he was going to high school. I dropped out of school in the eleventh grade myself to get married. But I always worked hard—not like some of these kids I hire to help me now. I'll give 'em a job and they'll only work a day or two, then quit. That's the trouble with the colored race out here in California—they want something for nothing."

George Adams, Eddie Taylor and Richard Crowder spent about an hour and a half in the Watts business district. "We just were looking at the burned-out buildings. Eddie and George each had a bottle up there and they each took a drink," said Crowder. "Me—I don't drink. On the way back we got stopped at a roadblock, but the police, they let us through. Eddie, who was drivin', said to George: 'I'm going to take you home now.'

"George, he said: 'No, Eddie. If I had a car, I'd take you anywhere you wanted to go.' But we went by George's house anyway."

George talked with his wife, then called his sister and told her what he had seen in Watts. He said, "Sister, I'm going to stay out of this thing."

She cautioned him: "Don't go back down there."

He said he would not, hung up the telephone and began playing with his children.

"He was teasing me and the kids. He kept putting on and taking off a pair of sunglasses one of the kids had," remembers Mrs. Adams, a portly woman with a pretty face. "Then his friends come back and he said he would go up to a barbecue stand he liked and bring me back some dinner. Beef or shrimp or something like that. He stood in the doorway and winked at me."

Crowder and Taylor were waiting outside in Taylor's 1950 Pontiac. "We headed for that barbecue at 75th and Main," said Crowder. "But when we got to 82nd and Main, we couldn't go no further because of a big crowd there. So we parked the car. We must have been there for about 20 minutes, standing around and talking. We each kept saying what a shame it was what was going on. We'd been saying that all day long. It was dark by then, but there was a street light illuminating the crowd."

Approaching the intersection at that time, 9:48 P.M., were two carloads of officers, city policemen, who had participated in the events following the Frye arrests. In one vehicle were Officer Gary C. Bebee and his partner, Sergeant Richard W. Rankin, driver of the police car that had been the first to be stoned on Wednesday night. In another were Joseph F. Scanlon, John L. Heene and William L. Davis, the driver. Also in the second car were three looters the officers had just arrested a block to the west.

"As we approached the intersection of 82nd and Main," said Scanlon, "we rounded the corner and the people were shouting and threw some missiles at us. Some rocks and bottles. All of a sudden, my partner Davis yelled: 'Look out. They are shooting.' "

The policemen saw a husky man of about thirty-five wearing "a wide-brim Panama hat" with a gun in his hand. Said Scanlon: "He was pointing a gun at our car and fired. I yelled for the prisoners in back to duck, and they all tried to get on the floor. Then my attention was drawn to the left, and there was a man on that side of the street in a T-shirt. He also was pointing a gun at our vehicle. At this time, I fired twice at him. Both shooters had hand guns."

Said Heene: "I saw flashes from a gun. The prisoners in back were terrified and immediately began to fight for cover."

The police car carrying the three looters was struck once by a bullet, but no one was hurt. The driver plunged the accelerator to the floor, and the car shot away from the scene. Sergeant Rankin stopped his car and fired once at the man in the Panama hat, who darted away.

Bebee got out. As he did so, a bullet whanged against the grill of a nearby pickup truck. Bebee, armed with a shotgun, ducked behind a fender of the truck as a man ran east along an 82nd Street sidewalk. Said Bebee: "I dropped to one knee and fired one shot from the shotgun just as he ran past the right front fender of a stake truck parked about 20 feet to the rear of the pickup."

Sergeant Rankin ordered Bebee to jump back into the police car, "due," he reported later, "to the gathering of a hostile crowd" and "fearing for our welfare."

Before the gunfire, Richard Crowder had seen no man in a Panama hat. But he did hear "a voice" bellow at policemen: "You better put that thing away before it is taken away from you." It was his belief that someone in the crowd was threatening to rush the police and try to seize their weapons. Then he saw "a flash of gunfire," and heard in quick succession what sounded to him "like ten or fifteen shots all at once.

"I think the cops just opened fire in the crowd. I saw only two cops shooting. The man with the gun had fired only once," said Crowder, who recalls he, Eddie Taylor and George Adams had begun to walk toward Taylor's automobile after being told by an officer: "Go home. Get the women and kids off the street."

After "bullets began flying around," said Crowder, "I got behind Eddie's car, holding my hands out to show the cops I didn't have anything. I didn't know George was hit. Then I heard him say to Eddie: 'Eddie, I'm hit.' Eddie asked a cop to help. 'Go on. Leave him there,' the cop said. Eddie said: 'No—he's a friend.'

"So the cop let us put George in the back seat and the cop told us which hospital to take George to. I can't remember the name. But it's a little one. On Broadway, I think."

On the way to the hospital, said Crowder, Taylor's car was halted by police at two different roadblocks. At one, he claimed, they were delayed 20 minutes.

"After the first roadblock," he said, "I just knew George was dead. He'd been shot in the chest. When we'd put George in the car, we'd propped him upright in the back seat. Before we hit the first roadblock, I heard him say: 'I'm cold.' I told Eddie: 'Hurry up.'

"As we drove, I asked: 'George, are you all right?' He just grunted. That's the last sound he made. Then his face fell in his lap."

When George Adams did not return home Friday night, his wife was less concerned than might be thought. One of their sons was visiting relatives in Long Beach. She thought George might have taken a bus there and planned to return with the boy on Saturday.

Saturday morning, as she was watching riot scenes and reports on television, she heard an announcer, in reading off the list of known dead from the previous night, say, "George Adams, forty-five, shot at . . ."

"That's all I heard," Mrs. Adams recalls. "I just went to pieces. I was hoping it was another George Adams. But deep down I knew. A little bit later, I called the kids and said: 'Your daddy's dead.' "

A few weeks later, George Adams' aged mother, Mrs. Estelle Taylor, who lives with Mrs. Hutson, received an envelope from the nation's capital. Inside she found a scroll, the type sent to relatives of deceased ex-servicemen. It bore President Lyndon B. Johnson's signature and the inscription: "The United States honors the memory of George Adams."

"That's all we've got left of darling Brother," said Mrs. Hutson.

16

THE ROARING BLAZE consuming a supermarket at 120th and Central Avenue was an unlikely place to find Engine Company 61. Its normal station was a prosperous neighborhood near Beverly Hills. Thus when thirty-one-year-old firefighter Warren L. Tilson had battled a blaze in the past, it often was at a smartly maintained home, certainly not a market in the heart of Los Angeles' Negro ghetto. But like other fire companies from throughout the city, even from as far away as the San Fernando Valley, the 61st had been thrown into the riot area.

Tilson, a native of Matador, Texas, and a Korean War veteran, rode to the Shoprite Food Market blaze accompanied by a police escort, armed with shotguns. The police soon left the flaming scene as they received other urgent calls for escort duty and for help.

Only the blazing shell of the market still stood when Tilson and fellow members of Engine Company 61 arrived. All he and others could do was seek to contain the flames. But once police departed, leaving them unprotected, even this was impossible.

Jeering Negroes bombarded the firemen with stones and bottles. Some whipped large sections of broken glass through the air like boomerangs, lethal missiles that could have sliced off a man's head if aimed more accurately.

Fire Captain J. Slade Delaney saw the futility of continuing the battle under such peril. Negro motorists raced their cars back and forth over the fire hoses, a newly discovered form of harassment. Delaney ordered his men to drop their lines. At that, the mob watching from across the street chanted: "You're not going to get out of here, white boy."

It was then, recalls Delaney, that "I heard a wall crack. I knew the whole wall was coming down. I ran diagonally to the left with my engineer. He was hit on the leg, but knocked free of the collapsing wall. But two other of my men weren't so lucky. Firemen Robert Laxague and Warren Tilson disappeared under 200 tons of concrete and steel, buried in the debris.

"Then a strange thing happened. Those same Negroes who had been taunting us, throwing objects at us—those same people who had been threatening us, suddenly were horror-stricken. They came rushing across the street and began tearing with their hands at concrete and steel, trying to free the two men beneath it.

"Two firemen began burrowing through the debris with their bare hands. They made a tunnel to where Laxague was. We could hear his cries. They got to Laxague. He was pinned and couldn't move. But he was only bruised."

But when the two burrowing firemen, one of whom was Frank Harrison, a Negro, reached Tilson, just three feet from where they had found Laxague, the circumstances were different. Dark-haired Warren Tilson, whose wife Carole gave birth to a baby boy, Warren, Jr., a month and a half later, was dead.

"A steel beam had crushed his head and chest," said Captain Delaney. "It took a crane to free the body.

"At that, I guess, we were fortunate. If that wall had gone four minutes sooner, 20 men would have been trapped beneath it." Then Delaney added: "By the time we'd gotten Laxague out, another mob had set a new fire right up the street."

Tales of heroism by firemen and their police, Highway Patrol and sheriff's escorts are legion. Many such acts went unnoticed at the time and the deeds, in many cases, never came to public attention.

Some men were too modest to talk of them. Some who talked of them did so grudgingly. As they reminisced, they discovered that what they did, saw and heard became almost too florid, wicked, absurd or gallant to actually believe any more.

But the memories of the firemen and police officers who were there are crowded ones. Some of the developments, because they were so grotesque, even inspired laughter later. There was no time to smile during the riot.

James Lawson, thirty-five, a fireman for seven years, found himself a long way from home on the night of Friday, August 13. Lawson, three teammates and an acting captain had rolled from their home station in Canoga Park in the vast San Fernando Valley to Watts, 23 miles away, at 9:30. Quickly the firemen unloosed the hose on the new pumper truck to work on a blazing store. Lawson stood atop the truck, priming the pumping mechanism.

From nowhere, a Negro man ran to the pumper, shoved a pistol at Lawson and pulled the trigger.

"I had my back to him," said Lawson. "But I heard the report. And what must have been a piece of wadding hit my coat. I'm sure the man must have had a blank cartridge in that gun. But if there'd been a policeman there, he'd have shot him dead for sure. After the man fired, he gave a crazy laugh and ran across the street into a crowd."

Later during the night, the pumper received some police protection. But, more often than not, the firemen were on their own.

"Let me tell you," said Lawson, "we were scared to death. When we'd go to pick up our hose lines, those people would dance around us. They'd taunt us by pointing at flames shooting up from an entirely different building. Then they would shout: 'Man, look what we got going down the street.' Those people acted like they'd never had so much fun in their lives. The whole thing was like a carnival to them."

At the scene of a liquor store blaze, Lawson and his fellow firefighters realized a flat above still was occupied. "So," he said, "we broke into it to try to save the occupants. The place was so smoke-filled, we had to wear masks. There were three Negroes inside, two men and a woman. They were all drunk and giggling. The woman was stark naked. Suddenly, however, it must have dawned on the men they were in danger of suffocating. They bolted for the door. But the woman wouldn't leave. We had a heck of a time with her. She refused to leave until she found her clothing."

Meanwhile, another fire crew was set upon by a flock of Negroes of all ages. To the relief of the firefighters, it was not an attack. The people beseeched the firemen to save a house which had caught fire when embers skipped to it from a torched commercial building. Firemen agreed, after first warning they would pull up their hoses at the least hint of harassment.

The firemen were given no trouble. They extinguished the blaze. Then they entered the dwelling to see if any mopping up remained. The firemen could scarcely get inside, so crammed was the home with merchandise from looted stores.

Nearby, another fireman saw a Negro man absconding from a pawnshop, carrying a saxophone. A policeman grabbed him.

"This is my horn," the looter protested.

"All right, play a tune," the officer said.

The man tried, but he couldn't blow a note.

Pilots and passengers passing over the riot area in planes landing and taking off from Los Angeles International Airport to the west that Friday night saw what looked like great blocks of the city in flames. Next day, large portions of neighborhoods would be obscured from the air by towering plumes of smoke. *Herald-Examiner* reporter James P. Bennett, after flying over South Los Angeles in a helicopter, made this observation about the firefighters' experiences: "It could easily be seen from the 'copters that firemen were being hampered in their attempts to quell blazes. As soon as engines would pull up, large groups of rioters would swoop in, throwing rocks at the firemen. In some instances, police would put up a cordon of protection around the firemen.

"From the air, the whole scene looked like a crazy patchwork of hatred and devastation. Looters were scurrying in and out of shops, carrying their booty to cars past beleaguered firemen fighting fires in other shops. As soon as one blaze would be put out, a new one would spring up in the next shop, obviously set by looters or the frenzied mob. At least three firemen were observed from the air to go down under a barrage of rocks and bricks. At one point, firemen turned their hoses on a charging mob.

"Flames could be seen leaping from rooftops of stores, with black clouds of smoke billowing skyward. At least three cars could be seen overturned by jeering and cheering groups, and then were set afire. Torches were lit from these fires and tossed through broken windows of stores along 103rd Street.

"Firemen were forced to abandon their efforts to put out the flames, in some cases, due to the rioters. They would retreat down the street until the roving mobs moved on, then come back to take up hoses they had left behind. In one case, several firemen tried to run to safety, leaving their equipment behind. Looters moved in and removed hoses from the trucks and did a snake dance with them as they chanted and raved down the streets."

Bennett reported that photographer Lou Mack, riding in the helicopter with him, shouted: "It looks like all the fires of hell down there." Observed Bennett: "And it did."

What Bennett saw from the air, Captain J. Slade Delaney of Engine Company 61 was continuing to experience on the ground, and he remembers: "We'd knock down one blaze, then just up the street another building would go up with a roar.

Some say that this was the work of about 200 rioters—but there were 200,000 people cheering them on."

No one was cheering when Fireman Gene T. Smart, forty-two, of Engine Company Four arrived in front of a flaming shop at 903 East Jefferson Boulevard, just a few blocks from Exposition Park, site of the Memorial Coliseum, the modernistic Sports Arena and the Los Angeles County Museums. A crowd of youths watched the dancing flames, wearing what Smart considered the "uniform" of many of the boldest young male looters and arsonists—"black pants and dark turtle-neck sweaters." It was 11:30 Friday night.

As Smart unwound hose, one of his partners, Harold Myers, Jr., thirty-seven, cried to him: "Watch out, Smart. He's got a gun."

Gene Smart heard a shotgun roar. He saw Myers sprawl to the pavement, wounded in the back, and felt buckshot tear into his own back and wrist. He turned angrily to face the young rioters and barked: "I'm a fireman. I get paid to fight fires. And I'll keep fighting them, just as long as you keep setting them."

Nervy Gene Smart did just that. Though wounded, he stood alongside other firefighters trying to control the blaze as police, having heard the gunfire, raced in and dispersed the rioters. An hour afterwards, when the officers left, so did Gene Smart, to seek hospital treatment.

But as he pulled his truck away, a new crack of gunfire sounded. Bullets splattered against the truck and splintered the windshield. Of the crew of five in Gene Smart's truck, only two were unwounded at the end of their tour of duty.

Another fireman compared getting to a burning store "like riding through a shooting gallery." He saw boys standing along one street with boxloads of bottles. Before pitching the missiles at passing firemen, the youths carefully broke each bottle.

One fire truck careened wildly down another street after a mob leveled a volley of at least 20 stones at the driver, knocking him unconscious. Up the same street, the crew of the truck saw two young men in Bermuda shorts and sandals dance past six stores and throw Molotov cocktails into each.

An unharmed gasoline station did "a fire sale business," selling bottle-and-jar-carrying boys the fuel for Molotov cocktails.

One fireman found a way of holding off rioters while his co-workers fought blazes without police protection. He took what firemen called a "Life Gun" from his truck. It resembles a sawed-off shotgun, but is a device used to fire an arrow-carrying rope used in rescue work. "I thought maybe they'd think it was a riot gun. And they did," said Fireman Bill Plotkin, who held one mob at bay for two hours with this ruse.

Negro reporter Robert Richardson of the *Times* roamed the riot area freely Friday night, after he had mastered a safety technique. He reported in the *Times:* "I had to do all my telephoning from street-corner gas stations. You have no idea how naked you feel in an exposed, lighted telephone booth. But I was hep by that time.

"Whenever a group of Negroes approached to look me over, I knew what to do. You open the door, stick your head out and shout: 'Burn, baby, burn.' "

Times photographer Cal Montney, arriving late Friday night at 43rd Street and Broadway with reporter Eric Malnic, saw what seemed to him "a block of buildings on fire along Broadway" and he thought the firemen's task hopeless. "The street was lit up like daylight and hot—glass would shatter and fly out into the street as plate glass windows burst from the heat. We saw only one fire truck and two policemen, doing the best they could. I got out by the fire truck and took some pictures as the officers protected us," Montney said.

Malnic remembers an eerie aspect of the fiery scene: "The street was filled with dismembered mannequins that lent an increased realism to the warlike scene. Every two blocks or so, groups of from 20 to 200 Negroes were looting systematically. Every time they saw us, they'd shout: 'Kill Whitey.' And the fun would start."

Adds Montney: "We wheeled our car around in the middle of the street and headed north along Broadway. There still were a lot of Negroes' cars on the street. And at 43rd, the whole intersection was filled with Negroes. They had seen us come in and now they were going to try to stop us. They ran out in front of the car, trying to make us stop."

Said Malnic later: "We hit no one—but we sped out of there."

Later the two-man *Times* crew returned to a nearby part of the riot area, in the belief that the first contingent of National Guardsmen had arrived there and were preparing to sweep through the neighborhood. But the Guardsmen were not there.

Montney stopped for a traffic light. "We were caught in a crowd of cars, all of them filled with Negro youths," he recalls. "We were scared. All of a sudden, I heard a crash. I looked across the street and saw a liquor store window cracked open. Within seconds the store was filled with people. A car pulled up in front of the store. A man jumped out, followed by a little boy who couldn't have been more than seven. The man ran to the back of the car and opened the trunk. They ran into the store through the broken window and were back within seconds, their arms filled with bottles. The little boy staggered under his load. They put the bottles in the trunk, slammed it and drove off.

"The signal changed to green. The whole episode had taken place just in the time it took the light to change from red to green."

Soon afterward the liquor store went up in flames, once the looters had satisfied their greed.

"We weren't trying to put these fires out. We simply were trying to knock them down," said Captain J. Slade Delaney.

"Our main concern was that the flames would get out of control. In which case, they could have swept westward all the way to the ocean. Thousands of homes could have been destroyed. Who knows how many might have lost their lives if this had happened? And it could have."

Delaney and other firemen had learned from harsh experience what a "firestorm" is. Even on a still night, when not even the faintest breeze ripples the air—nights such as these mid-August ones were—the possibility of a firestorm is to be dreaded.

Flames unite, creating a kind of fierce velocity of their own. Once out of control, a firestorm moves with hurricane force, consuming every structure and living thing in its path.

"We were prepared for such an eventuality," Delaney said. "If it happened, we would have had to dynamite a path to keep the flames from crossing the city. That barrier conceivably would have been a mile-or-more strip along Crenshaw Boulevard."

Crenshaw runs south from Wilshire Boulevard in mid-Los Angeles almost to the ocean and is five miles west of Watts. The area of which Delaney spoke is chiefly a neighborhood of business establishments and modern apartment buildings.

Dynamite had been used before for such a purpose. Five hundred miles to the north, as flames spread following the great San Francisco earthquake on April 18, 1906, the city's Committee of Safety met and reached a decision: the only way to check the flames was to blow up all residences on the east side of Van Ness Avenue, between Golden Gate and Pacific Avenues, a distance of a mile.

Shortly after the turn of the century, Van Ness was one of San Francisco's most fashionable streets, but because it was 125 feet wide, the Committee of Safety believed that if the east side were leveled, the flames would not leapfrog the street. A million dollars' worth of homes were blown to drifting dust, but the strategy, costly as it was, quenched the torrent of fire by sending the raging flames back across their own charred path. A crater a block deep was all that remained along 22 blocks of Van Ness Avenue's east side. The west side was intact.

Captain Delaney is among those who believe that, because so many holocausts were touched off so quickly and blossomed so rapidly, the real riot death toll may never be known. It is, he believes, considerably higher than what was officially proclaimed. According to the theory held by Delaney and others, many persons may have died in flaming structures, and the bodies, or what remained of them, never discovered amid the massive, sooty rubble. He recalled one instance in which his men had to cut through the roof of a burning store to save several looters trapped inside. Had firemen not reached them, he said, they "simply would have disappeared."

17

AT 5 P.M. FRIDAY, Lieutenant Governor Glenn Anderson signed the papers enlisting the National Guard on the side of law enforcement in the guerrilla warfare raging in Los Angeles.

In time, more than 13,500 soldiers would be patrolling the streets, off and on. When, at 5 P.M., Anderson signed the proclamation, 1,336 National Guard troops were assembled in armories, according to the McCone Commission. But the first thousand Guardsmen were not en route to staging areas until 7 P.M.—and not deployed from there into "postions for action" until 10:45 P.M.

As "the worst night" shuddered violently on, the Guard commitment continued to swell. By 3 A.M. Saturday, 3,356 Guardsmen were making massive sweeps through the sundered neighborhoods.

But, as the McCone Commission noted: "Despite the new tactics and added personnel, the area was not under control at any time on Friday night, as major calls of looting, burning and shooting were reported every two or three minutes. On throughout the morning hours of Saturday, and during the long day, the crowds of looters and patterns of burning spread out and increased still further until it became necessary to impose a curfew on the 46.5 square-mile area on Saturday."

Governor Edmund G. Brown, flying back to California from Greece, paused early Saturday in Rome to scan news reports from Los Angeles, and called what was happening in his state's biggest city—the nation's third largest—"a war. Terrible . . . unbelievable . . . absolutely beyond my comprehension."

Outbreaks of looting came that night, Friday, the 13th, in Los Angeles' old beach district of Venice and in suburban Pasadena and Pacoima, both of which have large Negro populations. Before the riot ended, other serious racial incidents occurred in Southern California cities from Long Beach to San Diego. And racial strife was occurring too in Chicago and Springfield, Massachusetts.

When Guardsmen did roll into the riot area, they were an impressive sight. Helmeted young soldiers from the 40th Armored Division moved in convoys led by Jeeps with mounted machine guns. "Sweep and clear" operations were handed the first troops. Police with bullhorns preceded them, warning looters and rioters to disperse. Command posts were set up at schools, while infantrymen, advancing with bayonets "at the ready," fanned out through the torn streets.

Police followed the reservists as the Guardsmen flushed out hard-core rioters. Police then herded Negro men, women and children into paddy wagons, many of these school busses pressed into service. Guardsmen strode curb-to-curb along the avenues and boulevards that had experienced the worst violence, the "hot spots." Some peeled off and set up barricades at intersections; others assembled .50-caliber machine guns on tripods.

Those first Guardsmen in the riot area were designated the Second Brigade and made up of squadrons and battalions from such close-by suburbs as Glendale, Long Beach, Inglewood and Burbank and Santa Ana in neighboring Orange County. They were placed under the command of Guard Colonel Irving J. Taylor, oddly enough, a mere patrolman in the Los Angeles Police Department.

The young reservists had no experience for what they would have to cope with, described by one of their superiors as being "like Vietnam," although each year they had been drilled to respond to such an emergency. But as Julian Hartt, a former war correspondent and *Los Angeles Times* military writer, would note later in the official magazine of the National Guard Association of the United States: "These [drills] were keyed chiefly to natural disasters, such as flood or earthquake, to which Southern California was prone. A major insurrection was almost unthinkable. There had been routine riot training for the troops, but nothing to match the scale they were to face."

Nevertheless, the young soldiers, with but few exceptions, responded coolly and bravely. As Major General Charles A. Ott, the 40th Armored commander, put it: "They became veterans in a hurry."

Hartt, a sophisticated observer of military response, commented that "the National Guard was always one businesslike step ahead of the anticipated demands put on it, for two major reasons." In the magazine *The National Guardsman,* he cited them: "One was the closely-knit relationship of the senior officers. Virtually all are combat veterans both of World War II and Korea. They had worked together as a team under the 40th's colors in the Korean conflict. For fifteen years, they have known how each other 'operates,' how each other thinks. Secondly, the Division already had 'steam up' logistically for the long-scheduled move on Friday night and Saturday, 13–14 August to Camp Roberts for their two weeks Annual Field Training."

When Ott was advised many hours earlier that Police Chief Parker might request the Guard, Hartt wrote: "General Ott decided to let the most distant units, such as those at Indio and San Diego, for instance, start their northward moves [to Camp Roberts] as scheduled. 'It will be quicker to halt them en route, if needed, than to hold them at their home armories,' he reasoned. He also prudently held back certain items from the packing, such as gas masks, tear gas, ammunition, so they could be quickly available, rather than lost for hours with advance parties."

It became obvious, soon after the first Guardsmen entered the riot area, that an even greater force would be needed. The call-up of troops quickened and eventually became a massive undertaking. Some units were "air-lifted" from Northern California. Others already north of Los Angeles on their trek to Camp Roberts got the call to pull back.

"Typical," wrote Hartt, "was the experience of Lieutenant Colonel William Geissert's 132d Engineer Battalion. En route to Roberts, they had just finished their noon meal break near Gaviota, a lonesome stretch of U.S. 101 north of Santa Barbara, when a Jeep from Ventura Battery A, First Battalion, 144th Artillery, roared up. The driver handed Colonel Geissert a scrawled note, misspelling his name, which read: 'Geyser call Turnage [Colonel Thomas K. Turnage, 40th Armored chief of staff].'

"The nearest farmhouse was occupied by an elderly Japanese couple who barely spoke English. But, from his Japan and Korea experience, he quickly negotiated use of the telephone. Within minutes, his convoy of forty-six vehicles, stretched out over five miles, was turned around and headed back."

In Los Angeles, the first Guardsmen committed to the riot area were quickly blooded—even before midnight Friday. A chain of Guardsmen was setting up a barricade at Santa Barbara Avenue and Avalon Boulevard, not far from where Fireman Gene T. Smart had been wounded earlier. Major Richard J. Marcell, a Guard information officer posted as a liaison for the Guard command post and troops in the field, remembers that Colonel Taylor, the policeman-Guardsman, "was concerned" about the reaction of his green troops in the face of mob violence.

The Guardsmen had been directed by police to the Santa Barbara-Avalon intersection because, at that time, it was considered one of the "hot spots." Taylor had warned his men "not to fire unless fired on." Marcell recalls that both Taylor and Chief Parker in earlier and later conversations "appeared concerned about bloodshed." Marcell recalls that the first two days he saw the chief, "Parker had not slept—he just changed his shirt. All during the time, I never saw him ruffled once: he held his meetings [with Guardsmen] in a very military manner."

Now at Santa Barbara and Avalon, Marcell saw an unlighted car bearing down on the line of troops. Guardsmen shouted for the car to halt. When it didn't, Marcell saw the young reservists "scatter instinctively—maybe if they had been seasoned soldiers, they would have held their ground."

One young Guardsman could not get away fast enough. Marcell saw him "bounce into the air." He saw the speeding car continue down the street, then strike what he took to be a sheriff's car parked in the center of the thoroughfare. He heard the crackle of gunfire from what he believed were deputy sheriffs and city policemen. "I never hit the ground so fast in my life," he recalls. "My helmet flew off and it started to roll on the ground. There I was, trying to stay flat and grab my helmet and get it back on my head."

No Guardsmen fired at the fleeing car, as were their instructions at that time, said Marcell. Local law enforcement officers seized the occupants of the car which had struck the young Guardsman. "He's lucky to be alive. He got a broken leg and a head injury," said Marcell.

As Guardsmen flocked into the riot zone, squads went from their own staging areas to similar posts set up for city policemen, Highway Patrolmen and sheriff's deputies, many established in schools. The 97th Street Elementary School, for instance, took on the appearance of a fortress, with 1,000 officers deployed there for riot assignment.

Medical and communications equipment were moved into the school. Neighborhood residents watched silently as the schoolyard swelled with squad cars, telephone company trucks, water and power vehicles and a self-powered searchlight. School busses, carrying weary-eyed uniformed men and escorted by motorcycle officers employing red lights and sirens, traveled in and out of the school grounds.

An emergency booking desk was set up to process arrested rioters. Technicians installed a police teletype machine in the principal's office. Policemen talked rapidly into red and yellow "hot line" telephones. In the school auditorium, a police captain stood on the stage behind a lectern. He read to several hundred policemen their assignments. Mimeographed maps of riot areas were handed to sergeants who would be leading groups of officers through the school gates. Officers were solemn, quiet. Once in a while one joked quietly over having to bend low to drink from the children's drinking fountains.

A first-aid center was established in a wooden bungalow, normally the school kitchen. An ambulance was parked beside it. Doctors and nurses stacked medical supplies.

Los Angeles hospitals were having their own problems at the time. Central Receiving Hospital, Los Angeles' chief public emergency clinic, was busy but surprisingly orderly Friday and early Saturday. Later the tempo there and at other hospitals would step up, but, for the most part, medical matters during the rioting went smoothly. Many of the cases handed to doctors and nurses were pathetic, like that of Richard Flores and his sons, Richard, Jr., fourteen, and Ronald, thirteen.

The family lived in Huntington Park to the north of the riot area, but Friday night the father, apparently unaware of the seriousness of the situation, drove his sons through the area on the way to a late evening snack. Near Will Rogers Park he apparently panicked and crashed through a National Guard barricade. Guardsmen fired. Bullets pierced the windshield of Flores' car and one wounded him in the chest. He lost control and his car struck a lamp post. The two boys were cut by flying glass. Guard Private Larry Mitchell, twenty-three, was clipped by a gunshot in the left hand. All were treated at Central Receiving.

Early Friday night, at Oak Park Community Hospital, at

Manchester Boulevard and Broadway in the riot area, a mob broke front windows in the hospital and threatened to storm it. The staff barricaded the front door with filing cabinets.

Later police arrived and, ultimately, National Guardsmen, but they were too late for a twenty-year-old Negro, dead with a gunshot wound in the head. When the youth had arrived wounded but still alive, the hospital was largely unprotected.

"We might have saved him if we'd had an anesthetist," said a staff member, Mrs. Gladys Monzetti. "But upon the arrival of the youth, attempts were made to obtain an anesthetist from several hospitals. None dared pass through the mob to reach Oak Park," she said.

More then 100 persons were treated for riot wounds at the small hospital during the night. Fireman M. J. Maddox suffered one of the most unusual. Mrs. Monzetti said it appeared to her his leg had been sliced open with a machete.

Later, hospitals asked physicians to return from their vacations. Many doctors and nurses put in long, grueling hours, especially at emergency centers set up by the Guard.

18

J.B., A JANITOR making $390 a month, father of two with a wife expecting a third child, always had been an honest, hard-working man. He wanted no part of the violence, but he drifted into the riot area Friday night because he felt a sense of identity with the mutineers and was "just curious to see what was going on." No sooner did he arrive than he saw plenty.

"I was on San Pedro and 105th. I watched rioters set fire to a big grocery store. Three men ran inside and lit it. Suddenly the place went up in flames.

"There wouldn't have been a riot, I was thinking, if the cops would have come out there in the beginning with guns. Later, anytime I saw police point their weapons at the crowd, the people would freeze. But at the start, at that time, the cops were running away. They were afraid of the people. That's what got things really going. The police didn't exert authority. The people were angry; they were in rebellion. When they saw they had the upper hand, all hell broke loose.

"No, I didn't throw any rocks. But I felt like it. I see the cause of the people who did. I'm with them in spirit. My wife doesn't understand. We live in a pretty good neighborhood in the West Adams section. She couldn't figure out why I was for these people. After the riot, I took her down to Watts to show her how the people lived crowded in substandard housing.

"This Friday night, I was standing in a phone booth watching. A little kid came by carrying a lamp he had taken out of a store. Maybe he was about twelve. He was with his mother. I remember him saying: 'Don't run, Mommy. They said we could take the stuff because they're going to burn the store anyway.'

"Then, suddenly, about five police cars stopped. There were about 20 cops in them and they all got out. One came up to the booth I was standing in. The cop hit me on the leg with his club. 'Get out of here, nigger,' he yelled at me. I got out of the booth.

"Another cop ran up to the boy and hit him in the head with the butt of a shotgun. The kid dropped like a stone. The lamp crashed on the sidewalk. I ran out of the phone booth and grabbed the cop by the arm. I was trying to stop him from beating the boy. Two cops jumped on my back. Others struck the boy with their clubs. They beat that little kid's face to a bloody pulp. His mother and some others took him away. That's when I thought white people are animals. They had no feeling, those white cops."

Later, J.B. returned to his own neighborhood. "Cops," he said, "came up and started chasing the people off the street. They weren't doing anything. One old man fell down. He pleaded: 'Please, mister, don't hit me.' A cop cracked him on the head with his club. Later, when the cops left, the people got mad and broke into a lot of auction warehouses along West Adams."

J.B., like many Negroes, is bitter about Negro-area merchants, many of whom are Jewish. Some of the rioters were openly anti-Semitic, feeling that the Jewish merchants contributed to their hopeless lot.

Speaking of Negro-neighborhood merchants in general, J.B. said: "If they give you credit, you can be sure they rob you on the finance charges. Negroes always pay more for everything. The merchants are all out to gyp us. We know it. But what can we do? We like to live decent like anyone else. We like good furniture in our apartments and homes. We like to see our kids dressed decently. We like to have a good car. What the hell is unusual about that? Isn't that what everyone wants? But go out and buy any of these things on credit if you're a Negro—they'll stick it to you good.

"A lot of people are wishing it will happen again. Next time, we'll have guns. We'll be able to fight back."

What percentage of the Los Angeles Negroes rioted or even passively sided with the rebellion, like J.B., is impossible to estimate.

Chief Parker guessed that only 1 per cent of the city's huge Negro population took part in the violence. So did Assemblyman Dymally. But there is no question that even great numbers of law-abiding Negro residents who kept to their homes felt a deep identification with the active rebels.

Yet among these, and among untold numbers of other Negro citizens who saw the riot as a setback to the cause of equality, there were many who performed acts of great courage during the violence.

A handful of residents of one huge housing project, for instance, banded together to persuade their neighbors to stay at home and away from the trouble. These few volunteers were surprisingly successful. In the few instances where they found project residents had taken merchandise from looted stores, they coaxed the conscience-stricken culprits either to return it or hand it over to authorities.

Negroes were among the Guardsmen who, finally, as the McCone Commission points out, were the effective instrument in quelling the insurrection. Many of these young citizen-soldiers were placed in a predicament. Some were residents of Watts or other Los Angeles Negro neighborhoods. It was conceivable they might look over their bayonets into the eyes of a neighbor, friend—or even relative.

One such was Private Bill Wilkes, twenty-two. When the rioting broke out, he sent his wife and seven-week-old daughter to stay with relatives outside the trouble zone. At a staging area, awaiting his riot assignment, he said: "I keep thinking that I might have to shoot a friend—someone I've grown up with. It'll be better once these people have worked the hate out of their system. The National Guard probably can accomplish more than the police. The people are prejudiced against the police because of brutality. Hostilities have been building up for years because police have a stereotyped image of Negroes. They think of us as brutes, dunces and hoodlums. That kind of attitude naturally builds resentment."

One of the four Guardsmen to receive the California Military Cross, of the more than 13,500 who participated in riot duty, was a Negro—Second Lieutenant Raymond O. Wrenn, a twenty-eight-year-old native of Texas and in civilian life a prospering young bank executive, a supervisor of loans. He won his award, according to the Guard citation, for his courage in protecting firemen from a "large hostile crowd." But Ray Wrenn did much more than that during the height of the fury.

Wrenn, a dark-complexioned man with pugnacious features but pleasant manner and voice, had attended both public schools and college in Los Angeles. He and his wife of two years, and their one small child, were in the process of moving into a new $33,000 home in an integrated Compton neighborhood that only recently had been developed. Ray Wrenn, the only Negro in his 30-man 40th Armored Division platoon, was its commander.

About 2:30 Friday afternoon he was alerted by his superior officer that his unit probably would be among the first called for riot duty. "I was packed and ready," he said. "About 5 P.M. I got another call—the Guard had been mobilized. My unit was the fourth to be called up." Wrenn reported to his armory and at 8 P.M. his unit received an order to "unpack and prepare vehicles for duty." This, he said, meant "we had to prepare light loads for combat duty."

At 10 P.M. came the order to move out of the armory. Highway Patrolmen escorted Wrenn and his fellow Guardsmen to their command post at Jacob Riis High School where they were briefed and instructed to await further orders. "Finally," he said, "we were told we were to give support to LAPD in quelling the riot. The area we were assigned to was bounded on the east by Main Street, on the west by Vermont, on the north by 79th and on the south by Century Boulevard.

"Friday night was hectic and everybody wasn't aware of what the situation was. Things were happening so fast we couldn't plan. Since my unit was a mechanized one, we canvassed the area quickly." At that time, Guardsmen had orders, as Major Marcell pointed out earlier, "not to fire unless fired upon." Wrenn's unit spent most of Friday night and early Saturday seeking out looters.

"Any looters we apprehended," he said, "we radioed LAPD and they transported them to 77th, and booked them. We confiscated Molotov cocktails, cigarettes, canned food and other items. The bulk of the night was spent doing this. We traveled east on routine patrol with two vehicles which had mounted machine guns."

After the first night's patrol, Wrenn's unit got about two hours' sleep. "Saturday," he said, "it was clear and the neighborhood around us looked like a war-torn area. But the hell was yet to come."

By dawn Saturday, Los Angeles could count ten dead in the violence: a sheriff's deputy, a city fireman and eight looters. Another 300 persons had been injured: 50 police officers from various agencies, eight firemen, two National Guardsmen and 240 private citizens, either innocents set upon by rioters, or rioters and looters themselves.

19

TWO OF THE DEAD were Leon Cauley, thirty-one, and Miller Chester Burroughs, twenty-eight, both born and reared in Alabama. Cauley had lived in Los Angeles only eight months; Burroughs, two years.

Both Cauley and Burroughs were married. Cauley's wife's name was Juanita; Marcella Burroughs, when she appeared a month later at her husband's inquest, would be sworn in while seated to accommodate the tiny baby she was holding. Cauley, a husky five feet nine inches, had only a trace of a police record as far as authorities were able to determine: he once had been convicted in Chicago of driving a car without the owner's consent. Burroughs, also five feet nine inches but slender, apparently had no police record.

Both had been drinking Friday night. Accompanying them were four other men of their own ages: Lewis Wharry, Aaron Bynum, Lawrence Jacques and Calvin Jones. Jacques later insisted he knew neither Cauley nor Burroughs; Jones that he knew only Jacques. But all were at 61st Street and Vermont Avenue at 5 A.M. Saturday.

On one corner of that intersection stood a ravaged appliance store. What was left of its merchandise was open to the still warm, predawn air. The store's windows were broken out, its front door smashed in. Appliances, clocks, radios and electric mixers lay in a jumble on the floor and atop counters inside. Just outside, on its side, reposed a grandfather clock. Near it sat a television set. Nothing more was needed to attract officers in two passing squad cars. But the movement of figures they saw helped.

The officers in the patrol cars, their nerves rubbed raw by a night of being sniped at and jeered at, were in no mood to continue on without investigating. They had begun work at 8 A.M. Friday and for more than 20 hours had been under steady harassment by rioters.

The cars passed the store, then pulled up sharp. As they made a U-turn, the officers saw what appeared to be a man putting a television set in the rear of a 1957 green Ford, while two other Negroes emerged from the store carrying a second set. Then the men scattered, "running in all directions."

One of the police cars was a radio car, the other unmarked. In each were three officers from the Los Angeles Police Department's Metropolitan Division, a far-ranging kind of task force. Louis Sale, driver of one of the cars, saw two of the men stop next to a pickup truck parked in the lot of a Shell Oil Station across the street. His fellow officers ordered: "Halt. Put your hands up."

But, said Sale, "Mr. Cauley continued to run and crouched down in front of the truck, out of my sight. I negotiated a hard right-hand turn, and attempted to cut him off, at which time, he ran again—westbound through the lot toward Vermont Avenue."

Sale heard an officer in the back seat call, "Police, halt," then the report of a shotgun. Twenty-five feet away, Cauley fell dead.

The fatal shot had been fired by Officer John T. Moroney, who pulled his shotgun's trigger when he thought he detected the fleeing man's hand "near his waistband." The blast struck Cauley in the back, perforating his heart and lungs.

"Moments later," said Moroney, "I got out of the police vehicle and ran over to him and stayed next to him."

Meanwhile, Officer Ronald McCarthy leaped from Sale's car and ran to the storefront to find Wharry standing alongside the green Ford in the custody of an officer from the other car. McCarthy dashed into the store and found a man he later identified as Calvin Jones trying to hide beneath a couch. The man beneath the couch was ordered to stand.

"He jumped from behind the couch," said McCarthy, "and grabbed a shotgun I was holding. We grappled for the shotgun." Another policeman reached McCarthy, and together the two officers subdued and handcuffed McCarthy's foe.

John R. Walton, another officer in the second car, saw a man he later identified as Wharry halt by the Ford at the command of one of his partners. But a second man who had been carrying a television set from the store with Wharry, he said, "continued to run."

According to Walton's recollection, "I hollered for him to stop, and, at this time, he darted behind a tree which was located approximately halfway between the sidewalk and the building. It was very dark back there—I could just see a silhouette. As he went behind the tree, I dropped on one knee and hollered: 'Police officer—come out.' He darted out from behind the tree in a crouched position; he was just beginning to move away. I hollered again: 'Hold it—police officer.' And as he was moving away, I shot."

Burroughs fell, mortally wounded by the pellets from Walton's twelve-gauge shotgun. The officer remained with him until an ambulance arrived and took Burroughs to Los Angeles County General Hospital, where he died at 6:35 A.M. Saturday. Buckshot had ripped through his back into his aorta and kidney.

Lawrence Jacques' story was that he was sitting in a small foreign-make car in the Shell Station parking lot when he "saw a fellow [Cauley?] run by." Said Jacques: "He ran by me and the police jumped out of the car and stopped him. At this particular time, he [a policeman] told me: 'Don't run, nigger.' I told the officer: 'I'm not going to run; I haven't done anything.' "

Jacques claims he was forced to lean against the pickup truck, then lie on the ground with another Negro. As he lay there, he said, he heard one policeman ask another: "How many did you kill?"

The other officer replied, according to Jacques: "I killed two niggers. Why don't you kill those two lying on the ground?"

The first officer's response was, said Jacques: "They won't run."

"One officer came up to me and put a shotgun at the back of my head," said Jacques. "He said: 'Nigger—how fast can you run the 50-yard dash?' I said: 'I can't run it at all.'

"He kicked me in the side two times, and the other officer put his foot on the back of my head."

The case of Theophile Albert O'Neal is a departure from the riot death pattern. Little is known about O'Neal, less about how he died. He was born in Louisiana twenty-three years earlier, had lived in Los Angeles sixteen years, was unmarried and worked for a distributor of linens.

Early Saturday morning, O'Neal either was inside, or in the vicinity of, a liquor store at 1650 West Jefferson Boulevard.

Late Friday night, two brothers clerking in the store had become apprehensive. At any other time, the source of their anxiety would have been ludicrous: parading in and out of the store were "customers," seeking to exchange cases of liquor for different brands. The brothers Ray and Herschel Davis could not help but think such barter suggested the possibility of more dangerous behavior.

Ray Davis telephoned the store owner, who instructed him to close the establishment immediately and to lock the doors and windows. Ray Davis did so, but wise as the precaution was, it proved of no merit at a time such as this. Not long after the store was shuttered, looters reopened it with a brick here, a stone there, and a well-thrust foot-fall. They entered and made off with beverages and stock worth an estimated $20,000. Simultaneously, police received reports of sniper activity there.

At 2:30 A.M. passing firemen saw a man lying about 150 feet up the street from the liquor store and notified police. Officers arrived to find on a sidewalk at the corner of Jefferson Boulevard and Denker Avenue the body of Theophile Albert O'Neal, dead from a .38-caliber bullet wound in the back of the head. Blood led from the body back to the liquor store. The "physical evidence," scuff marks and abrasions of the face, indicated to police that O'Neal had been shot, then dragged some distance.

Who killed Theophile O'Neal? And why? Was it a sniper taking potshots at a crowd gathered around the looted store or at persons roaming inside? Was he murdered by an intoxicated or bloodthirsty rioter? Police were not able to determine. Probably no one ever will. Or try to.

Pathos was commonplace during the dark days of hate, fire, destruction and bestiality that was the Los Angeles riot of 1965. But few experiences matched that of twelve-year-old Larry King. He saw his father shot to death.

William Vernon King, thirty-seven, was a widower who also used the name William Caston—the way he was first listed in riot death records. As a youth of seventeen, he had been convicted of burglary and larceny in St. Louis. He was sent to prison in Nebraska in 1944, again for burglary, and in 1946 for auto theft. He also had a Los Angeles arrest record. Yet none of these blots against his father's character prepared Larry King for what he was to experience at 9:45 A.M. Saturday.

Larry, his cousin Henry Burroughs and Larry's father were in a Compton Avenue liquor store when police passed it. William King was holding a revolver.

"I got the gun in the liquor store," said Larry. "The rest of the stuff was mine," he said of a watch and money found on him by officers.

Young Burroughs told police: "I went into the liquor store

with my uncle and Larry. We went in to steal stuff. My uncle found the gun inside and then the officers came and shot my uncle. My uncle was holding the gun in his hand and, I guess, trying to get away."

Officers Nicholas Bakay and Charles Hudson, in passing the liquor store, could see through a broken front window three persons inside. One, they said, was crouched with a revolver in hand.

"Drop that gun," yelled the policemen.

Instead of doing so, said the officers, the figure with the gun raised the weapon; Hudson fired his service revolver. The officers entered the store and found the boys and Larry's father. The latter lay dead on the floor, a .38-caliber revolver in his hand. The gun held six rounds of ammunition.

Larry King sat silently through the inquest a month later and heard a coroner's jury rule his father's death "justifiable homicide," as similar panels would rule in cases of all slain rioters.

20

DURING THE DAY Saturday, a huge section of Los Angeles' Negro area was in flames. By Saturday night, more than 20 persons had died. The riot continued to spread north toward the Civic Center ten miles from 116th and Avalon and west toward the integrated Crenshaw Boulevard district. In Pasadena, another ten miles beyond the Civic Center, more than a hundred Negroes were arrested when buildings were stoned and a liquor store and two gun stores looted.

By now, Guardsmen, who continued to arrive in the riot zone in ever-increasing numbers, had been given authorization to load their rifles. Mobs continued to attack fire trucks. Black-gray smoke hung over much of the city. Police were forced to flee some pockets of heavy sniper fire. Commercial aircraft flying in and out of Los Angeles International Airport altered their flight patterns to avoid the riot zone, where police and news helicopters earlier had been fired upon.

Combat-equipped Guardsmen swept through neighborhood after neighborhood in skirmish lines, providing greater and greater support for policemen who, by now, had confidence enough to counterattack. "We want to put as many people as we can in jail on bona fide arrests," proclaimed Deputy Police Chief Roger Murdock at the 97th Street School command post.

Guardsmen also offered stronger and stronger protection for weary firemen, and some streets where the worst rioting had occurred Friday night were deserted. But no sooner was one "hot spot" erased than a half dozen others developed.

"This situation," said Police Chief Parker, "is very much like fighting the Viet Cong. We haven't the slightest idea when this can be brought under control."

To make matters worse, Saturday was a day in which reports reached police of impending raids on white neighborhoods and the downtown business district. Typical was: "Men with red armbands heading toward downtown in trucks." This, and other such reports, proved false. But they were unnerving to police and to the public who heard them on radio and television.

The reports, like one that the Shrine Auditorium was being burned, seemed to follow a calculated pattern of terrorism. A charity professionel football game scheduled between the Los Angeles Rams and the Dallas Cowboys at the Coliseum Saturday night and two circus performances in the nearby Sports Area were canceled. Both actions were unprecedented.

More and more Negro-owned stores were hit by rioters. Store owners fought back. One, defending his shop with a shotgun, forced a mob to back off by warning: "You may be my brother, but you're going to be my dead brother."

Persons in high places spoke of their distress over the happenings. The state's senior Republican Senator, Thomas Kuchel, expressed dismay over "The rule of the jungle," and appealed to "all citizens involved in this frightening and bloody breach of peace to become law-abiding and rational." Freshman Republican Senator George Murphy, the former movie actor, pledged his support to those seeking to put an end to the lawlessness.

Mayor Samuel W. Yorty inspected the riot zone from a helicopter. His brow was deeply furrowed and dark circles were noticeable under his eyes. "It must make those policemen feel pretty good to have those troops behind them," he said during the two-hour inspection. "It's a damn shame to let those crowds stand around down there," he said, and he asked the pilot to radio his observations of mob movement to the ground.

Back at City Hall, about 30 Negroes, anxious to find a solution to the continuing riot, showed up at a meeting called by

Negro City Councilman Billy G. Mills. Three other councilmen also attended.

The 30 Negroes had this message for Mills and his colleagues: some way must be found to communicate with the rioters; otherwise, "they could see little likelihood that the violence would cease soon. They conceded a major problem was finding responsible Negro leaders capable of commanding the rioters' respect. But they blamed persons in government who had failed to recognize the problems of Negroes for not doing something 'realistic' about them before the eruption.

"If you had just been around enough, if you had gone into the area, you could understand what's happening. But it's impossible for you to understand it because you've never experienced it," the councilmen were told by Felix Bell, the Negro policeman whose dress store had been looted.

"Some type of curfew should be put into effect immediately," Charles Grindel, member of a neighborhood coordinating council in the riot area, suggested to the councilmen. "Some type of martial law has to be initiated if you're going to stop this thing," he warned.

At that very moment, such a plan was being formulated. Saturday afternoon, Acting Governor Glenn Anderson imposed an 8 P.M.-to-dawn curfew making it illegal for anyone to be on the streets during those hours in a nearly 50-square-mile area of the city. The curfew was necessary, said the proclamation establishing it, because of a state of "extreme emergency in Los Angeles County."

"Anyone found in the street in the curfew area will be subject to immediate arrest by police," said Anderson, adding: "I implore everyone in Los Angeles to stay off the street tonight."

The curfew zone was bounded roughly by Washington Boulevard on the north, 120th Street on the south, Crenshaw Boulevard on the west and Alameda Street on the east.

About the time Anderson was signing the curfew order,

Governor Brown arrived by commercial aircraft in New York. He held a hurried conference with Leroy Collins, former director of the Federal Government's Community Relations Service, and White House Assistant Lee White, dispatched there by President Lyndon B. Johnson to offer California whatever federal cooperation might be needed.

The governor appeared haggard. Before taking off for the West Coast in a military plane, he termed the rioting in Los Angeles a "state of insurrection."

At his Johnson City, Texas, ranch, meanwhile, the President himself branded it "tragic and shocking." Mr. Johnson added: "I urge every person in a position of leadership to make every effort to restore order in Los Angeles." And he warned Negroes: "Rights will not be won through violence."

Lieutenant Governor Anderson went on television that evening to explain the curfew and the necessity for it to a jittery Los Angeles, where rioters, swept from many of their early arenas by Guardsmen and resurgent police, sought to regroup elsewhere—some in widely separated areas as far as ten miles from the original battleground.

It was a time of panic, and the jitters of frightened white citizens throughout broad areas of Southern California were understandable, even though the reaction of some was beyond logic. Many normally sober-minded fathers and husbands continued to queue up at sporting goods and hardware stores to buy guns. "They're buying every kind of weapon—guns, knives, bows and arrows, even slingshots," said Bob Ketcham, owner of an Inglewood store, who reported selling seventy-five shotguns and rifles in a single day.

One who bought was John Riley.* On Friday, the 13th, he purchased an M-1 carbine. On Saturday, from his home in the Crenshaw district of Los Angeles' Southwest Side, he could see a

* John Riley is a fictitious name. He asked that his identity be kept secret.

layer of smoke from a hundred blazing structures in the south-central city thickening; it seemed to him to be expanding toward his attractive, single-story stucco home, a structure indebted for its architectural style to the Spanish influence of the 1930's.

Riley sat in the living room of the home, rubbing the breech of the carbine with an oily rag and talking with a neighbor. The neighbor, though concerned himself, questioned Riley's need for a gun. The latter's comments in response explain more than just why a white man bought a gun during the riot. They also reflect and bring into focus some subtle circumstances regarding the white and Negro relationship in Los Angeles in August, 1965.

"The last time I used one of these was in North Korea during the fall of 1950," said Riley, a Marine veteran of both World War II and the Korean strife; now he was a successful import-exporter of forty-seven, with a wife and three children. Rumor had spread Friday that rioters planned to invade and sack stores in the Crenshaw business district not far from his home. The rumor struck Riley with sufficient logic so that he had purchased the carbine.

He explained to his neighbor: "Those people are burning up a section of this city. I don't care what their grievances are; it's no excuse for their defying law and order. So here I am, sitting around armed, expecting that some gang of terrorists will come any minute, invade my neighborhood and attack my home. Who knows how many other persons in this town are going to be waiting behind locked doors tonight with guns in their hands—like me, maybe jumping at the slightest sound, watching from the window for a strange car?

"Did you ever think what's happened in this city the last few years? Take this neighborhood. I've got Negroes living close by me here. And, hell, say I did pay only $17,000 for this house 20 years ago—it's worth $30,000 or more today.

"Don't think Negroes were welcome here at first. The white

people wanted to keep up the value of their property. They didn't want Negroes for neighbors. Some realtors here tried to keep the Negroes out—but it didn't work. Soon one family would give up and sell to a Negro, and suddenly, before anyone realized what had happened, Negroes were all around us. More and more white people moved away.

"For a long time this didn't bother me. Most of the Negroes kept up their property. I found no objection to them as neighbors. I made a trip through the South a few years ago and I didn't like what I saw, the way Negroes there were forced to live, the segregation, the Jim Crow treatment. It sort of reassured me to think that out here in Los Angeles these people were better off, that we didn't discriminate against them in restaurants and other public places.

"But now it seems that they don't live so well in Watts and places like that, after all. I wouldn't know. That's the other end of town. And I don't think many whites got over there to find out how the Negroes do live. Watts always has been the 'other side of the tracks,' the place where the poorer-class Negro lived. As soon as one got a decent job, he moved out. The more affluent ones come to neighborhoods like this and some of the homes they buy are pretty expensive."

The sound of a car outside interrupted Riley. He jumped up and squinted through the window drapes. "My neighbor's daughter," he said with a sigh of reassurance. "That must be her new boy friend."

He reseated himself, looked levelly at his companion and said: "That's another thing. I have a daughter who will be entering high school soon. Before the war, the high school in this area was predominantly white. Today it is just the opposite. Most of the pupils are Negroes. Sure, they say the kids get along. Maybe they do. I've heard some other stories.

"A guy down the block sent his boy to that high school for his first year. A nice quiet little kid, but kind of frail. He told his father that the colored youths ganged up on the white boys, pushed them around. Whatever truth there was to the story, it was enough for his father to sell their home and move out to West Covina.

"And another thing, we have a rising crime rate in this district. Lots of homes have been burglarized. The police say they get more calls than they can handle about prowlers in the neighborhood at night. Women have had purses snatched from their hands and have been beaten by young hoodlums. Despite what anyone says, the ones committing these crimes are mostly young Negroes. They don't have jobs, so this is the way they obtain money.

"I'm certain of one thing, I don't want my daughter to go to a high school that has mostly colored students. And I have the two smaller ones to consider. We've been looking at other property in the suburbs. You hate to give up your home, something you've worked hard for, just to go and move someplace else and start all over again in another community. But I guess we'll join the exodus."

The acquisition of weapons by rioters and the general public alike was a matter of concern both during and after the riot. Pawnshops were an early target of looters. Exactly how many guns were obtained from them never will be known. But police estimated the number in the thousands and felt certain that substantial numbers fell into the hands of would-be snipers. Snipers, for the most part, proved sorry marksmen. Otherwise, the riot death toll might have been far higher.

According to the McCone Commission, law enforcement officers recovered 851 weapons during the riot. Many policemen wondered later where the remaining stolen weapons had gone and for what purpose they were being stored away. Vice Squad Sergeant Lou Bonanno put into words what many of his colleagues thought when he said that he feared that someday "these weapons will be used against us or innocent persons."

Gunshops experienced a heavy run on supplies by citizens who lived in suburbs miles from the riot area. The City Council took note of what it deemed a sudden rash of advertisements by dealers in guns and ammunition, and passed a resolution urging gun dealers to "desist" from sales until calm was restored. "Such advertising could only serve to stimulate activity that could worsen the already tense atmosphere in Los Angeles and lead to further violence and bloodshed," said the resolution introduced by Billy G. Mills, the Negro councilman.

Governor Brown took the view that white citizens arming themselves was "a very dangerous thing to do." But Chief Parker said: "It is their right if they want to arm themselves. After all, the looters have guns. It's not up to me to tell the public to buy or not to buy a gun. There are a lot of terrified citizens in this community who have weapons and are buying weapons to protect themselves and their homes."

What problems and grief may have been caused by the stolen guns and weapons and those hastily purchased by inexperienced persons remains uncertain. But a week after the riot began, three-year-old Steven P. Parker was killed instantly when struck in the right eye by a bullet from his mother's pistol.

Mrs. Sue Parker, thirty, who lived in an apartment on the fringe of the riot area, said that, after putting her son to bed, she had gone to sleep herself. The little boy apparently got up, clambered onto a cupboard, found the gun on a high shelf and began playing with it. The sound of the shot awakened Mrs. Parker, a waitress. She had taken the gun from a suitcase and loaded it a few days earlier. She had become fearful when the tempo of the rioting stepped up.

The international press gave prominent display to stories about the Los Angeles riot.

Communist newspapers and press agencies, of course, took it as an opportunity to criticize the United States. Communist

China's official New China Agency described the violence as "a general outburst of their [Negroes'] pent-up dissatisfaction."

Tass, the Soviet news agency, said: "Los Angeles literally has turned into a battlefield between the Negro population protesting against racial discrimination and the police. The police and units of the National Guard have resorted to arms against the demonstrators, but they were unable so far to 'restore law and order' and make the Negro population buckle under."

In race-conscious South Africa, riot stories received splash treatment. And in London, a city becoming more and more sensitive to its own "colored problem," the stories commanded page-one attention.

"Race Fury—Troops Face 8,000 Rioters," was the headline in the *Daily Mirror*.

"Los Angeles Calls in Riot Troops; Shots Fired at Police as Looting Spreads," proclaimed the staid *Times* of London.

Later the United States Government found it advisable to make available to Americans abroad a four-page memorandum to guide them in answering embarrassing questions about what had happened in the City of Angels. The 2,000-word guide appeared on tables in U.S. embassies where travelers and American citizens domiciled in alien lands could easily lay hands on them. The obvious assumption was that many Americans abroad were ill-equipped to help repair the damage done by reports in the foreign press, especially that of Communist-oriented nations.

The tract, in question-and-answer form, suggested many causes for the riot, but it stressed unemployment and economic despair in the neighborhoods of the eruption. It was critical of California and Los Angeles authorities, saying both were tardy in summoning adequate force to put down the rioting once it broke out and suggesting that Los Angeles leaders had failed to react wisely to apparent frustrations in Negro communities. The guide also chided Los Angeles administrators for haggling over how federal funds for school and job projects might be disbursed, thus blocking the implementation of anti-poverty programs which, according to the authors of the memorandum, might have staved off the uprising.

"Much of the Saturday morning burning had been along Central Avenue. Again using sweep tactics, the Guardsmen and police were able to clear this area by 3:30 P.M.," the McCone Commission reported. "Guardsmen rode 'shotgun' on the fire engines and effectively stopped the sniping and rock throwing at firemen. Saturday evening, roadblocks were set up in anticipation of the curfew. The massive show of force was having some effect, although there was still riot activity and rumors spread regarding proposed activity in the south central area."

Among those not merely proposing activity, but purposefully engaged in it was Curtis Lee Gaines, no relation to Joyce, the young woman barber.

21

CURTIS LEE GAINES, though a young man, was almost as broad as he was tall. He was twenty-four, weighed 198 pounds and wore a goatee. He had been born in Arkansas. Since arriving in Los Angeles a year earlier he had experienced no trouble with the police.

But late Saturday afternoon he was inside Gold's Department Store, then in the process of being stripped by looters. Gold's faced Washington Boulevard and stood between Central Avenue and a short street called Essex. It was about a mile east of the Harbor Freeway and less than two miles south of Los Angeles' Civic Center, the city's pride, from which, now, the sky to the south appeared a dark gray patch from melding towers of smoke. On the Central Avenue side of Gold's, windows were smashed and most of their displays gone.

Police cars passing at the time saw shadowy figures moving inside the store and, at a loading door on the Essex side, a crowd of people stashing merchandise in cars and trucks. Negroes were pouring from the doorway, booty-laden. One man was burdened with two satchels filled with the components for an entire hi-fi set.

The passing police cars swung around on Washington and parked at the curb by the loading door. People ran blindly, some not fast enough. Those the officers intercepted were lined against the building. Other looters darted back along a narrow passageway into the store. Sergeants Glen Bachman and Len Leeds followed them. Across the street, flames from a blazing Thrifty Drugstore lighted their passage.

The late afternoon sunlight from the street also cast a glow into the long hallway, down which Leeds and Bachman followed what appeared to be several dark figures heading toward a storeroom. Leeds, armed with two .38-caliber revolvers and a twelve-gauge shotgun, yelled: "Come out. You're under arrest for burglary."

As the officers moved along the hall, Sergeant Leeds in the lead, two men burst past them and out the loading door. They did not follow, but proceeded on until they reached the total darkness of a storeroom. Bachman assured Leeds he was just behind him, then asked if Leeds thought a looter or looters were hidden in the room.

"I don't know. But I think so," Leeds replied.

Bachman paused to listen, then told Leeds: "Yes, I know there is. They are on my right."

Bachman, his eyes now accustomed to the dark, saw a man's figure uncoil from a shelf about three feet above the floor. Then he heard scuffling and Leeds call out: "You're under arrest."

Bachman could make out Leeds struggling with the man who had been hidden on the shelf and could discern that his fellow officer's assailant had one hand just in front of the trigger guard of Leeds' shotgun and the other hand on the policeman's which grasped the barrel. A tugging match ensued. The pair swung in a complete circle, battling for the gun. As they did so, Leeds felt the stock of the shotgun shatter, either against a wall or his antagonist's body.

Then Leeds pulled sharply and flew backwards with the gun in his possession. He saw the man moving toward Bachman and the exit from the storeroom. He recalled later that he was afraid the man was armed and that Bachman was in danger of being shot. "As he [the man] crossed in the silhouette of the door, I fired once with my shotgun from the hip, and at the same time I saw a flash to my right and rear, coming from a second gun," said Sergeant Leeds.

Bachman had not seen Leeds regain control of the shotgun during his struggle for it and when he saw the outline of the man in the doorway he thought the man had seized the weapon from Leeds. "At this time," said Bachman, "I was in fear that Sergeant Leeds' life was in danger, as well as my own. . . . I reached around Sergeant Leeds with my pistol and fired one shot. At the time I fired my pistol, Sergeant Leeds fired his shotgun. Both shots appeared to go into the back of the suspect. The suspect fell in the passageway. I looked at the suspect and I could see he was still alive."

Curtis Lee Gaines was taken to Central Receiving Hospital, then transferred to Los Angeles County General Hospital where, as the phrase goes, "he expired on arrival." At the inquest his death was ruled justifiable homicide.

"When the curfew started at 8 P.M. [Saturday], police and Guardsmen were able to deal with the riot area as a whole. Compared with the holocaust of Friday evening, the streets were relatively quiet. The only major exception was the burning of a block of stores on Broadway between 46th and 48th Streets. Snipers again prevented firemen from entering the areas, and while the buildings burned, a gun battle ensued between law enforcement officers, the Guard and snipers," reported the McCone Commission.

While many streets where rioting had raged previously were deserted, few Guardsmen, officers and newsmen remember Saturday as a night of "relative quiet."

"Saturday," as Lieutenant Wrenn remarked, was "clear but the hell was yet to come.

"Main Street," said Wrenn, "was densely populated by Negroes, most of them just kids, just kids looting, ages eight to seventeen, I'd guess. We were cruising along Main, and the whole place was on fire. We were told that the fire department was having trouble getting into the area and we were instructed to assist them.

"At 111th and Main, our two vehicles [machine gun-mounted Jeeps] paused where there was one fire truck. I noticed a TV store there. We cleared a path through the crowd so the firemen could get through. People in the crowd harassed us. There were only six of us, and a crowd of 500 people, and four firemen on the truck.

"As the truck got to the TV store, the building started to burn. We kept people away. As we did so, I could see four people running out of the back of a clothing store down the block. LAPD officers fired at them, then two more people ran out."

Over the Jeep's radio snapped a brisk warning: 50 gasoline drums were stored inside the second store. Wrenn and his fellow soldiers acted swiftly to disperse the crowd, fearing its members would be endangered by exploding drums if the four persons seen running from the store were arsonists. Their worst fears soon were realized.

"Suddenly," said Lieutenant Wrenn, "the building burst into flame. Next, two stores, then four buildings were on fire. And five minutes after we had dispersed the mob, the people were back."

No one was injured as flames gushed from building to building. Firemen put out the fires, but for four hours, Wrenn remembers, a wearyingly similar pattern was repeated: gathering mob, fire, returning mob, firemen fighting fire.

"The crowd," he said, "grew to 3,500. The Uncle Tom comments—such names as 'white nigger'—were thrown at me.*

* Sheriff's Lieutenant Don Torbert remembers that one Negro deputy in his flying squad took worse vilification than any of his white teammates. "He caught more than us," said Torbert. "They thought he was worse than the white officers—they accused him of 'trying to make his skin white.'" Other Negro officers who performed conspicuously valorous acts during the riot were exposed to similar verbal castigation.

Some in the crowd were drunk. They spurred the others on. We had rifles and mounted machine guns. But I didn't have enough people with me. I gave the order to load rifles after the crowd got so big. All rifles were pointed toward the sky; my intention was to fire in the air.

"But I managed to get some of the people in the crowd to help disperse it. I radioed for help and all I got was a major and a captain armed only with pistols." The young Negro lieutenant, all of whose subordinates were white, paused and said: "None of my men was disobedient; they were alert and responsive to military precision. About 3:30 [Saturday afternoon] we got things quelled."

The McCone report noted that this was the time the sweeps by Guardsmen were proving effective.

But calm was a chancy commodity that turbulent Saturday. Soon Lieutenant Wrenn and his men found themselves amidst a new frenzy.

"A black and white car [Los Angeles Police Department] appeared and things became fierce," said Wrenn. "The police were blocking off both sides of the street, when a blue pickup truck with two Caucasian fellows in it came through the intersection. They began shooting. They fired six or seven times at us. The heavy crowd prevented them from getting through the intersection. They stalled. One of the white fellows tried to start the truck, while the other one tried to reload his pistol. I couldn't fire back because of the crowd. But I told the men in the truck to dismount, and they did. They told police they wanted to help them. The police were pretty upset with them.

"Fire trucks again came into the area to put out a fire. And a panel truck came in, and when the driver, a Negro, saw the crowds, he panicked. His truck went wildly across a porch where some people were standing. But he didn't hit anyone, and his truck kept going and ran headlong into a palm tree.

"The fires never were completely out. Saturday night we continued to round up looters—then the snipers came into play.

Just as we left the area, we were fired upon. We found one fellow using a .22 rifle with .30-caliber ammunition. He and the others didn't seem to be doing much harm."

Lieutenant Wrenn's low regard for the snipers' marksmanship supports the observation that had not the Negroes firing from ambush been so lacking in skill, the riot death toll could have been enormous. The fact that Deputy Sheriffs Paul W. Wilson and Jack W. Innes are alive today is a case in point.

A fleeting encounter Saturday night between two young men whose lives never had touched before, who would never say a word to one another nor look directly in each other's face, left Joe Nelson Bridgett, twenty-two and a Negro, dead and Paul W. Wilson, twenty-nine and a Caucasian, crippled.

Two more totally unlike American males in their twenties would be hard to find. Paul Wilson, a Los Angeles County deputy sheriff, possessed nearly all the qualities found admirable in a young man. Joe Bridgett, alias Joe Horn, young though he was, already had acquired enough of a record, police believed, to bear watching.

Joe never was close to his mother. His grandmother reared him and took him to Los Angeles from his birthplace in Shreveport, Louisiana, when he was twelve. "He was a good child," said the grandmother, a worn-looking, heavyset woman. "I should know, because I took care of him all his life."

"I had my problems with Joe; he just couldn't stay home," said his estranged wife, a healthy-looking young woman who bore him two children. "He had to be out in the street all the time."

Whatever it was that Joe Bridgett did "out in the street," it got him in trouble with police the first time when he was only sixteen. He was arrested on suspicion of auto theft and the case disposed of through juvenile channels. As an adult, he got in trouble with narcotics officers, and was convicted, at least once, on a narcotics charge. He worked in a laundry for a time, said his grandmother, but by August, 1965, he was one of the thousands of idle young men populating Los Angeles' South Side.

Paul Wilson differed from Joe Bridgett in far more than his skin complexion. Six feet two, 210 pounds, he knew little of the tough street background in which Bridgett grew up until he joined the sheriff's office in 1962 and learned about that kind of life from the other side of the fence.

Paul Wilson was born and grew up in southeastern Oklahoma. Even as a boy he was industrious. No sooner was he graduated from Central High School in Marlow than he was busy working in a variety store. After two years in the service, he rejoined his family, which by then, 1957, had moved to California. He got a job first as an expediter in a small engineering plant, then went to work for General Motors as a tool crib attendant. Meanwhile, he was saving money to attend junior college in Compton, where he lived.

By November, 1961, he had worked up to administrative assistant with a showcase and fixtures firm—but by then he had been bitten by the law enforcement bug. The father of a friend was a sheriff's captain, and Paul Wilson enjoyed stopping by the station to visit with the elder man. He liked what he saw.

When rioting broke out in Los Angeles in mid-August, Paul Wilson for three years had been assigned to the Firestone Station, where his friend's father had been captain. Deputy Wilson escaped the first gusher of violence; he had been on vacation and was out of town. He reported for riot duty, however, on Saturday evening, August 14. At 8:30 P.M., whatever physical, mental and emotional renewal Paul Wilson, married and father of a seven-year-old daughter, might have derived from his holiday was spent in a brief moment.

Wilson and three other deputies, Jack Innes, D. J. Kennedy and Brian Keenan, began their tour of duty that night traveling together in a squad. Their job was to flush out looters and protect business establishments. Innes drove.

As he poked the patrol car's nose out of an alley and onto

Miramonte Boulevard just before 8:30, all four officers noticed a brown 1956 Pontiac parked on the west side of the street, about 100 feet south of Florence Avenue. The car was pulled alongside a curb at the rear side entrance to a Thrifty Drugstore. One man sat on the passenger side of the front seat. Another stood outside the Pontiac, handing a case filled with liquor bottles—four fifths of vodka, one fifth of Johnnie Walker Black Label Scotch and three half pints of Johnnie Walker Red Label to the seated man.

The deputies stopped, alighted and seized both men. As they were advising the two Negro men that they were under arrest on suspicion of burglary, the officers heard a racket coming from around the corner on Florence. Keenan remained with the two suspects. Innes, Kennedy and Wilson went to the drugstore's front entrance.

Through the smashed front door, the deputies saw two other male Negroes carrying what appeared to them to be boxes of liquor and cigarettes. The deputies ordered the pair to drop the boxes and come out of the store. The two men put the boxes down and began to emerge. At that moment, the intersection exploded with gunfire. To the startled deputies, it seemed to come from all directions.

Keenan left the two suspects he was holding and ran toward the front of the store. The two men who had been inside continued coming through the doorway. Deputy Paul Wilson felt what seemed at the moment little more than a "stinging sensation in the leg." Then he staggered toward the curb, crying to his companions: "I'm hit." What later appeared to have been a high-velocity bullet fired by a sniper, possibly from a moving vehicle, had struck Wilson in the groin.

Deputy Innes caught a slug in his upper left thigh during the volley of gunshots. The two men in the doorway charged onto the sidewalk. Another blast of gunfire narrowly missed the four deputies.

Deputies Kennedy and Keenan opened fire with their shotguns. One of the two men racing from the drugstore entrance collapsed on the sidewalk. The other staggered momentarily, wounded, but he got away. Kennedy and Keenan did not pursue him. They stood their ground to protect their injured companions in the event of new sniper fire.

In the glare of the light from street lamps overhead, they stood out like whitened figures in a shooting gallery. All four officers realized their peril. Wilson, lying almost directly beneath one light, fired at it, trying to black it out. He smashed the glass shield but could not knock out the bulb. Kennedy peppered the street lights with his shotgun, darkening the corner. Innes limped to the squad car and radioed for assistance.

Other officers quickly arrived. They found the two original suspects had fled. A dead man lay on his back on the sidewalk, his chest torn by eight shotgun pellets. He was Joe Nelson Bridgett, alias Joe Horn. The young man whom his wife remembers as a street roamer was only five blocks from his home when he died.

Sheriff's officers put his body in an ambulance. Then they tried to telephone the County Road department to advise officials in charge of street lighting that some repairs would have to be made at the intersection of Miramont Boulevard and Florence Avenue. The road department was closed.

22

REPORTER ROBERT RICHARDSON, a Negro newspaperman, remembers how it was that Saturday night, the first night of curfew, and how he asked himself, then others: "Why the riots?" Some of the answers, he recalls, were "like a slap in the face." One, he said, was "a scream":

"We are going to put the fear of the Negro into these white people because they do not have the fear of God."

After nightfall, Richardson roamed the area with friends in a car, seeking to piece together from the confusion of the night information for his newspaper. He carried press identification, but the scrap of cardboard did not alleviate his sense of peril.

"Out of the streets behind us—where there had been a deceptive silence—a hostile crowd begins to form," he wrote for the *Times*. "Suddenly, police officers with raised shotguns come striding toward us. 'Out of your car. Hands up—high!'

"We do not know what to do. But we get out, all trying to say at once that we are working newsmen. 'Get the hell out,' is the reply from the officers.

"We do. We get back into the car, make a U-turn and drive through the restive crowd that stares at us. Five police officers, helmeted and holding shotguns, watch us warily as we move away.

"At 120th and Central Avenue, I am stunned by the sight of the demolished supermarket that once boasted of its equal hiring practices. I get out of the car and look at the rubble, thinking, this was the store where I came with my mother as a little boy . . . where I met with other neighborhood kids and drank soda pop and talked about football. I am trying to think about that when someone shouts and footsteps come rushing toward me.

"The other guys in the car yell: 'Move, man, move!'

"Then there is a shotgun in my face and a policeman says: 'Move on, mister. Let's go now. Move.'

"In the policeman's face there is no awareness that I am trying to see my childhood in the charred wreckage of a supermarket. His eyes are only the eyes of a man with a job to do. . . .

"We cruise through the dark streets, empty except for an occasional caravan of police cars and busses. There are the sounds of sporadic shooting and we don't know whether to turn out our lights or keep them on.

"In the Watts area, we can see the flicker of flames and we head for it. But suddenly we see helmeted men running across the street with rifles and ducking behind buildings. Out of the darkness comes the command: 'Get out of here!'

"Guardsmen have their rifles pointed at the car. There is a sign in the street: 'Turn left or get shot.'

"We turn left.

"On Manchester Avenue, traveling west from Alameda Street, we find a service station open and pull into it. Three or four Negro men are crouched behind cartons of motor oil watching us. They are scared and so are we. We get out of our car slowly, seeing no weapons but taking no chances. The men come out from behind their barricades just as slowly—and suddenly there is a handshake and we are treating each other like old friends.

"No one has ordered them to close, so they have stayed open—the only service station for miles around. We get smokes and Cokes from machines and move out, following screaming fire engines.

"At Manchester and Broadway, we are stopped by a command post and checked out. I look across the street at a store where only Tuesday I bought a new pair of shoes. Now there is only smoldering rubble.

"Going up Broadway from 85th Street, we see the sky lighting up with orange. Fire trucks are coming from everywhere. Police caravans are crisscrossing the area. About ten officers have two Negro teenagers on the corner, searching them.

" 'Halt!' comes the bellow under a bullhorn.

" 'Halt!' A second time.

"I shove the brake to the floorboards. We are ordered out with our hands up.

"We shout: 'Press.'

" 'OK, get back in your car.'

"The Negro boys are being turned loose and ordered to run double-time away from the area. They move. We head for the fire.

"We get there and find a complete block of stores ablaze. Flames are boiling up and thick smoke is spilling into the sky. But the firemen are hiding under their trucks as the buildings burn. Police are scattering, seeking cover. There are shots.

"A store window crashes in near me and my friends are making it back to the car. A policeman charges toward me with a shotgun in one hand, a revolver in the other.

" 'Who are you people?' he demands.

"I show identification. Another window shatters and the glass falls at my feet. We duck. I run for the car. We make another fast U-turn and we're on our way home. It's time to go home."

The nostalgia felt by Richardson, born and reared in Los Angeles, was something considerably less than a universal sentiment among the young in the city's Negro neighborhoods. Indeed, if anything, it reflected merely a minority feeling, a small minority at that.

No ghetto can be satisfactory to those living in it, and little exists in a ghetto, as a result, for residents to wax nostalgic about. The prevalent sentiment among the vast majority of the young and embittered in the neighborhoods on fire was articulated by the strident voices calling: "Burn, baby, burn."

The grievances of the rioters and those who tacitly applauded their conduct will be picked apart, held up to the light and agonized over in ponderous sociological tomes as yet unwritten. The authors of these volumes will find the beginnings to the answers they seek in such voices of protest and dreams gone sour as these:

A twenty-two-year-old male Negro—"We went into the stores and took the clothing we needed. Man, some of the people don't have jobs, and they don't have money and they needed clothes. So they took them after the windows were broken. Me, personally, I was angry about this whole police thing. I saw a whole lot of police brutality in my time in Watts.

"Police brutality is like when they arrest you where it can't be seen and whip on you. They grab you when you walk down the street. They pull you over and beat on you. That ain't right. Man, I was born in California—in Long Beach. But I'm a Negro, so I been arrested.

"I was out there in that thing [the rioting] for three days. Yeah, I took things. Hell, I know what it is to do without. There was no leaders; the burnings was done by everybody. I threw bricks and rocks at white people in cars, and I'm sorry I missed now because I wanted to hurt them.

"I was a car wash until two days after the riots started. The guy that owned the car wash came over and asked me, while I was working, if I lived in Watts, and I told him I did, and he said: 'You're fired.' I asked him what for and he told me he didn't need a reason.

"That night I was right back out there in it. I got arrested after that night [Sunday] for burglary, but they released me afterwards."

A middle-aged female cook—"I don't feel anything about the burning—we didn't have the guts to do it when I was young. Johnson [President Lyndon B. Johnson] signed a bill to fix up this area and the white people downtown there are fighting like cats and dogs over it. All we got around here is a nasty filthy market."

A thirty-year-old Watts tavern owner—"It was a revolt. Every man wants to be a man; nobody has a right to deprive him of that. What can a man do with $1.15 an hour? Police don't care about us. We had a colored policeman down here that made life hell for the people. He ran a make* on everybody in this community, up until two weeks before the riots. We put together a petition against him—but we don't need that any more.

"It was a hell's pit down here before the riot. What was put on us we had to accept. The colored cop told us he was down here to clean up the hell's pit.

"Stores didn't do anything for us. We made a survey last week and found that for $2.77 you could get the same goods elsewhere that sell for $3.00 in Watts. And most of the goods down here are 'seconds' and 'thirds.' "

A thirty-two-year-old racetrack groom—"Police brutality has been going on for years. I remember the time they would take you in a back alley and whip you before they took you to the police station. One time they caught me out behind Santa Anita Race Track and whipped me something terrible. I wasn't doing anything. I was just out of my place—so they thought. Nobody wants to be jacked up all the time, when you haven't done anything."

A sixty-year-old disabled veteran of World War II—"The riots came because there was no work, and when people went down to the stores for a loaf of bread, the owners and clerks they treat them like dogs. But I believe now this has happened, it's going to be better. The younger generation wants more now and they better get it or it's going to be hell down here."

A neighborhood association leader—"Man, I want everything the whites got."

* Checking with the Los Angeles Police Records Bureau to ascertain if the person had been arrested previously, or if there were any outstanding warrants calling for his apprehension.

An unemployed twenty-year-old male—"Yeah, I was out there looting with the rest of them. The temptation was too much. The police passed by and people were taking things and they didn't say nothing, so why the hell not? I didn't break any windows. But I got two television sets and sold them."

A forty-six-year-old father of six—"The cops grabbed me by the collar and shot me in the side at 46th and Central on Friday. A friend of mine who was with me asked me, was I shot? and they jumped on him and beat him up. On the way to jail, they was steady-loading the bus. Every time they saw a crowd standing on a corner, they would jump off the bus, those cops, and shoot their rifles. Before they put me on the bus, a fireman jumped me. I wasn't doing anything. I was just watching and there were a lot of people just watching.

"If I ever made enough money, I would move out of Watts like all the other big shots. So I'm here, so what the hell. Los Angeles isn't all it's cracked up to be. Wherever you go, you're black—that's all there is to it."

A twenty-seven-year-old man—"Jobs are poor, for the simple reason the white society doesn't want the Negro to get a good job and become part of the structure. I've had two years of college and I have a scum job.

"The white merchants have extracted everything from this community and given nothing back. We are charged high interest. Those people live in Bel-Air and Beverly Hills. They won't hire you unless you work for less than minimum wages.

"Then they take their money and run off to a Beverly Hills bank. They keep those places clean and smelling sweet and no Negroes. Man, I came from Mississippi. This ain't supposed to be Mississippi, but I run into damn near the same kind of treatment."

A twenty-four-year-old father—"Have you tried to look for a job day after day and the man tell you no? Then a white boy come out and tell you he got the job?

"Man, you walk the streets all day and half the night, then

you got to go home and tell your wife and kids you can't find a job. On your way home . . . some cop want to crack your skull or put you in jail for vag.

"Man, they can go to hell. Look, I'll hustle first. I'll get me some money the best way I can. I've had it with equality and all these lies about opportunity."

A twenty-year-old mother of three illegitimate children—"Whites have everything. If Negroes try to go into business, they're told they're not qualified. There's always something to keep Negro men down—always some excuse to keep Negro men from getting ahead, from getting a break."

An unemployed father of two who was getting help from the Travelers Aid Society—"Some people say they would be too proud to accept this aid, but not me. When your stomach starts pushing your backbone, you forget about being proud."

A twenty-five-year-old Air Force veteran, unemployed for five months—"Some people get into trouble with the police when they see something that looks easy. So they try to get away with it and get caught instead. But, man, it's very hard to avoid having an arrest record in this town. The police are on you every minute."

A thirty-year-old Los Angeles–born man—"Pressure, man, pressure. Negroes have been through so much pressure—low-paying jobs, bad housing. . . . The average Negro has been arrested. They may use police brutality as an excuse, but actually it's a lack of knowledge. It's easier to blame someone else. The Negro here has it easier than in the South. Here, he thinks he is being done wrong. He thinks this because of a lack of leadership. Hell, man, there ain't no leadership."

A twenty-six-year-old Navy veteran, recently arrived from Gary, Indiana—"I want a job and all that, but I'm telling you like it is. I want some employment and I don't want to beg. I done took part in civil rights demonstrations and right now all I want is a job.

"I live right around the corner from where the rioting all

happened. I didn't break any windows, but I ran with the crowd. I had to, or I might have been shot.

"I don't hate white people, but I do understand that they live off the sweat of the Negro. We came out here because we thought we might be able to get jobs, but it's hard, man, real hard."

Then there was the twenty-year-old rioter who insisted he be known as "Joe," jobless and the archetype of the frustrated young adult Negro who saw the riot as a civil uprising against the city's white establishment. His is a voice those who write scholarly tomes dissecting the causes of the troubled six days in Los Angeles would do well not to forget.

Joe, born in San Francisco, but a Watts resident since he was a year old.

Joe, whose father left his mother when he was two.

Joe, who didn't know whether his father was dead or alive, who knew only that his mother worked in a fish cannery to support him, an older brother and a younger sister, but some days didn't make it to work because the family's twelve-year-old car wouldn't start.

Joe, who had worked a total of four months since getting out of high school three years earlier; who three times had enrolled in junior college, but each time had quit because the money ran out, what little there was of it.

Joe, who believed white policemen "were always stopping me," and delivered this commentary on his personal experiences with officers: "It seemed like they always were trying to see if they could make me break, make me do something that would save them time. It seemed like they figured they'd eventually have me in jail and they wanted to save time.

"I remember one night [months before the riot] a cop stopped me and said: 'I've seen you before. You've been in jail. I'm gonna check on you, punk.'

"That night I really wanted to do something—something to that white face. But I kept thinking about my mother, how she always had told me to stay out of trouble. I figured I'd gone this far without trouble, so I held back. My mother really takes things hard."

After the riot began, Joe remembers: "I didn't realize what they were doing when the looting began. I didn't understand the object of the looting. At first it just began with people breaking windows and taking nothing. Then I realized the object of the looting: it was to move all the whites out of Watts. We don't want white people in Watts.

"When they first began breaking windows, it was to drive the whites out of business. Then the people began grabbing food and things they don't normally have. They decided as long as we drive Whitey out, there's no use letting the stuff just lay there. Take it.

"TV made it look like the Negroes were a disgrace to LA during the riot, like everything bad that was happening was happening to the police."

Joe, his past a festering sore that burst with the rioting, believed that the trouble would come to Los Angeles again, and, perhaps, again after that. "Maybe it's all in my mind because I still feel something about it," he said. "But I know it can explode all over again. All that has happened is not something me or my people are likely to forget.

"Would I riot again? I just don't know. But I know the slightest thing could touch me off.

"If it comes again? I guess I will be there. Everybody has to be willing to sacrifice something for what he believes in. I'd be out of place, wouldn't I, if my race was out there fighting and I wasn't?

"We really don't live alike, the whites and the Negroes. As long as the whites keep trying to brutalize my people, I'll have to be out there trying to stop them."

In the Watts in which Joe lived, in the almost entirely Negro neighborhood of Marquette Frye and in the other broad black belts and swatches of Los Angeles, the word "brutality" had a very real meaning. And almost always it was coupled with another word, "police."

Whether or not Bill Parker's police force of 1965 deserved the epithet, the expression "police brutality," nonetheless, had foundation in fact. Police, not merely in Los Angeles alone but in many, many American cities, had compiled a past history of mistreatment of the Negro.

"Police brutality is really an ancient image that hasn't been washed away," a Los Angeles Negro patrolman, Norman Edelen, commented. "It takes time. The Negro community has a hard time accepting the fact that things have changed.

"Today, it's the rare cases of brutality, like all things that are bad, that get all the notoriety. But really, few officers overdo it. . . . I would not characterize the LAPD as brutal. It's just the victim of the history it has done nothing to change."

But even if police brutality were rare in 1965, as Edelen believed, instances of it were enough to provide Negroes with a reason for keeping the expression alive. It supplied a shelter under which Negro resentment against the white establishment thrived. And, after all, most Negroes' only contacts with whites were with police. The policeman, to them, represented the white establishment.

The subtle signs of racial contempt Negroes sensed in experiences with even the best white officers represented what they, at least, believed to be the attitude of Los Angeles' white community, an attitude which, in their eyes, had stripped them of one of man's dearest possessions: his dignity.

It was no secret, or at least a poorly kept one, that even in 1965 Watts and other Negro neighborhoods were known as "duck ponds," where policemen, without giving their action a second thought, continued to use expressions like "boy" or "nigger." In these neighborhoods, too, officers freely conducted what were known as "FIs"—or field investigations. Some officers were notorious among Negroes for the practice of what Joe described as "always stopping me."

Those checked out by police during these random investigations were required to supply information which was entered on a 3″-by-5″ field-interrogation slip. These slips later were put in a master cross file designed to keep track of possible troublemakers and wanderers with prior criminal records.

To the young Negro walking home from a movie or date, with no thought of wrongdoing on his mind, undergoing an "FI" was a commonplace experience. One policeman, in an off-guard moment, explained the practice by saying: "If a certain station feels that it has not made enough arrests for a month, it turns to the local 'duck pond.' In this way, many individuals are caught on minor charges, like failure to appear on traffic warrants and things like that."

To Negroes humiliated by "FIs," mainly young adults and teenagers, the practice was simply police brutality in an artful disguise.

Something more than oil must gurgle deep beneath the Red River country soil around Shreveport, Louisiana. Whatever it is produces a contagion among many people there. They hear music and they want to sing what they hear.

George Adams, the forty-five-year-old father of 15 children who died in the crossfire of a police-sniper gun battle Friday night, was born and grew up on a tiny farm near Shreveport. He sang because he loved to, but not many people heard his voice.

Charles Patrick Fizer, born a generation after George Adams in that cotton-corn-and-oil metropolis of northwestern Louisiana, also sang because he loved to—and for money. People paid to hear Charles Fizer sing. For a brief time, he made it big.

Charles's family called him Sonny. Others sometimes called him Charles Patrick Smalley, Smalley being the last name of a father who was almost unknown to him. Fizer was the maiden name of his mother, a member of a proud family which, even in Louisiana, disdained "Uncle Tom" customs.

Most of the Fizer family migrated to California during World War II to take jobs in the buzzing Los Angeles area aircraft plants and shipyards. In 1944, when he was only three, Charles Fizer was taken there by his grandparents. He lived with them for a time. Then, when he was seven, he moved to Watts with his mother.

The Fizer family was a religious one. Charles attended the Sweet Home Baptist Church and became an enthusiastic choir member. He had a good voice. By the time he was fifteen, he was singing in night clubs. He quit school in the eleventh grade, and his family worried about the gamy, after-dark element he hung out with. His relatives' concern was justified: when he was seventeen, he was hit by an errant bullet while watching a gang fight; he was picked up for smoking marijuana.

But Charles Fizer shook off these troubles. He became part of a successful group of entertainers. He broke in singing second lead with the Olympics, as the group was known. Then he advanced to first lead. Using his gift for humor, he developed a comic patter to go with the act.

Came the Olympics' recording of "Hully Gully," and Charles Fizer was something to be reckoned with as an entertainer. The record sold nearly a million copies. The Olympics won television guest shots. Charles came up with a snaky dance to fit the "Hully Gully" music. Other hit songs followed, and it seemed nothing could stop Charles Fizer from reaching the top.

But Charles Fizer had known what it was to be a second-class citizen of Los Angeles, and later he learned the indignity of being a Negro entertainer on tours of the South. Friends and his family sensed a change in him as he began remarking more and more bitterly on the difference between the lives led by whites and Negroes—not only in the South, but in the supposedly enlightened City of Los Angeles. His luck changed, too.

Charles became restless. With his fellow performers, he became impatient. His testy attitude and souring views cost him his job with the singing group. He and another entertainer formed a night-club duo, but it flopped.

The summer of the Los Angeles riot, he hit bottom. He

served six months at hard labor on a county prison farm after being arrested with illegal barbiturates.

He was released Thursday, August 12. The riot already was in progress. But Charles Fizer, under the influence of a scholarly white prisoner he had met while serving his sentence, had resolved to make a new start.

Even as the violence spread in Los Angeles, Charles Fizer wakened early Friday, went job-hunting and found work as a busboy. He worked the night shift that very day. But there would be no work Saturday—the restaurant manager decided to close until peace was restored in the city.

Charles spent Saturday talking with his family about what was happening in Los Angeles. Then he spruced up, borrowed an uncle's 1955 Buick. He planned to visit a girl friend, and return home before the 8 P.M. curfew.

But that night Charles Fizer drove through Watts after the curfew hour. In the center of the fire-blackened community, he stopped short of a National Guard roadblock at 102nd and Beach Streets.

Inexplicably, he backed the Buick away from the barricade. Suddenly, he turned on the car's headlights and shifted into forward gear.

What compelled him to jam the accelerator to the floor only he could say—and soon he was past explaining. Too many white faces challenging him? Perhaps. A white man giving him an order? Perhaps.

In any event, he pointed the car straight for the roadblock. Guardsmen cried to him to halt and fired warning shots into the air. Then came the roar of M-1 carbines. The Buick spun crazily and rammed a curb.

Charles Fizer never realized his resolve to make a new life. Inside the car he lay dead, a bullet in his left temple. The time was 9:15 P.M.

23

RUMOR OF IMPENDING ATTACK on police and sheriff's stations proliferated Saturday. Extraordinary precautions were taken.

Ten miles from the original riot area, in the heart of the megalopolis, heavily armed policemen patrolled boundaries of a parking lot separating Los Angeles Police Headquarters from the street. Other officers, stationed atop a balcony, commanded an elevated view of comings and goings. Every entrance to the "Glass House" was covered by weaponry. Inside, for the first time in the memory of Caroll (Spud) Corliss of the *Times,* dean of the police press corps, policewomen took their guns from their handbags and strapped them on.

Officers reported for duty carrying their own shotguns and hunting rifles, at their superiors' suggestion. These supplemented their standard service revolvers, the only weapons with which they normally were armed.

A not uncommon sight was a motorcycle officer scooting along with a shotgun or rifle strapped to him or his machine. Some wore hunting jackets over their official blues. These held the shells for their personal weapons. No one quibbled about a policeman being out of uniform during this turbulent time.

A request for short-barreled riot guns went out over the statewide police teletype. Response came from as far away as San Francisco 400 miles to the north.

Most frequent reports of forthcoming strikes by rioters centered on the Firestone Sheriff's Station and the city's police substation in Watts. As early as Friday, extra shotguns were dispatched to stations in sensitive areas. Deputy Sheriff Robert O'Sullivan remembers that, before being summoned to the scene of the Ronald Ludlow shooting, he had helped carry a fresh inventory of such weapons into the Firestone Sheriff's Station. Because of rumors that the building faced a siege, Acting Commander Isom Dargan and other superior officers had ordered that all exterior lights there remain dark at night and that those inside, wherever possible, be dimmed.

Times reporter Eric Malnic recalls "finding the place dark" upon a visit to the station at 10 P.M. Saturday. "Some distance from the building," he said, "deputies suddenly sprang up from cover, shotguns ready, and ordered us to cut the car lights and back out slowly.

"We phoned from a booth and got permission to approach again and enter the station. We returned slowly, lights out. The place was surrounded by deputies, armed with shotguns. People were advised, once inside, to stay clear of windows. Snipers were reported nearby. Scouting parties of deputies were sent out to 'case' nearby streets for them.

"While we were in the station, deputies brought in three women, all accused looters, all in their thirties and all neatly dressed. One laughed defiantly, one sat in numbed silence and a third put her head in her folded arms and cried softly.

"When we left, deputies told us we were on our own—that they couldn't guarantee our safety in any direction. We hit Florence and ran all the traffic lights."

Good reason existed for the precautions taken by Firestone officers. Earlier the Watts substation had been a snipers' target. A man lay dead in the morgue as proof. The victim may have been guilty of nothing more than standing in the doorway of a nearby hotel. But Andrew Houston, Jr., forty-one, was beyond saying whether this were so or not.

Across the street from the hotel and the Watts police substation—an intermittent object of sniper fire—a young National

Guardsman surveyed the 4 A.M. darkness from a second-story rooftop. The bespectacled young soldier, Douglas W. Mercer, heard shots below him. He ran to the front of the roof and "scanned the surrounding area." Below him, policemen pointed guns toward the second floor of the hotel across an alley from the station. Mercer's eyes traveled in the direction the police guns were aimed. He saw a man "standing in the doorway leading to a balcony on the second floor" of the hotel.

"I fired a warning shot against the side of the building," said Mercer. "He [the man on the balcony] moved out of my sight and then reappeared and I believed he was going to shoot the police in the street. I shot him."

Mercer's aim was amazingly accurate, considering the lack of light and the fact that his only target was a patch of white shirt he glimpsed across the darkened street. Or his shot was a lucky one. It tore into Houston's head, killing him at once.

At the sound of Mercer's gunfire, Guard Lieutenant William C. Johnston strode toward the hotel and, once inside, found police already there. The officers told Johnston they had discovered a .22-caliber pistol and a .22-caliber sawed-off rifle in the manager's office on the first floor. Both weapons, they said, were loaded. No other guns were found in the hotel, and no weapon near Houston's body.

Testifying at an inquest which resulted in a coroner's jury ruling that Houston's death was "justifiable homicide," Mercer said: "I saw only his white shirt. I could not say if he was holding a gun or not."

Law enforcement now had on its side crude but effective roadblocks and imposing weaponry—M-1 carbines, machine guns, shotguns—plus a preponderance of well-equipped manpower. But the snipers still had on their side stealth and the terror produced by sudden ambush—or at least the panicky sensation the threat of it posed.

With these as the distinguishing elements on the opposing sides, the warfare raged through Sunday and into Monday and Tuesday. Even with the lifting of the curfew Tuesday, uneasiness persisted throughout Los Angeles. And the city's citizens continued to die from riot-induced causes—if at a slower pace.

During Sunday, Monday and Tuesday, police and Guardsmen acted with mounting force in flushing suspected snipers from hiding and intercepting intruders at previously contested intersections where now stood barricades.

"One move and I'll kill you," rasped an officer as a suspected sniper tentatively reared his head from a gutter in which he had been ordered to lie.

"Shoot one, shoot one fast, if they don't come out," instructed another, as his squad headed toward a building believed to be a snipers' nest.

A Negro policeman, searching a youth he suspected of looting, scolded the young man for "the way you've screwed up this town." He punctuated his instructions to the young Negro with a jab of his gun and a slap of his hand: "Look straight ahead, goddamit. You gonna loot any more? You're goddam right you're not gonna loot any more."

Outside a Central Avenue apartment, where police had routed residents with gunfire, a man and two women were forced prone on the lawn, face-down. One of the women whimpered: "Ain't nuthin' here but babies and one or two half-husbands. You shot right into a houseful of babies. Just because I'm a Negro doesn't mean I don't love my black babies just as much as you love your white ones."

A pedestrian objected to being halted by police; he claimed he was going innocently home from work. "Don't yell at me; you lost your rights a couple of days ago," snapped an officer in reply to his protests.

The pedestrian snapped back, directing his remarks to two other policemen: "He thinks everything black is wrong. Well, you ain't the man no more. Who are you to judge any black man?"

But if law enforcement sometimes was heavy-handed during its time of trial in Los Angeles, some of its harsh response frequently was deserved. Trigger-happy snipers, all else aside, were provocation enough to warp the enforcers' conduct on many occasions, especially since officers and Guardsmen alone were not the only targets. Newsmen also experienced the trauma associated with sneak gunfire.

Three such newsmen were Eric Malnic and photographer Cal Montney of the *Los Angeles Times* and Roland Faure of Paris' *L'Aurore,* a French journalist with jet black hair and the slender, supple physique of a ballet master.

The Frenchman wheedled the Los Angeles pair into letting him accompany them into the riot area late Saturday night. They agreed to let him go along in the photographer's radio-equipped car, but they had the gravest misgivings. They feared Faure underrated the danger of such a venture.

"It was eerie," Malnic wrote in next day's *Times* of their journey through the curfew zone. "A large segment of a great city was silent and deserted—except for alert men in uniform who stood watching, waiting, searching. The silence of the empty streets seemed more terrifying than the howling mobs. . . . On a rooftop or behind a window, eyes might be watching and a hand might squeeze a trigger to shatter the silence—or a life."

On the preceding night, Malnic had learned such a possibility was not idle speculation. As the three newsmen cruised, they heard a report of a shooting on Florence Avenue. Speeding toward the scene, they ran into what appeared to them a blazing gun battle about half a block away.

"We stopped right there, dead, and pulled to the side of the street and turned off our lights and hit the floor of the car," said Montney. "We crouched as low as we could get. We could see sheriff's officers on both sides of the street, firing east up Florence. They were crouched behind cars and around corners of buildings. During a lull, one of the officers hollered from where he'd come alongside of us: 'Get your ass out of here.'

"We did. We backed up down the street for a block and parked behind another car, out of range of the gunfire. Then we headed back to the Freeway, but we got a call from the office radio that a man had been shot at Vernon Avenue and the [Harbor] Freeway off-ramp.

"We got to a checkpoint at Grand and Vernon. We were talking to a National Guard captain there, and he said we were nuts for being out there. We agreed.

"Then it happened. It was 11 P.M. An old Cadillac roared west on Vernon Avenue at Figueroa. National Guardsmen opened fire at the vehicle when the driver refused an order to halt. Both front tires were punctured. Bullets riddled the car body and the middle-aged Negro behind the wheel.

"The car careened across the Harbor Freeway overpass and came to a halt 100 yards away. *Times* photographer Cal Montney, French journalist Roland Faure and I pulled up near the riddled Cadillac. A helmeted police officer shouted to us: 'Get out of here. You're taking your life in your hands. We haven't got this area controlled.'

"But like other newsmen that night, we ignored the danger; we got out of the car. I started walking toward the Cadillac. A shot rang out. The bullet struck the ground a foot from Montney and Faure. We dashed for cover and flattened out on the pavement.

"Many shots rang out. Police and Guardsmen converged on the area. Machine-gun bullets and rifle fire zipped through the air. The sniper seemed to be firing from a building on the northwest corner of Vernon and Broadway.

"I was lying beside the Cadillac near an officer firing at the sniper's nest. Amid the sporadic firing a police ambulance rolled up to take the unconscious driver to a hospital. The two-man ambulance crew crawled up to the car and pulled the wounded man out. Then, ignoring the sniper, the ambulance attendants stood up, fully exposing themselves, in order to place the wounded man in the ambulance. Quickly, they drove off.

"During a lull in the firing, the Guardsmen leaped back into their trucks and prepared to move out. The young soldiers sat in silence, guns poised and ready, faces pale and expressionless.

"A young officer cursed and shouted orders to hurry. In a moment, the small convoy had disappeared around a corner. The police slipped from their cover and began to move up the street in groups of two and three. Slowly, zigzagging from doorway to doorway, they hunted the unseen sniper."

Montney, flat beneath his automobile with the French newspaperman, heard what he took to be "several hundred rounds" of machine-gun fire passing over them. "For some reason, they aimed low, because the shots hit a chain link fence across the street—and the bullets began ricocheting back and hitting the curb around us," said the photographer. "The only thing I can recall was that it was like a small-scale war and the Frenchman and I, for some reason or other, were grinning at each other.

"I don't know what was funny, because we really should have been scared stiff. When the policemen went into one building looking for the sniper, Eric asked: 'Shall we follow them in?'

"I said: 'No. Let's get out of here.'

"We did."

When Montney, a trim, youthful-looking grandfather, and Malnic returned to the Times building in the Civic Center with Faure, they looked at their begrimed clothing. "We were filthy," said Malnic, a cool twenty-nine-year-old California-born Ivy Leaguer. "We were covered with wet ashes from fires, oil from the street in which we lay, and sweat—of the cold variety. Then we looked at Roland Faure. His perfectly tailored suit still was pressed and clean, every slicked-down hair on his well-groomed head still was in place. And he had ducked into every ruin, and had scuttled, belly-down, on every street that we had."

Faure calmly sat down to write a story for his newspaper, *L'Aurore,* which would headline it in bold type: *"Roland Faure a veçu au plus dur des batailles de rue."* And beneath that, in even blacker type: "LA REVOLT DES NOIRS à LOS ANGELES."

As Faure wrote for Frenchmen, Malnic and Montney produced material for their own paper, while trading recollections of grotesqueries that they had encountered during the dangerous night. Montney could not forget what he had observed at one liquor store: looters cleaned the shelves of beer and cheap wine, but left untouched the good bonded bourbons and expensive scotches for which, apparently, they had cultivated no taste.

As for Malnic, he recalled that "at the peak of the shooting, a San Francisco reporter backed up his car to leave the scene in a hurry. But he neglected to close both right-hand doors of the auto. He got away safely enough—but he left the car doors behind. They dangled from our rear fender on which they'd caught when he backed away so furiously."

Charles Fizer, creator of the "Hully Gully," died Saturday night at a barricade of garbage cans. No fifes and drums for him. This is the way it was during the riot.

Death came coarsely, without even a wisp of glory. The blockades thrown up by Guardsmen and police were ugly reminders of death's contempt for human dignity during this time of chaos.

Days later, Lieutenant Colonel Thomas T. Haykin of the California National Guard described the crude construction of a roadblock: "You take whatever you have available—a garbage can, sign, broken glass, any refuse you can find to cause the vehicle to slow down or for it to hit prior to getting through the block. In our particular case, we had to make available any obstacles we could find to throw in. We used some automobiles after they were shot up, dragged them into the intersection to slow people down. We had people positioned at the roadblock, however, ahead of the roadblock in each case, people to warn the occupant to go back."

Lonnye Lee Cook didn't slow down, she didn't go back.

24

TO ALL OUTWARD appearances, Lonnye Lee Cook was a swinger. But to her eternally patient husband of more than twenty years, she was a woman with troubles who tried to lose whatever was gnawing at her in alcohol.

Clayborne Cook, fifty-two, never was quite certain exactly what bothered his wife. Sometimes he thought it was the "fast" home life she knew as a child; sometimes he placed the blame on himself, or rather on the fact that he was a staunch Baptist and she was a Catholic. But whatever it was that troubled Lonnye, Clayborne Cook was certain that it killed her just as surely as did the National Guard machine-gun bullets which tore into her tiny body (five feet, 100 pounds) just before dawn Sunday.

Lonnye Lee was tough; it took her almost three days to die. "I was just driving home and they shot me. I don't know what I'm going to do," she moaned as her husband sat at her bedside in Los Angeles County General Hospital.

Lonnye Lee Cook was a beauty, with big brown eyes and creamy chocolate skin. Maybe that was part of her trouble. Men liked her. And one woman, in particular, liked her too.

Lonnye Lee grew up in Cleveland, Ohio. "When she was a child," said Clayborne Cook, "her family had money. Her real father was an auto mechanic. But her stepfather, he had something to do with numbers. He was big in it. Her family was a fast crowd. But they sent her to school in a convent."

Lonnye Lee married the first time when she was in her early twenties. She had a son. The first marriage didn't last long. Then she met Clayborne Cook, sober-minded, hard-working. "I told her my birthday was coming up," he said, "and she told me she would bake me a cake. And she did." They were married and in 1952 moved to California.

Clayborne Cook prospered; Lonnye Lee drank. "She was all right until she drank," her husband said. "Her problem was drinking—it always got her into trouble. That's the way the thing with this other woman started. Started with her drinking.

"We separated about four years ago [in 1961], and she went to live with this woman, this girl friend of hers. It was one of those kind of relationships. You know what I mean—not the right kind. After it started, she was scared of this girl, and every once in a while she'd run away. But she couldn't make it stick. She was scared. But the girl kept after her.

"I know how it was for her. We kept in touch. She told me everything. And from time to time, I'd help her along with a little money when she couldn't get work [as a maid]. When she worked, she supported her and this other woman."

During this relationship, Lonnye Lee was arrested on a prostitution charge. But Clayborne Cook never believed that, despite her love of good times, his estranged wife would have stooped to whoring—even if she needed money. "A drinker, yes. A prostitute, no," he said. "It was—what do you call it? Entrapment? Here's what really happened—she told me all about it herself.

"One night a colored cop came over to her house and they were sitting there having a few drinks. You know, the way it happens when you go over to see a girl. You have a few drinks. Well, this guy was a colored cop. And she knew him. But the next thing that happened, he pulled a badge and said she was under arrest. Yeah, it was entrapment. They put her on probation. But she was no prostitute."

In June, 1965, Lonnye Lee—"Cookie" to many of her friends

—broke off her relationship with the woman. According to her husband, she got the strength to do it from another man.

"She met this big developer from Pasadena. A white man. He was married, but separated. He told me once his wife would kill him if she ever found out about Lonnye. He set up an apartment for Lonnye. I never went over there, but I'd talk to him on the phone. It was a nice building, but one of those places where nobody minded what anyone else did because they were doing the same thing themselves."

Clayborne Cook, the very soul of forbearance, approved of Lonnye Lee's new liaison: he believed it would mean the end of her long affair with the woman, which he bitterly opposed. But he was wrong. And, in fact, because she could not fully break away from the woman, Lonnye Lee perished.

"The Pasadena man really liked that girl," said Clayborne Cook. "But he would get mad with Lonnye over the other woman. He would give her money and find out she had given it to the woman. But she realized she had a good thing in him, and, well, she decided she would straighten up and go back to him after they split up. On that Friday before she got killed, he gave her the money to go and get a new apartment, and she did.

"I spoke to her on Saturday. We talked about the riot. I said to her: 'You mean you ain't gonna get out there in it?' And she said to me: 'No, I got some ironing to do.'

"This Pasadena man told me he came home about seven Saturday night with a bottle. Lonnye was ironing. He said she stopped ironing and said she was going out because she needed cigarettes. He told her she had cigarettes. But she said she would need some in the morning.

"The way I surmise it, the woman picked her up in an old 1951 Chevrolet she and Lonnye had bought together. She must have picked Lonnye up outside the new apartment and took her over to her apartment to do some drinking. And she must have gotten Lonnye drunk. But Lonnye must have woke up and had sense enough to know she had to get back home. So after everyone who was partying at the woman's apartment was asleep, she must have took the old Chevvy and started home."

A National Guard and police blockade was set up at Vermont Avenue and 62nd Place, along the route Lonnye Lee Cook chose to travel, at what witnesses said was a high rate of speed, possibly 50 to 60 miles an hour. A police car with its red light flashing already was chasing her because this was in the curfew area and the sky still was dark.

Corporal Horace Speiss of C Troop, 1st Reconnaissance Squadron, fired a warning shot. The car continued on. From another roadblock two blocks north on Vermont, Speiss heard rapid bursts of gunfire. Bullets tore into Lonnye Lee Cook's back. The time was 4 A.M.

"Man, they riddled that car with bullets," said Clayborne Cook. "I went to the inquest because I wanted to clear her name. I told them she was a drinker but she wasn't one of them out there that night rioting and looting. A police lieutenant told me that when the National Guardsmen found that she was just a woman, they broke down and cried. He said evidently she just got scared and didn't stop. At the inquest, I told those boys in the National Guard that I didn't have any hard feelings. And I shook hands with them.

"I found out she was shot by phoning a woman friend who is a deputy sheriff. You see, I was looking at television and I heard about this unidentified woman who had been wounded by National Guardsmen. And I called this friend, because I had a feeling, and she checked up on her and called me back and told me it was Lonnye.

"The Pasadena man never knew she was dead until he met me two or three days later. He told me he had been looking all over for her. He went to the rosary and cemetery. He told me he was going to keep the apartment. I went to him and asked him if he would help me pay for Lonnye's burial. He told me he hadn't known her long enough."

Lonnye Lee Cook died Tuesday, August 17, 1965, at the age of forty-seven. "It was almost the exact day I met her twenty years earlier. I remember because I buried her on the 22nd—and that's my birthday," said Clayborne Cook.

Except for scattered incidents, battle-scarred South Los Angeles was quiet Sunday morning. Some of the brave and devout even ventured from their homes to attend church. But attendance was far below normal in houses of worship.

In residential neighborhoods within the riot zone, August 15, 1965, was almost like any other Sunday. Residents sat on their front porches, watered their parched lawns and watched their children at play.

The sniping and fire-bombing resumed, however, as the day wore on. Military guards continued their wary patrols. Police stations throughout Los Angeles County, and even in neighboring Orange County, received telephone calls warning of new bombings and fires. "An organized campaign of terror," was how one public official described the pattern of these calls.

Rioters monitored police calls on transistor radios. Some even went so far as to "test" police capability to respond. They telephoned a report of a fire or a shooting at a certain distant address in the trouble zone, then determined by listening to their radios how long it took officers to reach the scene of the phony alarm.

A new specter reared its head in the plundered curfew area: hunger, and its ally—disease. Reports spread that, because of the burned and sacked markets and the closing of other food shops in the area by frightened owners, residents were having difficulty finding food to buy. Drugstores being a favorite target of looters, fear developed that medicine also would be difficult to obtain.

Many persons in the area owned no cars—and, as noted earlier, busses simply weren't running. So Negro leaders appealed for help in alleviating what was believed at the time could become an even greater menace than the lawlessness that had gone before. Warned the Reverend H. H. Brookins: "If you get these people hungry, you haven't seen anything yet."

As a result, Governor Brown, who toured the riot area Sunday until sniper gunfire a block away prompted National Guard officials to cut short his survey, instructed the State Disaster Office to assume the responsibility for distribution of food and other necessities. Other agencies also sent provisions to centers in the Negro neighborhoods.

As it turned out, the shortages proved overstated and the threat of a food rebellion never materialized. At one distribution center, a belligerent male Negro accepted a package from a volunteer worker, looked at it and threw it to the ground. "Look at that—they give us TV dinners," he snarled.

On Sunday "Major fires were under control," reported the McCone Commission, "but there were new ones and some rekindling of old ones." The Fire Department reported that between 8 A.M. and 5 P.M. Sunday as many as 200 new fires erupted in the curfew zone.

And night was yet to come. To Chief Ken Long and his 50 Battalion 8 firemen it came with a deceptive quiet that soon was shattered. Here is his account of Battalion 8's experiences that Sunday night, as it appeared in the Monday, August 16, *Los Angeles Times:*

> Everything seemed in good shape.
>
> To the south of the burning building [a structure in the riot zone where Battalion 8 had been called to battle a blaze], there was a two-story apartment building, to the north a gutted building and to the west a two-story frame house. We thought we could save them all. So we went to work on the thing.
>
> All of a sudden gunfire started.
>
> It was difficult to tell where it was coming from. It was

dark. There was a lot of noise amidst the real gunfire—popping bottles, exploding cans.

There might have been three snipers. We couldn't tell. It seemed as though one was on top of a building. More gunfire seemed to be coming out of a group of houses in the middle of the block.

We could tell from the radio that the National Guard and police were coming. So we kept on fighting the fire, trying to protect ourselves at the same time.

But there was too much gunfire. Finally we had to pull back to the command post until they could clean out the snipers.

It was very discouraging. This is my district. These were all professional firemen. We knew we could beat this fire if we had the chance. We all felt very bad.

A short time later, we got the OK to come back again.

By this time, the apartment house was beginning to burn and so was the building next to it.

We were still sure we could save the private house on 48th Street. The people who lived there were standing outside waiting for us.

We had to hook one pumper up to a fire hydrant. A sniper began shooting at the engineer. More shooting came from an alley west of us.

For a while they had my men pinned behind a concrete wall.

We had to pull out again. The people whose house was burning just stood there looking at us.

By the time the police gave us the OK to come back again, the first apartment house was gone. Flames were coming from a structure behind the second apartment. The attic was beginning to go on the family's house.

We did the best we could, but the gunfire was increasing.

At that point, a police tear gas grenade, meant for a rooftop sniper's nest, bounced off a wall and exploded amid the firefighters. Five were overcome by fumes and were evacuated by ambulance. All were reported in good condition later.

Finally the chief [police commander at the scene] told us to pull out.

Lieutenant Ray Wrenn, the National Guard platoon leader, spent much of the night with his men seeking out snipers. It was a frustrating experience, he remembers. The men with guns were elusive, their movements almost impossible to follow. Wrenn's men began hearing radio reports of a new terrorist tactic: a black Chevrolet was speeding through streets, bearing occupants throwing acids at Guardsmen.

Then came an incident which, while involving no peril at all, set Wrenn's teeth grinding. "A white man came to our field headquarters," said the lieutenant. "He was in his late forties. He was driving a late-model Cadillac. My commanding officer instructed us to escort him to his home. The man would not divulge what he needed protection for.

"I got four vehicles and three were mounted with machine guns. Everybody had a rifle. I had a pistol and we had two radios.

"We were ten minutes away from where the man lived. It took longer to reach his home because we were cautious. He lived in the Baldwin Hills [a prosperous residential neighborhood]. When we arrived at his home, he asked us to wait while he got this thing out of his car."

"This thing" proved to be sackfuls of money. The blasé selfishness of the white man left Wrenn "flabbergasted."

"He called his son and another man," said the lieutenant, "and he opened the car trunk and they took out nine bank sacks." At that very moment, when the Guardsmen might have been needed elsewhere to prevent death and injury, looting and sniping, they had just completed a mission that amounted to nothing more than escort duty for a rich man's wealth.

Anger surged through Lieutenant Wrenn, and he remembers

feeling like "I wanted to kill that man. After he carried the money inside, he turned to us and said: 'Thank you.' "

The young Negro lieutenant estimated that 75 per cent of the men in his all-white platoon never before had been in the neighborhoods where the rioting occurred. For them, it was an eye-opener. "One of my fellows asked me," said Lieutenant Wrenn, " 'Do they sell this stuff?' He meant the rotten foodstuffs we had come across in some of the markets. The food was of an inedible quality.

"Some of my men asked me: 'Do people live in these houses?' I know one thing: everybody learned a lot they hadn't known before."

Wrenn said that his relationship with officers of the Los Angeles Police Department during the riot were unmarred by disagreeable incident. "But I remember a seventy-year-old gentleman who we literally had to hold onto—he was so beside himself at something he had seen," the young Guard lieutenant said. "This elderly man said he saw the CHP stop this one fellow who was driving to work and tell him he would have to leave his vehicle where it was and go home and get his driver's license, which he had forgotten. On the fellow's way back home, which was about two miles away, he was stopped by the LAPD, according to the old gentleman. The fellow told them what he was doing—going home for his driver's license—and they knocked him down and kicked him. Eventually, the man went home and got his license and walked back and showed it to the CHP, so they would release his car. The LAPD provoked the situation which disturbed the old man so. But I don't remember a CHP officer being rude to anyone during the riot."

Burning, looting and sniping. Each continued to exercise its own special terror throughout Sunday night, and would continue to do so Monday, Monday night, Tuesday and Tuesday night. But on each succeeding day, an ebbtide was noticeable. Still, more dying remained to be done.

25

JOSEPH IRVING MAIMAN, a gentle, middle-aged milkman, was the only civilian Caucasian to die by gunfire from harried men in uniform.

Gray, balding and fifty-six, Joe Maiman was no looter, no rioter. Quite the contrary. Few men living in Los Angeles were less likely to defy the law or behave violently than Joseph Maiman. He was a devoted family man with a pretty, dark-eyed wife, a twenty-two-year-old son, and a twenty-one-year-old daughter studying to teach the handicapped to speak correctly—an interest probably inspired by her father's defective hearing.

He had a pleasant home in the pleasant neighborhood of Westchester, not far from that of Jesse Unruh, politically powerful speaker of the California Assembly. Joe Maiman delivered milk to the Unruh home and liked to swap political chitchat with the speaker.

Joe also was a proud man, and he had reasons for being proud. He was descended from a famous family of Jewish scholars, craftsmen and artists; one of his ancestors was Moses Maimonides, or Moses ben Maimon, a twelfth-century rabbi, physician and philosopher who was one of European Jewry's most celebrated figures. Joe Maiman's nephew, Dr. Theodore H. Maiman—son of Joe's brother Abe—had become in years just past one of the most-talked-about men in science. Dr. Maiman was developer of the laser, that slender ray of light from which untold scientific wonders are expected.

Finally, Joe was intensely patriotic, though his poor hearing, the result of a bout with diphtheria when he was eight, kept him from military service in World War II. "When he was a little boy," said his brother Abe, "he was very concerned about the First World War. He wrote Woodrow Wilson, asking the President to send him a flag. 'I don't care how big it is,' Joe said, 'just as long as it's from the President.' I can't remember whether Joe got an answer or not."

But Joe Maiman was not entirely a flawless man. He did have the hearing defect, and he would have had to plead guilty to being a man of strong principle and a creature of habit. Because of these qualities, he died in a quick burst of machine-gun fire before sunup on Monday, August 16.

Because he was such a creature of habit, Joe Maiman unquestionably awoke at 3:30 A.M. that fateful day before setting out across town for the main office of the Foremost Milk Company, for which he had worked nearly thirty years. "He always set his clock for 3:30. Joe was a punctual man, always on time. It was a matter of principle with him," said his brother Abe. "But he was puzzled why, during the riot, the company wanted deliverymen to come to work as early as usual. He told me on Friday he couldn't understand, since they couldn't drive the milk trucks into the riot area until after daylight.

"Anyway, Joe's coffee would have been ready for him when he awoke that Monday. He always prepared it the night before—it was a habit with him. As a matter of fact, if it weren't for habit, he never would have driven through the curfew area that morning. He could have used the Freeway and gotten to work faster. But for years before he got the Corvair, he had an old Chevvy. He wouldn't trust it on the Freeway because it wouldn't go more than 30 and he always was afraid it would conk out on him. So when he got the new car he still drove the same surface streets he'd always used."

Joe Maiman's milk route during the riot took him, as it had for many years, into the heart of Negro neighborhoods. He had formed close bonds with many of his customers, associations which stood him in good stead when the trouble broke out. His Negro patrons stood outside their homes to make certain he made his deliveries unharmed. But his family noticed that by Saturday night, Joe Maiman appeared shaken by what he had seen and heard since mid-week. He talked with his brother by phone and told him that evening that his employers wanted deliverymen to check periodically with the main office until the violence ended. "What do they want to know—whether I'm still alive?" he asked. It was an unusual show of petulance for the normally gregarious, good-humored little milkman.

The time was 4 A.M. In one Jeep were Corporal Robert Kaufman and Private Louis DeToskey. In a second Jeep, a short distance behind the first, were Corporal Robert Edwards, Specialist Fourth Class Ronald Shlesman and Private First Class Gary Rogers. Three days earlier, each of the young National Guardsmen had been preparing to leave for summer camp, along with thousands of other citizen-soldiers. But they discovered summer camp would have to wait. The five young men received word of their call-up Friday, but did not move onto duty in the riot curfew area until Sunday.

Now, before dawn Monday, they were traveling north on Degnan Boulevard. At the boulevard's intersection with Stocker Street, they saw a red Corvair stopped for a traffic light. Inside, alone, was Joseph Maiman. It was a dangerous place for him to be. The sun would not rise for another two hours; this was a curfew area and unauthorized travel within it was forbidden.

But Joe Maiman had passed untroubled through this checkpoint on the two previous mornings. So as he sat in his car, with the windows rolled up (to hear better), listening to the radio news—as he always did on his way to work—the fact that he may have been acting improperly by being at the intersection probably was the farthest thing from his mind. He had become deeply concerned about what was happening to his city, and, no doubt, was absorbed in the latest reports about the rioting.

Corporal Robert Kaufman knew none of this. But he did know he could chance no risk. Throughout the curfew area, looters, rioters and even normally law-abiding citizens—inflamed by alcohol or infected by the lawlessness around them—were ignoring the ban on unauthorized travel. Even worse, the lives of Guardsmen and peace officers remained under constant threat, not just from snipers, but also from auto-borne terrorists bent on challenging and smashing roadblocks.

So when Kaufman saw Joe Maiman's red Corvair stopped at the intersection he was approaching, he ordered DeToskey, the driver of his Jeep, to stop. DeToskey angled the Jeep to a stop about six feet from the right front fender of the Corvair and the corporal stepped out to inspect the automobile. With his M-1 held at port arms, Corporal Kaufman approached the car and said: "Halt." As he did so, it appeared to him "the driver just started taking off . . . nearly running over me. . . . I jumped quickly to the side, missing being hit by the vehicle." Private DeToskey thought the Corvair had "headed straight toward" Corporal Kaufman before swinging north from Stocker onto the "wrong side" of Degnan Boulevard, which is divided by a grassy rise planted with trees.

"I called 'halt' again," said Kaufman, "but the car kept going. So I fired one warning shot into the air. Then I proceeded back to my vehicle and we started pursuit." The Jeep bearing Edwards, Shlesman and Rogers had continued north on Degnan through the Stocker intersection when Kaufman's stopped. As the red Corvair passed, the occupants of the second Jeep heard Corporal Kaufman's warning shot and picked up the pursuit.

Young Gary Rogers later testified at an inquest: "The commander of our vehicle fired a warning shot over his head when we were about a block and a half away. Then he ordered me to load and fire the .30-caliber machine gun. It wasn't even loaded at the time . . . the first time I shot over his head—a burst of approximately 15 shots."

The Corvair continued on, at a speed which Private Rogers estimated to be "at least 45 miles an hour—maybe faster."

Rogers did not check the Jeep's speedometer, but sensed "the Corvair was pulling away from the Jeep." It was then that Rogers "took aim and fired." As he watched, the Corvair "went out of control, up over the left curb and back down over the curb . . . down the street another 100 yards and over the curb on the right side of the street, and upon a lawn, and stopped."

From the trailing Jeep, Corporal Robert Kaufman heard what he thought were "a few sounds going off from an M-1," then "the .30-caliber machine gun being fired." He arrived at the intersection of 39th Street and Degnan where he found "this Corvair's back window all shattered and in somebody's front yard"—two blocks from where the brief chase had begun.

Inside the red Corvair, Joe Maiman's white milkman's uniform crimsoned rapidly. He was dead, a copper-jacketed machine-gun bullet having ripped into his skull.

Not long after learning of his brother's death, Abe Maiman, a retired telephone company engineer, wrote Governor Brown, asking his aid "in clarifying the paradox" of Joe Maiman's death. In the letter he said: "How was my brother to have known whether these men who were chasing him were bona fide soldiers or hoodlums? I know if someone started shooting at me at 4 o'clock in the A.M. on a dark and lonely road during a period of rioting when lawlessness reigned supreme, I would have run just as fast as I could. You probably would have done the same. . . . Why, oh, why didn't they merely fire a tear-gas bomb instead?

"I know it is too late to do anything about this. I am not bitter against the police, the National Guard or anyone else. We are all victims of a lawless age. Now there is nothing left except to attend his funeral and listen to condolences from all who knew him. . . ."

A month later, Abe Maiman, musing on life's ironies in the living room of his home, remarked: "Years ago in Colorado [birthplace of the Maiman brothers] I went through another time of disaster—a flood. We phone company men were called in to repair damaged lines. I worked with lots of National Guardsmen, right alongside them. For what I did during that emergency, I got a medal—all my brother got was a bullet in the head."

26

ON TUESDAY, Governor Edmund G. Brown considered the riot sufficiently under control to end the curfew. On Wednesday, the National Guard pullout began.

Tuesday also was a day for funerals. Funeral services were held for Ronald Ludlow and Warren Tilson, among others.

Ludlow was the deputy sheriff slain Friday night, the first person to die in the riot. Tilson was the fireman killed later the same night when he was trapped beneath a crumbling, fire-weakened wall of a store which had been set afire.

Among the mourners at Tilson's funeral was Robert Laxague, who had been trapped with him but who had escaped with his life. Laxague had just been released from the hospital. He sat with other firemen, many of whose haggard faces were wet with tears as Fire Department Chaplain Robert Gaar delivered the eulogy.

Chaplain Gaar finished by saying: "I would to God that we as a people, white or black, could look each other in the eye and say: 'You are my brother.' "

In the annals of officialdom, the rioting ended Tuesday night with the lifting of the curfew. Los Angeles' six days of hell were past.

But the appetite for violence still demanded more satisfaction. Carlos Cavitt, Jr., eighteen, was Wednesday night's sacrificial offering.

Carlos Cavitt, a slender, dark-skinned youth, was in an ill-humor Wednesday evening. "Carlos said he was mad, because he hadn't got to take anything from any of the stores," explained his fourteen-year-old friend, Nelson Chew.

Nelson had run into Carlos while visiting his grandmother who lived not far from the eighteen-year-old. They also met another boy of fourteen, Mitchell Wilson.

Carlos got his mother's automobile and suggested that the two young boys accompany him. The two fourteen-year-olds agreed.

Carlos pointed the car in the direction of the Allied Furniture Company at 4705 S. Broadway, several blocks away. That store had been burned and looted Friday night and a woman resident of an apartment above it had lost her life in the blaze, though this was not known at the time. Even as Carlos, Nelson Chew and Mitchell Wilson approached the furniture store her body still lay somewhere amid the rubble of the ruined building.

There was a grisly irony about the three youths' choosing for their misadventure the devastated furniture store whose ruins concealed the charred body of the missing woman. It was as if death sought to tie up the riot's loose ends in one final package.

Once they arrived at 47th and Broadway, Carlos Cavitt parked his mother's car and the three youths got out of it. "We looked into the store, and saw some marble tables," said young Wilson. "Carlos said: 'Look at those tables. You watch for the National Guard.' "

There is little reason to doubt Mitchell's version of what happened in the ruined furniture store. For Carlos Cavitt was no stranger to this sort of escapade. He had a juvenile record for burglary, theft and receiving stolen goods.

Inside the store, the three youths trod across blackened debris toward the marble-top tables they had seen from the sidewalk. Mitchell Wilson, however, balked at going further. But Carlos threatened to drive away and leave him unless he helped carry off a table, Mitchell claimed.

After one table was deposited in the trunk of the automobile, Carlos returned for another, said young Wilson. This time, he added, Nelson Chew was his helper. "Carlos said he was going too slow," said Wilson. "So Carlos took it from him."

As Police Sergeant Ronald M. Lopez and his partner, Joseph Sonlitner, drove past the burned-out Allied Furniture store at 7:30 P.M., they sighted a young man standing on the sidewalk outside the store, looking "furtively" up and down the street. This presumably was Mitchell Wilson. Two other figures were emerging from the broken doorway, a marble-top table between them.

The officers halted their car and got out. "Stop," yelled Lopez. "Hold it."

The three young men scattered along the sidewalk. The table hit the pavement with a thud that snapped off its marble top.

Again Lopez called out: "Halt, police officers."

Nelson Chew and Mitchell Wilson obeyed. The third youth continued to run toward an alley even though Officer Sonlitner heard one of the other two youngsters call out: "Carlos, halt."

Sergeant Lopez raced after the fleeing figure which appeared to him to pick up speed after his second warning. "He began to outdistance me," said Lopez. "I again called: 'Halt, or I'll shoot.' He failed to halt and, as he began to turn into the alley, I fired one shot and observed the 'defendant' [*sic*] fall to the ground, partially disappearing from view." A bullet fired from a distance of about 25 to 30 feet had struck Carlos Cavitt above the left ear.

Sergeant Lopez and Sonlitner handcuffed the fourteen-year-old boys and called for an ambulance which carried Carlos Cavitt, Jr., to Orthopaedic Hospital. There he died the following Friday—about the time the body of the unidentified woman

Charcoal Alley. Midnight along 103rd St. in the Watts business district, which was almost totally burned to the ground by rioters. An uneasy calm prevails as members of the California National Guard deploy along the street to restore order.—John Malmin, *Los Angeles Times*

Hundreds of cars were stopped by police during the rioting and their occupants searched for concealed weapons. Many of the guns looted from pawnshops have never been recovered.—Don Cormier, *Los Angeles Times*

A National Guardsman escorts an elderly woman across a debris-littered street in Watts as order was finally restored. Many residents of the community, fearful of their lives, had remained in their homes during the days of rioting.—Bruce Cox, *Los Angeles Times*

There were hungry to be fed, when people were finally able to venture into the streets with safety. Here, members of the California National Guard distribute food to the needy.—John Malmin, *Los Angeles Times*

California's Governor Edmund G. (Pat) Brown visited the riot area on Sunday, August 15, to view the damage and listen to the complaints of residents. Guardsmen, fearful for his safety, cut short his stay in Watts when sniper fire broke out in the vicinity.—William S. Murphy, *Los Angeles Times*

Reverend Martin Luther King, Jr., *center,* expresses his views on the causes of the riot at a press conference held at a Los Angeles hotel, while Governor Brown listens at left. King received a cool reception from Watts residents, where his philosophy of nonviolent resistance was widely ridiculed.—William S. Murphy, *Los Angeles Times*

Roadblocks were established surrounding the Los Angeles City Jail, as hundreds of prisoners arrested during the riot were being processed. Here, a police officer explains to a woman how to locate a missing relative she believes is being held, as National Guardsmen stand by.—William S. Murphy, *Los Angeles Times*

Looters on the loose—Young plunderers make off with lampshades from furniture store at 103rd St. and Wilmington Ave. on Friday, August 13. Dick Gregory, who played a prominent part in helping to restrain the rioters, is seen at the right.—*Los Angeles Times* photo

Having the appearance of a bombed-out block in a war-ravaged land, this is the heart of Watts following the August holocaust.—William S. Murphy, *Los Angeles Times*

The Central Ave. district showing the ruins of burned-out store buildings before the lots were leveled and cleared by bulldozers.—William S. Murphy, *Los Angeles Times*

There was work for some of the unemployed in Watts during the aftermath of the riot. This man was hired to help clean the rubble from the devastated community.—William S. Murphy, *Los Angeles Times*

Looters are shown running through the streets of Watts, carrying merchandise they have stolen from plundered stores.—*Los Angeles Times* photo

A home fire that occurred in September revealed a storehouse of stolen loot in a small home on West 60th Place, when firemen responded to the blaze. A kneeling detective checks for fingerprints. The items had apparently been taken from stores that were looted during the riot. Three trucks were needed to haul away the merchandise. The occupant left in such a hurry that he failed to turn off the color television set at upper left in the picture.—John Malmin, *Los Angeles Times*

was discovered by firemen in the ruins of the Allied Furniture store.

The riot began with one Rena—Rena Frye. The dying ended with another Rena. Her last name was Johnson.

As firemen poked through what was left of the Allied Furniture store at 11:20 A.M. Friday, no more marble-top tables of the kind that had proved a fatal attraction for Carlos Cavitt, Jr., remained there. But searchers, trying to tidy up the blackened mess, did find what was left of Rena Johnson. It wasn't much—the pitifully burned body, a scrap of red shirting, a ring, a watch embedded with red stones, some of which were missing, and a money order for $7.40 payable to Bekins Van & Storage Company. Strangely, the slip of paper had withstood the flames and was intact.

The coroner affixed a tag to the remains of Rena Johnson, which read "Jane Doe No. 24." She lay unidentified for several days and the "Jane Doe" tag signified hers was the 24th unidentified female body recovered in Los Angeles County in 1965. Riot statisticians would provide her with a more enduring distinction: when she ultimately was identified, hers would be the 35th and last death to be recorded in their logs, even though she had died five days before young Cavitt.

Who was Rena Johnson? She was born in New Orleans. Other than that, her past is as obscure as that of thousands of other migrants to Los Angeles from the South. How she got to California from the Louisiana metropolis is unknown.

"No known relatives," reads her death report.

That wasn't quite true. For nearly seven years, Rena Johnson had lived with a man named Leroy Robinson. During that time, he discovered surprisingly little about her. But then Rena Johnson was a strange one.

She told Robinson that she had been married once before, but not to whom. As for her age, he could guess it only as "a little over forty."

Like Lonnye Lee Cook, the woman shot Sunday morning by National Guardsmen, there appears to have been something in her past that had twisted her. To neighbors she appeared infected with a sense of hopelessness—and the hopelessness was reflected in her strangeness.

For one thing, Rena Johnson hid from people; they seemed to frighten her at times. "She wasn't crazy or anything," said Robinson, "but she was mentally disturbed."

He can remember her walking down the hall and hearing other persons walking up the steps. "She'd duck back, just the same as if she thought they were after her," he said. Sometimes Rena Johnson even hid in closets. "Just all of a sudden," said Mrs. Birdie Lee Pagoda, a neighbor who escaped from the fire which killed Rena Johnson, "it seemed like something had happened to her; she just cracked. When she would see you coming, she would break and run and hide."

About a week before the rioting began, remembers Mrs. Pagoda, she noticed the knob on her own apartment door slowly turning. She watched for a moment with fascination; then suddenly she reached for the knob. "When I yanked the door open, it was her. When she seen me, she started to run," said Mrs. Pagoda.

"Come here," Mrs. Pagoda ordered Rena Johnson, who obeyed, returned to the former's apartment and sat on a couch.

"She had a book in her hands," said Mrs. Pagoda. "She would lay the book down and pick it up."

Finally, recalls Mrs. Pagoda, Rena Johnson exclaimed: "I want to say something, but I don't know how to say it."

"Well, come on and tell me. What do you want to say?" asked Mrs. Pagoda. "If you want to say something, say it."

Then, remembers Mrs. Pagoda, her visitor gave "just a little 'jibble,' just like a child. You know—when he is trying to talk and doesn't know how."

A silence followed, and that was the end of it.

Some nights were bad for Rena Johnson. Tenants began to

complain to Mrs. Lilly Celeste Pollard, who managed the apartments. "She ran up and down the hall late at night, screaming and carrying on," said Mrs. Pollard. Mrs. Pollard once thought it wise to suggest that Robinson take Rena Johnson to a doctor.

Rena Johnson, a stubby little woman, almost always wore the same costume—sweater and skirt and a handkerchief, tied bandanna-style over her head. She didn't seem to care much about her appearance. But, it appears, there was something she did care a great deal about.

After moving into the apartment at 47th and Broadway, she went to great pains to store her belongings. She had some nice things, Robinson remembers—furniture, dishes, clothing and a hi-fi set. Perhaps, she was so careful about them because they reminded her of a finer time in her life, a happier one that, somewhere, somehow, she had misplaced. In any event, she carefully kept up her storage payments, and it is perhaps only poetic justice that the money order she was preparing to mail defied the flames in which she died.

Arsonists set fire to the Allied Furniture store shortly after 7 P.M. Friday. Robinson remembers he had gone to a nearby drugstore and purchased dinner for Rena Johnson and had taken it to her. He watched her while she ate, then he left the apartment to visit nearby.

Two distinct blazes were touched off in the furniture store and quickly flames shot into the living quarters above. Residents ran through the halls, urging their neighbors to flee. As far as firemen knew, the building had been evacuated shortly after they arrived, and Rena Johnson had gotten out with the other tenants.

When Leroy Robinson heard the building in which he lived was aflame, he hurried back. He began searching in the crowd for Rena Johnson. He couldn't find her.

Other tenants told him they had seen her leave the apartments on the second floor when they did. Then a woman spoke up: "Your wife went down the alley."

Robinson walked through the alley and stopped suddenly. He stood before a door which once had led to steps—and the steps once had led up to the second floor, directly to his and Rena Johnson's apartment.

Though Leroy Robinson continued to search for Rena Johnson, and even filed a missing persons report with police, it was all too apparent what had happened: she had returned to the building and died when the second floor collapsed into the furniture store.

Because little but a blackened waste was left by the fierce flames, the truth would not be known for five days, and it would take even longer to establish for certain that the corpse found charred beyond recognition in the rubble once had been Rena Johnson.

Why had she returned to the flaming apartment and certain death? There seems but one answer.

The jostling residents of the building, some of whom had assisted her from her apartment and down the steps, were people. People frightened her—so much that sometimes she had to run and hide.

"Jane Doe No. 24." Thirty-fifth victim of the Los Angeles riot of mid-August, 1965. Rena Johnson.

At last, the dying was done.

27

SUNDAY, AUGUST 15, 1965, another sun-drenched, cloudless day, was a time of paradox. It was a time of soul-searching and prayer—but continued violence. It was the beginning of an end that still would be marked by additional deaths, injuries and many arrests before order would be restored.

Thousands of residents of the 50-square-mile area devastated by four days of rioting began to emerge from their houses and apartments to survey the holocaust that hate had brought to their community. No longer congregating in groups on street corners, they moved hurriedly to perform their various errands. Sometimes they glanced briefly at the burned-out shells of store buildings which left their black scars on every block.

For many persons, this was their first appearance since the grisly carnival of looting, drunkenness, fire and disorder had commenced. These were the law-abiding citizens who had remained in their homes fearful for their own safety. Some gazed at the wanton destruction in dismay, but many were apathetic. Life resumed. Many had jobs to go to, and with the relaxed curfew they were glad to be able once more to move freely on the streets.

The parking lot of a Central Avenue supermarket that had escaped the flames and had not been broken into by looters was crowded with automobiles. Inside, patrons lined up before check stands with wire carts filled with groceries. Two National Guardsmen drove up in a jeep. Casually, they studied the impassive faces of the shoppers. Several clerks busily punched the keys of their cash registers, tallying up the purchases. The market was busier than usual. Many of its competitors had gone out of business after their shelves had been stripped of merchandise and Molotov cocktails with burning fuses had been left behind to complete the devastation.

There were some who attended church services, although the attendance of major congregations was down 80 per cent. In the Grant African Methodist Episcopal Church on Central Avenue, its pastor, Reverend Henry W. Murph, gazed out at the somber faces of his flock. Normally, nearly 900 persons gathered in the church on a Sunday morning. Today, there were less than 200 present. They shifted restlessly in their seats. The day was growing warmer. Already, the heat inside the large hall was oppressive. An elderly man mopped beads of perspiration from a balding head with a large white linen handkerchief. The Reverend Murph cleared his throat and began his sermon in a soft, restrained voice.

"I'm sure all of us are sick in our hearts at what has transpired these few days," he said. "I recognize there are many injustices heaped on people of our color. But no amount of police brutality should cause a man to steal guns and beds. The majority of Watts residents are decent, law-abiding citizens. It's so unjust for newspapers and officials to stigmatize our whole community for what a few people do who are misguided."

"Amen," his congregation chorused.

At the 103rd Street Baptist Church, the Reverend Bobby Newman selected his sermon from the 12th chapter of the Book of Romans, as National Guardsmen patrolled the street outside, their bayonets glistening in the morning sunlight.

"Let love be genuine; hate what is evil . . . love one another with brotherly affection," he read to a tiny gathering. He was disappointed that there were many who still feared to venture into the streets.

"Never flag in zeal, be aglow with the Spirit, serve the Lord," the Reverend Newman exhorted his listeners. "Bless those who persecute you; bless and do not curse them. Rejoice with those who rejoice, weep with those who weep. Live in harmony with one another. . . ."

At Muhammad's Mosque No. 27 on South Broadway, the Black Muslims were gathering for services which would commence at 2 P.M. There would be no philosophy of brotherly love in the sermon. The Muslims preach hate. Ushers stood outside greeting members as they arrived. A procession of white-robed women filed through the doorway. A small boy rode by on a bicycle carrying a bundle of handbills the Muslims had been distributing since the first night of the riot, which urged people to attend their meeting at the Mosque the following Sunday.

"Stop Police Brutality," the leaflet proclaimed in large type. "We want an immediate end to police brutality and mob attacks against the so-called Negro throughout the United States. We believe that the Federal government should intercede to see that black men and women tried in white courts receive justice or allow us to build a new nation for ourselves, dedicated to justice, freedom and liberty.

"We believe that we who declared ourselves to be righteous Muslims, should not participate in wars which take the lives of humans. We do not believe this nation should force us to take part in such wars, for we have nothing to gain from it unless America agrees to give us the necessary territory wherein we may have something to fight for.

"As long as we are not allowed to establish a state or territory of our own, we demand not only equal justice under the laws of the United States, but equal employment opportunities—NOW! We do not believe that after 400 years of free or nearly free labor, sweat and blood, which has helped America become rich and powerful, that so many thousands of black people should have to subsist on relief, charity or live in poor houses. We want the government of the United States to exempt our people from ALL taxation as long as we are deprived of equal justice under the laws of the land."

Across the street, down the block, a police car was parked in the shade of a building. Two officers sat inside, their backs to the Mosque. They were watching the traffic pass along Broadway. Most of the cars were filled with Negro sightseers. They were silent, well behaved. For the tired police officers, their conduct was a welcome sign. It could mean that the crisis had passed.

A white man walked by. He leaned into the car window and spoke to the patrolmen, his eyes on the Mosque down the street. "That's my store next door," he said, gesturing toward a building with a large sign over the front window announcing that he dealt in surplus goods.

"They didn't burn me out. I've been in this neighborhood for a long time. Everything I've got in the world is tied up in that place. No, I don't live around here. My home's across town in Hollywood. Why do I have my business in this location? Well, mainly because the rent is cheaper. Low overhead." He paused, his eyes scanning the occupants of the passing cars, as though he momentarily expected a recurrence of the violence that had shattered his business district.

"I've got two guys from a protection agency inside the place, watching the store. They've been in there since the rioting started. If any of the mob had broken in, well those guys are armed with shotguns. Sure, they'd use them. That's what I'm paying for—protection. I'll be glad when this all settles down and gets back to normal. It's costing me a fortune keeping those guys inside the store."

Attending the meeting in the Mosque was Marquette Frye. He spoke before a gathering which subscribes to the tenets of a belief that writer Louis E. Lomax says has but one message: "The white man is by nature evil, a snake who is incapable of doing right, a devil who is soon to be destroyed. Therefore, the black man, who is by nature divine and good, must separate from the white man as soon as possible, lest he share the white man's hour of total destruction."*

Young Frye informed the meeting that Muslim Elijah Muhammad "has been teaching the doom of the white man for a long time and now we understand. . . . These troops don't mean a thing. They haven't seen anything yet."

John Shabazz, minister of the Mosque, later denied to reporters that the Muslims were in any sense responsible for the rioting. "All this is part of the general awakening," he said. "Some are responding in one way and some in another. Some are trying to destroy the whole image before them and others are following the only man they know—Elijah Muhammad—who can free them."

Three days after Marquette Frye appeared there, the Mosque was the scene of a furious gun battle. Miraculously, no one was injured. At 1:43 A.M. an anonymous caller informed police that guns were being taken in or out of the temple on South Broadway. When officers arrived, they believed their cars were hit by pellets fired from within the Mosque. Muzzle flashes, they said, were observed from a second-story window.

The police opened with a barrage of fire from rifles, shotguns and pistols. They shot out every window in the building, and when they charged inside, they discovered Muslims crouching on the blood-soaked floor, many cut by flying glass. Fifty-nine members of the sect were taken into custody. No guns were found inside the Mosque.

California's governor, Pat Brown, had expressed a desire to visit the riot area the Sunday afternoon Marquette Frye spoke at the Muslim Mosque. A 15-car convoy of National Guardsmen escorted him on the tour. The governor later remarked that he was appalled by what he had seen.

"The five days of violence were caused by a hoodlum gang

* *When the Word Is Given* (New York: New American Library, Signet Editions, 1964), p. 19.

element," Brown told newsmen. "Here in California, we have a wonderful working relationship between whites and Negroes. We got along fine until this happened. This is the first trouble we have had."

The governor's first stop was at the Jacob Riis High School in an all-Negro neighborhood in the heart of the riot zone. A crowd of children and adults gathered. Guardsmen with fixed bayonets and uneasy expressions formed a cordon around the state's chief executive. Brown, however, shook hands with many residents, patted youngsters on the head and disappeared inside the school to lunch with his troops in the cafeteria.

An hour later, the motorcade raced off to the Watts business area, which if he had seen it would have presented the most shocking sight of all. For here an entire block of stores and office buildings had been burned to the ground. The procession paused first, however, at a fire station at 103rd Street and Success Avenue, then being used as a command post by a unit of the National Guard's 49th Division. The governor went inside to shake more hands.

An officer standing outside the door said: "I wish he hadn't come here. The governor is a friendly man. He likes everyone, and he wants people to like him, and I wouldn't say that it's just the fact that he's a smart politician. He's sincere. Pat Brown's a good governor for my money, but he doesn't understand these people. It only took one crazed fanatic in Dallas to kill the President. There could be someone else down here whose mind is just as distorted."

Other National Guard officers shared the same fear. When the governor emerged from the fire station, all of the automobiles had been turned around facing the direction from which they had come. The Watts business district was just a short distance beyond. Governor Brown expressed surprise.

Lieutenant General Roderic L. Hill, state adjutant general, informed him that shots had been fired seconds earlier, a half-block ahead, and live electric wires were lying on the street. The governor returned to his Los Angeles office in the downtown Civic Center, where he met with a delegation of 50 Negro leaders. There, as noted previously, he was told: "The immediate need is for food for these people. If you get these people hungry and without food, you haven't seen anything yet."

As Governor Brown listened to the complaints of the delegation in the State Building, a force of 13,500 National Guardsmen and 1,000 police officers were still working to bring an end to the violence. Reports still were being received of sniper fire. Four fire stations were set on fire that day, and motorists were warned to stay off the Harbor Freeway which runs from downtown Los Angeles to the Port of Los Angeles, San Pedro.

For Los Angeles Police Chief William H. Parker, it had been a long ordeal. Ailing, he would soon undergo major heart surgery. The Negro community was clamoring for his ouster, and the oft-repeated charge of police brutality now reached a crescendo. Some Negro leaders demanded that he be removed from office.

Many white citizens of Los Angeles rallied to the chief's support. It had been clearly evident that, as disorder and destruction spread throughout the southern section of the city, Parker appeared to be the one man in civic government whom the people looked to for leadership. National Guard officers who saw him in action during the crucial hours were amazed at his calmness in making decisions under combat conditions. He—or his top lieutenants—made tactical errors at the outset of the riot, but these were counterbalanced by the fact that officers under his command, augmented by National Guard troops, isolated the riot in one section of the city and prevented it from spreading into other areas where the death toll and loss of property would have been drastically increased.

On Sunday afternoon, Chief Parker reported: "We had lost control, but the power is now back in the hands of the police and the military. However, it doesn't mean that it is over."

Disorder continued to spread to distant sections of Los Angeles. Venice, on the oceanfront bordering the city of Santa Monica, has a sizable Negro community. Its members live in antiquated houses, decaying apartment complexes and deserted store buildings alongside their white brethren, mainly social misfits who once tried to establish the beach town as a mecca for beatniks. The movement failed due to the pressures of property owners, some of whom can recall the town's days of grandeur, when it was a popular seaside resort with gondoliers poling their boats through myriad canals designed to resemble the Italian city from which local promoters borrowed the name.

Most of the beatniks moved away in disgust, but a small colony clung to a fringe near the oceanfront which they call Venice West. On a quiet night you still can hear the thumping of bongo drums or the chords of a guitar.

Sunday night, August 15, a police lieutenant stood in the middle of a darkened Venice street with a loudspeaker in his hand. He had arrived with other officers to protect firemen, whose truck had been stoned as they answered a call in the district.

"I'm ordering you people to disperse and return to your homes," his voice boomed over the loudspeaker. The crowd scattered, disappearing into the night. Screen doors slammed. A young officer holding a carbine turned to a newspaper reporter standing beside him. "We're pulling out of here now. You'd better leave," he warned. "One of our men was shot at here last night."

The reporter nodded. All the house lights in the neighborhood were turned off. He wondered how many people were watching them as they stood on a corner illuminated by the overhead glow of a street lamp and pinpointed by the glare of a police car's headlights. The officer's white helmet was a perfect target.

In Long Beach, violence erupted briefly and with tragic results. Eight city patrol cars rushed to Anaheim Street and

California Avenue, where a disorderly mob had been stoning passing automobiles. Officers Richard LeFebre and George Medac attempted to push back the crowd. Another patrolman, Stuart C. Gordon, was holding a shotgun when, he said, three Negroes grabbed him from behind. As he turned to defend himself, the shotgun discharged, wounding Medac in the arm. LeFebre fell. He died as a force of 350 Guardsmen and 100 officers were rushed to the scene to restore order. The Long Beach officer was twenty-three years old.

28

ORDER WAS CONSIDERED sufficiently restored in Los Angeles to permit the departure of 10,500 National Guardsmen on Wednesday, August 18. They left for summer training exercises at Camp Roberts, near Paso Robles, California. This contingent represented the entire 40th Armored Division. A greatly reduced detachment remained to aid police. During the peak of the disorders, 13,500 National Guardsmen had patrolled the riot zone.

As the long columns of troop-filled trucks exited, city officials were completing their tally of the destruction. More than 600 buildings were damaged by burning and looting. Of this number, more than 200 were totally destroyed by fire. Markets, liquor stores, pawnshops and firms dealing in furniture, appliances and clothing had been the principal targets.

There were exceptions. A revival center at 621 E. Vernon was burned. A county library at 2326 E. El Segundo Boulevard was put to the torch by arsonists. The destruction of this library was particularly reprehensible in that its primary purpose in the neighborhood was to provide a means and stimulus for youngsters to study and learn. Twelve thousand volumes were reduced to ashes, and the loss was estimated at $95,000.

There were also the human statistics. Thirty-one persons had been fatally shot by law enforcement officers, National Guardsmen and "persons unknown" during the riots.* It is the opin-

* The McCone report lists the death total as 34 persons killed. Of these, one was a fireman, one was a deputy sheriff and one a Long Beach police-

ion of many that there were additional deaths which may never be determined. It is conceivable that some individuals were trapped inside some buildings that burned and their remains never recovered. Firemen reported instances in which they pulled looters from stores the looters or companions had set fire to. If firefighters had not discovered the looters in time, they would have been consumed by fire—and firemen were frequently blocked by enraged mobs as they sought to approach a blaze, much less fight it. They were stoned, fired upon and harassed in dozens of ways.

"What a strange quirk it would have been," a newsman remarked at the time, "if some poor devil was inside one of those burning markets being roasted alive because his cries for help couldn't be heard above the wild screams of the barbarians on the outside."

Inquests into the riot deaths were held in September by the Los Angeles County Coroner's office. The setting for these was a hearing room once used by the Los Angeles County Board of Supervisors in the antiquated Hall of Records between Spring and Broadway in the downtown Civic Center.

On the walls of the room are murals painted during the WPA era, which depict scenes of California's past. Directly behind and above the chair occupied by Coroner Charles G. Langhauser is a large garish painting portraying the founding of Los Angeles on September 4, 1781, by the Spanish governor, Felipe de Neve. He is shown reading the royal proclamation while surrounded by Spanish settlers from Sinaloa, local Indians and a Franciscan padre. History records that only two of the settlers could claim to be of Spanish blood. The rest were *mestizos.*

---

man. There were 1,032 reported injuries, including 90 police officers, 136 firemen, 23 persons from other governmental agencies and 773 civilians; 118 of the injuries resulted from gunshot wounds. Bobbie Cannon, a 14-year-old girl crushed to death in a loot-filled car, was not considered one of the riot victims by the McCone Commission. Most unofficial statistics included her, making the generally accepted death toll 35.

There were also several Negroes among these first families who founded the pueblo. The artist refrained from painting them into the picture.

The death list shows that all but one of the victims were from minority groups. The vast majority were Negroes, three were Mexican-Americans, one was a Japanese-American and one was a Caucasian. Sixteen had police arrest records. Twenty-six were born outside of California, and most of these came from the South. Those who had jobs were in low-income brackets. Thirteen, autopsies disclosed, were under the influence of alcohol when they were killed. None had less than .15 per cent alcohol in his blood, which is a state of "acute ethanol intoxication"; to put it more bluntly—they were roaring drunk.

The death reports all had a dreary similarity. The fact that many of those who were killed had been arrested previously for other offenses is significant, but relatively unimportant. Among those jailed for participation in the riot, 500 had criminal records.

Mayor Samuel W. Yorty made much of placing the entire blame for the riots on "criminal elements who hate the police who restrain them and protect us from them to the best of their ability." It was tempting to place the blame for the riots on a criminal element—particularly for those holding political office who must watch the barometer of the Negro voting community in Los Angeles, which is becoming a more powerful bloc with each passing year.

The fact remains that hundreds of others who ran with the mob had never been in trouble with the police. Many were juveniles. Certainly the crimes committed by those who died were no more serious than any acts of many other participants.

Some were killed because they were slow on their feet. Where others escaped from pursuing officers, they were the last over the fence. Others who lost their lives were innocent victims. George Adams, a sightseer like hundreds of other Negroes, was felled by a slug from an officer's shotgun. Joseph Maiman,

Caucasian, a frightened milkman, ran a roadblock and was shot to death by National Guardsmen. Probably the most tragic of all were the youths who died violently.

There was Bobbie Cannon, a fourteen-year-old girl, who was crushed to death when a loot-filled car in which she was riding crashed into a parked truck. Ramon L. Hermosillo, nineteen, died from gunshot wounds when he tried to run through a roadblock. Elliott Carlton, seventeen, was shot to death at Griffith Avenue and Jefferson Boulevard. There was Frederick Maurice Hendricks, nineteen, a Negro with a juvenile record for burglary dating back to when he was twelve years old. Caught while smashing into a liquor store at 1st and Utah Streets, Freddie made the mistake of trying to run. A police officer shot him in the back.

One of the looters killed was Eugene Tikuro Shimatsu, eighteen, a Japanese-American. The Nisei community in Los Angeles prides itself on the behavior of its youth. They are seldom in trouble with the law. With few exceptions, Japanese-American children are raised in homes with strong family ties where there is respect for parental authority. A maverick in the Japanese-American community brings dishonor to all those of his ancestry. Such a boy was Eugene Shimatsu. His grieving parents wrote to the district attorney requesting that there be no public inquest into their son's death. They knew he had been guilty of whatever he had been caught attempting to do—in his case, looting a liquor store. He had, they wrote, always been a bad boy. The inquest was not held.

One inquest that did take place was that into the death of Aubrey Gene Griffin, thirty-eight, Negro, shot in his home at 314 W. 93rd Street early Monday morning. The details of his death were slightly unusual.

Mrs. Renee Griffin, his widow, was first to testify. She said that she and her husband were in bed. They heard a noise. Aubrey got up, slipped into a pair of trousers and went to the front of the house to investigate. Their son, Aubrey, Jr., was in the living room watching television. Mrs. Griffin heard the front door slam. There was the sound of gunfire. She ran from the bedroom and found that her husband had fallen by the front door. He told her to call the police. Her son knocked her to the floor in the kitchen to protect her from shots crashing into the house. He testified: "I was sitting down watching TV. Mom and Pop had gone to bed. I heard shots. Some time elapsed. There were more shots. One hit the house. The door closed. I went into the hallway. My father had been shot. I had seen him walk outside, then return to the house. A volley of shots followed. They came through the door."

There was conflicting testimony when Police Officer Roy Mazingo took the stand. He related that he had been in his police vehicle near 93rd Street chasing a car. The driver yelled to him that his wife was having a baby. Mazingo escorted him to a hospital at 94th and Broadway. Here, he heard shots. He encountered two National Guardsmen, who told him that a man with a white T-shirt had fired at them. Mazingo, accompanied by two other officers, moved on the house that the Guardsmen had pointed out as the one where they had observed a man run from a car in the driveway through the front door. There was a light burning on the front porch. Other officers were arriving rapidly. Soon, about 15 surrounded the residence. One shouted: "We're police officers. Come out with your hands up."

"Fuck you. Come in and get me," a voice yelled from within the house.

Police opened fire. A fusillade of bullets tore through the front door. One officer ran to the rear and gained entry, injuring himself in the process. He could see both Mrs. Griffin and her son in the front room. He ordered them to sit down in chairs. Aubrey Griffin was lying in a pool of blood by the door.

Lieutenant Pierce R. Brooks of the LAPD homicide division told the coroner that a thorough search had been made of the house following the shooting. Officers found a .32-caliber Spanish pistol with three live rounds in it, but a ballistics test showed that it had not been fired recently. The autopsy report stated that the victim had not been drinking. He died of massive shotgun wounds with multiple tracts in his right limb, his stomach, chest, heart and right hip.

The jury deliberated longer on this inquest than any of the prior ones before they returned to the hearing room. The case had an unusual aspect. If Griffin had fired on the National Guardsmen and had run from his car to the house, where was the weapon he had used? The gun was never found. If he had one, certainly neither he, his wife, nor his son would have had time to dispose of it. The verdict of the coroner's jury, nonetheless, was justifiable homicide.

Each inquest had its own element of personal tragedy. There were bereaved parents and widows present, some who would testify, others who would listen silently to the tragic accounts of violent death, as a procession of police officers took the stand to relate how, in the performance of their duty, it had been necessary to shoot down a number of the rioters.

29

LINCOLN HEIGHTS JAIL is a cold, austere four-story building between Avenue 19 and the Los Angeles River. At one time, in the early days of the city's history, the river had actually coursed through the old pueblo. *Zanjas,* crude but effective aqueducts, siphoned water from this swift-flowing stream to irrigate vineyards, groves and fertile fields, which extended as far as the eye could see. Today, the river is a giant concrete moat. Most of the time it is dry. Freight trains clatter by on their way to the rail yards in the city. For some time the jail had been closed, superseded by a larger hostel for lawbreakers built near the Union Station to keep pace with the city's ever-climbing crime rate.

It had been necessary to reopen Lincoln Heights to make room for the tremendous influx of prisoners taken during the riot. Nearly 4,000 persons had been arrested. They arrived at the lockup in busloads. The street around the old jail was cordoned off. National Guardsmen and police officers carefully checked everyone coming near the jail. Patrolmen with rifles stood guard on the Santa Fe Railroad overpass which crosses the street adjacent to the jail building. They were taking no chances on a possible mob effort to attack the jail and effect the release of the hundreds of prisoners.

The majority of people who converged on the old building were Negroes searching for sons, husbands and wives reported arrested. Inside, officials faced a mountain of paperwork as they attempted to process those who had been taken into custody. It was soon apparent that it would be days before there would be any hope of untangling the legal snarl that the mass arrests had precipitated.

Across the street from the jail stood a row of buildings occupied by the purveyors of freedom—bail bondsmen, who for a fee arrange for the release of a prisoner pending his trial. The fee generally is 10 per cent, plus the $50 cost for a writ. They were now besieged by telephone calls from relatives seeking to free those being held. Other relatives sat disconsolately in bondsmen's reception rooms, for it was obvious that those charged with felonies would have a lengthy stay in jail. Bail had been set for those accused of burglary and looting at $5,000.

A number of relatives could raise the $550 for a bond, but another stipulation blocked most. Underwriters for the bondsmen insisted that security be offered for the balance of the bail, with the only collateral acceptable being a trust deed for real estate. Few of the prisoners owned property, so they remained in jail until a later date, when the bail was reduced to a lower figure—$1,650. The police and district attorney's office had sought to prevent any bail on a felony charge. They didn't want the rioters back on the street before order was finally restored.

Each visitor to the jail building was carefully searched before being allowed to enter. One tired officer standing at the front door remarked: "Some of the attorneys object to being frisked. That's too damned bad about them. I've been down in Watts for three nights. They figured I'd had enough of that kind of duty and sent me up here for a change of scenery. Listen to those guys yelling up there in those cell blocks. Some change.

"I took this public relations stuff serious. I've tried to do the best job I know how in that respect. But you know something, I've just about had it. I'm tired of being a target. So is every other police officer who worked down there in the area. One of those rioters had me pinned down. Zeroed in on me from a hotel window. I couldn't move. All of a sudden, a National

Guardsman raised his rifle and fired. He got the guy in the window. That boy saved my life."

Seconds later, a tall, proud man with a pencil-line mustache strode with dignity up the steps leading into the jail. Two police officers armed with rifles halted him. They volleyed questions, then searched him for weapons. Finally, he was permitted to enter the building. His name was C. J. Fitzpatrick. He smoothed the rumples in his neat green suit and straightened his dark tie. The forty-five-year-old Negro was not angry with the policemen. He understood what they had to do.

This was Monday, August 16, and since Friday—when he last saw his eighteen-year-old son, Ralph—he had come to understand that many things people do they might not wish to do. He arrived at Lincoln Heights Jail, the last stop in a long search. He had been told he would find his son there, and he waited for him to appear in the makeshift courtroom hurriedly set up to process the hundreds of persons arrested for felonies during the rioting.

Ralph, a Los Angeles City College student, did not return home Friday night from his job in a paper plant. "I work nights, too," said his father, a foreman in a fiberglass plant. "Ralph and I eat together every night when we get home. But when he never came Friday, I figured they kept him at the plant because of the trouble."

The elder Fitzpatrick did not sleep Friday night. He spent the time trying to find out what had happened to his son. He did not sleep Saturday or Sunday night either, but by then he learned that his son had been arrested. He could not learn why. He trooped doggedly from one public building to another during the weekend, trying to find out where the boy was and what he had done wrong—if anything. "No one could tell me," Fitzpatrick said.

His was a story repeated by many other relatives searching for arrested persons, by relatives believing some way, somehow, there had been a mistake, by relatives wanting to get their loved ones home. Fitzpatrick finally learned Monday morning that his son was jailed at Lincoln Heights on a burglary charge. The father drove to the jail for the court session there.

One felony prisoner after another passed before Municipal Judge Maurice T. Leader for arraignment. Bail of $5,000 was set for each. Fitzpatrick's son had not appeared by recess, nor was his case called later. It was put over to another day. But his predicament had made Fitzpatrick a patient man—almost.

"One minute I am thinking honest to God, I'll be able to do something for my boy," he said. "The next I am frustrated because I can't. It's hard to even picture my son behind bars. He's a good worker, good student. Never been in trouble. I know it's going to cost me and him something if he's not locked up for nothing.

"You know how kids are. I'm not stupid. He might have had something in his hands. If what he had in his hands was his own, then I'm going to be angry at someone. If he had something valuable in his hands that wasn't his, then after he is all through here, with this court and all, he's still going to have to answer to me, his father. But I still don't think my kid has done anything wrong."

On saying that, Fitzpatrick nodded toward the jail blocks beyond the temporary courtroom, and said, "But I guess everybody in that place over there figures they have done nothing wrong, too." Fitzpatrick wearily rubbed his temples. Then he added: "My wife Ruth, Ralph's mother, hasn't left the house since this rioting started. I just didn't know what to think of until my son was arrested. All that trouble just sounded like another time and another place."

Newsmen were not permitted to enter the jail. They gathered on the front steps listening to the uproar in the caged floors above them. It was an angry cacaphony of shouting and cursing. Later, those inside would recall what it had been like in Lincoln Heights.

Richard Crowder was one. He and Eddie Taylor had been

driving George Adams to a hospital. Adams was the bystander hit by a police shotgun slug when officers fired at an unidentified assailant who had shot at them.

George Adams died in the back seat of Taylor's car. When police discovered his body at a checkpoint, the two men with him were arrested. Crowder recalls that they were first taken to 77th Street Station, and from there transported to the "Glass House," the focal point for all activities conducted by LAPD.

"I asked the man what they was booking us for," Crowder related. "He said it was murder. 'Murder,' I replied. I couldn't believe it. But that's just what happened. The next thing I knew I was in the Lincoln Heights jailhouse. It was Friday, the 13th. I wasn't permitted to make a phone call until the following Tuesday. Everyone thought I was dead. Even my mother. What was it like in that jail? I'll tell you. There were four of us in the cell. I slept on the concrete floor. I didn't even have a blanket. I finally got out on September 10th. The judge threw the case out of court, but it hasn't helped me much. Before, well, I was an interior decorator, but now my business has gone up in smoke.

"The paint store where I used to get credit was burned," he continued. "I can't find another that will extend me credit. They ask me where I was during the riot. I tell them I was in jail. Now, I'm considered a bad risk."

There were tired lines around his eyes. He sat back in a chair and reached for a cigarette, striking a match. "I've done a lot of other jobs. Why, once I was even a chef—and a good one at that. But there's a lot of houses here that have got to be painted. I'm a good painter. Let me do the walls and ceiling of a room, and you won't find a drop on the floor. That's the mark of a professional. Somehow, I'll make it. There's bound to be work. There's a lot of fixin' up that has to be done down here if people are going to be able to live decently."

Walter Crawford, thirty-nine, is heavy-set with a muscular body and a broad face. He arrived in Los Angeles from Tulsa in

1961, and he speaks in the soft drawl characteristic of many native Oklahomans. His wife works as a caterer, and when he can find work, he is employed as a cement mason. The apartment they live in is across the street on Avalon Boulevard from where the Fryes were arrested. As noted earlier, he witnessed the incident, as did most of the people in the block. But it was not until Friday, August 13, that Crawford himself got into trouble.

"I had been helping my brother work on his car," he began. "Later, I was walking down 92nd Street about two miles from my home. There were no busses running. All of a sudden, a policeman came up to me. He told me to lean against the wall. I had just passed a store that had been looted.

"I told the cop: 'Hell, man, I've got nothing on me but my personal possessions.' I had $50 in my wallet. It didn't make any difference. They took me down to Lincoln Heights Jail. I'll never forget that place. They put me in a bull pen with 32 others. The room had two toilets. There were no baths. You can imagine the stench of human sweat in that goddamn place.

"The beds were double-decker bunks. They were just steel springs without blankets or mattresses. I caught cold because of this, but who the hell didn't. We got no water, no coffee. When they fed us, the guards would simply take TV dinners and kick them under the barred doors of our cell.

"You know, when you feed an animal—a pet, like a dog or a cat—why, you place the food in front of them. It's a loving gesture. But when they kick it at you under the grating of a cell door, it made you hate those people. It was like they were feeding swine."

30

THE ASHES HAD BARELY cooled in Watts and in other burned-out neighborhoods before a new controversy was ignited. Accusations flew through the air like firebrands, and in this instance it would be the body politic that would be scorched.

Following a disaster, it is a fundamental concept in our society to affix responsibility. Charges are often levied in the heat of the moment that are unfounded and later cannot be substantiated. Those who serve the public in some official capacity often are singled out for attack. Sides are taken; accusations of negligence are made by one faction and denied by another.

The aftermath of the Los Angeles riot was no exception. In this case, however, the elected officials themselves were divided. What had initially been a local disturbance became, because of its size, an occurrence not only of statewide significance, but one which spotlighted Los Angeles in the eyes of the nation and the entire world.

In this charged atmosphere, it was inevitable that political leaders throughout California would utilize the catastrophe to heighten issues placed before the electorate.

Governor Edmund G. (Pat) Brown must run for reelection in 1966, if he is to remain in office. There were many who hoped to see him replaced. The top aspirant within his own Democratic Party was Los Angeles Mayor Samuel W. Yorty, who announced early in March that he would oppose Brown in the June Democratic primary election. As the political rivalry between the two was intense, the campaign was a lively one.

Republicans were envisioning a return to power at the state capital, pointing to the 1964 success of their candidate, actor George Murphy, when he bucked a national trend by defeating Democratic Senator Pierre Salinger. The former press secretary for Presidents Kennedy and Johnson had been appointed to the office by Governor Brown following the death of Senator Clair Engle.

Principal Republican challengers for the governor's post in California were actor Ronald Reagan and George Christopher, who had served as mayor of San Francisco. He fired the opening salvo of the post-riot verbal skirmishing.

Democratic Governor Brown's administration "fiddled while Los Angeles was burning," Christopher charged. "There was too much delay in ordering out the National Guard to halt rioting. We should know what motivated the lieutenant governor to procrastinate."

The McCone Commission report, released on December 7, 1965, had indeed expressed the belief that Anderson did not respond with sufficient speed on Friday, August 13, when Chief Parker asked for National Guard support. Lieutenant Governor Anderson defended his course of action. "It's a serious thing to call the National Guard," he stated. "Especially when I had been told only four hours before that the riot was contained."

Administration officials denied that there was any delay in getting troops to Los Angeles. In the chronology of events they prepared for August 13, the timetable went like this:

6:45 A.M.—Anderson, acting chief executive while Governor Brown vacations in Greece, was at home in Los Angeles. He phoned John Billett, an aide, in Hollywood. He instructed Billett to get a report on the riot from Los Angeles Police Emergency Center.

6:50 A.M.—Billett spoke with an officer he identifies as Sergeant Eberhardt. The officer reported that there had been 88 injuries, 77 arrests, 25 known crimes, and stated that the riot apparently can be "contained and handled."

6:58 A.M.—Billett relays report to Anderson, who decides that situation allows him to attend University of California regents meeting at Berkeley as planned.

7:25 A.M.—Anderson flies to Berkeley.

10:30 A.M.—Winslow Christian, Brown's executive secretary in Sacramento, calls finance director Hale Champion in Los Angeles to say Parker has asked for troops. Champion puts in a call to State Attorney General Thomas Lynch, who must prepare the formal call-up proclamation.

11:15 A.M.—Anderson is told that Chief Parker wants the Guard. He asks for conference with Guard commander, Lieutenant General Roderic Hill, and a plane for a flight to Los Angeles. Newsmen are informed that the lieutenant governor will decide on Guard call-up after meeting with local officials in Los Angeles.

12:45 P.M.—Anderson's plane detours to Sacramento for airport conference with Hill. The general informs him that Southern California's 40th Armored Division is scheduled to assemble at 7 P.M. that night for two weeks' active duty. Also, he advised that it would be difficult to get men mobilized much sooner under any circumstances, because most are at their civilian jobs. Anderson instructed the general to attempt the assembly of three infantry battalions at 5 P.M. under provisions for early drill. Hill issued the order.

Champion reached Governor Brown in Athens, Greece. He described the Los Angeles situation as being rough. Brown favored an immediate call-up of the Guard and perhaps a curfew. Champion tried to reach Anderson with the governor's recommendation, but Anderson was in the air en route to Los Angeles.

3:30 P.M.—Anderson arrived at the Van Nuys airport, where he received a message to call Champion, who in turn notified him of Governor Brown's recommendation. Anderson left for his office in the State Building. At 5:05 P.M., he signed the proclamation. Troops began moving into the riot zone.

Los Angeles Mayor Samuel W. Yorty was criticized for leaving the city on the morning of Friday, August 13, to deliver a speech in San Francisco. The mayor toured the Watts area by helicopter, but unlike Governor Brown, he refrained from making a personal appearance in the community.

Yorty has often been called a political maverick. His policies have on occasion confused both liberals and conservatives. While in office he has demonstrated a shrewd judgment in fiscal matters, which has won him strong support among the taxpayers—that segment of the population which owns property within the city, and is faced with an ever-spiraling annual tax rate. When Yorty declared that financial help to aid the Watts area must come from the state or the Federal Government, because the local citizens are practically being taxed off their property, there were few home owners in the city who wouldn't have agreed with him.

At one time in Los Angeles, the primary requisites for the mayor's position were a jovial personality and a sizable wardrobe. He was the city's official greeter—a hearty handshaker of scores of visiting dignitaries, including kings and queens who arrived to view Hollywood and other local wonders. Today, the job is much more complex. The mayor's chair is the hottest seat in Los Angeles. Pressure groups labor night and day to obtain benefits from City Hall. The Negro problem is not the only ethnic headache confronting the city's highest elected official. On the East Side there is a Mexican-American community living in a slum area which in some sections is more hideous than Watts.

The Mexican-American community had long been divided into too many opposing factions to make itself heard as a sizable voting bloc. But recently, taking a lesson from the more militant Negroes, the Mexican-Americans were exhibiting signs of a more united front. At the same time new leadership was replacing the torpor-bound elder statesmen who for years have helped to perpetuate the image of the carefree *vaquero,* with his broad sombrero, jingling spurs, and melodic guitar, who lounged around the pueblo with seemingly nothing better to do than sing his head off. The Mexican-Americans in East Los Angeles have little to sing about. They know poverty, and they have also experienced discrimination, particularly when it comes to jobs.

Sam Yorty was elected to office in 1961 after defeating the incumbent mayor, Norris Poulson. He has had a long political career, beginning in 1936 when as a twenty-seven-year-old attorney he was elected to the state legislature. Here he became the sponsor of such legislation as an anti-sweatshop act, amendments liberalizing the state old-age pension act, a slum-clearing and housing act, and legislation to curb loan sharks.

In 1949, following service as an Air Force captain during World War II, the voters sent him to Washington as a Congressman. He was re-elected in 1952, but then lost a campaign for U.S. Senator against Thomas H. Kuchel. James Roosevelt attempted to unseat Yorty as mayor in 1964, but the people of Los Angeles re-elected him by a large margin.

For nearly a year prior to the riot, Los Angeles had been unable to qualify for the federal anti-poverty program, which would have given jobs to many young people in the Watts-Central Avenue district. In Harlem, federal funds had put 4,000 youths to work, thus removing them from the streets and averting a possible riot.

The federal Office of Economic Opportunity, which R. Sargent Shriver directs, stipulates that the board which approves anti-poverty projects in each city must be broadly representative. In particular, it stressed that there be representatives of the impoverished themselves on each board. The Youth Opportunities Board in Los Angeles did not have these qualifications. Local public officials declined to add new members to the organization, and insisted that the spending of funds should be administered by elected officials, who would control the board. Critics of the mayor saw this as a move to control patronage, for with millions of dollars in federal money available to be spent, not all of it would reach the poor. In a bureaucracy it costs money to give money away. In any such government-administered program, there are always a number of administrative jobs created. These are the political plums.

Yorty, already at odds with Governor Brown, directed his attack against Washington following the riot. He charged that Sargent Shriver's agency had deprived Los Angeles of funds, and that this was one of the riot-inciting factors. He sent California's junior Senator, George Murphy, a telegram which read: "There has been a reckless effort to incite the poor for political purposes. The funds cut off from the poor in this area are our tax funds. Please demand that Shriver process our programs and release our funds while we reorganize. . . . There is no excuse for continuing the inciting tactic of trying to publicly strong-arm us into complete submission to federal whims which are confusing, changing and arbitary."

The mayor stated that other large cities had not been subjected to such strong-arm tactics, and that efforts of local anti-poverty officials to organize a federally acceptable community action screening board had been hindered by what he termed "chameleonic Office of Economic Opportunity criteria."

Senator George Murphy asked Shriver to visit Los Angeles in order that the "confusion and political nonsense" could be ended. California's senior U.S. Senator, Thomas H. Kuchel, who may or may not have shared the feeling of many fellow Republicans that the administration's anti-poverty program was riddled with politics, declared in the United States Senate: "Housing programs, aid programs are for naught unless finally free from any venal political concern, organized government in this country is able to raise up the standards of those, it may well be, whose deprivation may have contributed to the holocaust which we face in the state from which I come."

In Washington, Sargent Shriver declared flatly that Los Angeles officials had failed to get the understanding of groups who participated in the bloody rioting. When interviewed, he said: "I'm sorry Mayor Yorty made this intemperate and unfounded charge against the war on poverty, because we have not changed our criteria since that program was first founded."

The anti-poverty chief stated that when federal funds were first given to Los Angeles in November, 1964, the mayor had agreed to seek a greater cross section of representation on the community action screening board, but following his re-election, he failed to carry through his announced intention. Shriver also claimed that the attitude of local officials in Los Angeles seemed to be one of "we and they."

"This was a complete failure to get representation and understanding of the poor people, particularly Negroes," Shriver said. "Los Angeles is the only major city in the United States that does not have a well-rounded community action program because of the failure of local officials to establish a broad-based community action board representing all segments of the community."

At a press conference the mayor related that he had been trying for months to end what he termed a senseless controversy. He linked the lack of poverty funds to the riot when he declared: "The people in the poverty areas have been led to believe the money was forthcoming. They were upset over their failure to get it."

The controversy was only beginning, and as the recriminations grew in intensity, they not only involved the mayor, the governor of the state, the city council and federal authorities, but the one man in Los Angeles who carried the difficult responsibility for maintaining law and order in the entire community—Los Angeles Police Chief William H. Parker.

PART TWO

31

WILLIAM H. PARKER was born on June 21, 1902, in Lead, South Dakota. His father was a miner. After graduating from high school, he moved to Los Angeles in 1923. One of his first jobs was as an usher in a downtown theater. Parker joined the Los Angeles Police Department in 1927 as a patrolman. When not on duty, he studied law, receiving his degree from the Los Angeles College of Law in 1930. He was consistently the top scorer in examinations for promotions, including the one that led to his appointment as chief in 1950. Since that time, he has built the Los Angeles 5,000-man police force into one of the finest in the nation.

Potential recruits are carefully screened before being accepted. A candidate must pass a rigid examination—mental and physical—as well as demonstrate his psychological aptitude for law enforcement work. An intensive recruitment program is in progress to encourage young men to join the department, which because of an ever-increasing population within the city must necessarily have additional personnel. When Chief Parker was asked if he would lower educational requirements for applicants, as a large Eastern city has done by waiving the need for a high school diploma, the chief retorted that he wouldn't have dropouts on his force.

Many members of the Los Angeles Police Department complete their college education on a part-time basis, and there are numerous instances where officers emulate their chief by graduating with law degrees and are admitted to the California bar. A number of them remain with the department, completing 20 years' service which qualifies them for retirement, and then enter private practice. The opportunities for advancement are many in the LAPD. The pay is good, and the retirement benefits, particularly for those who move up the promotion ladder, are excellent. There are drawbacks. In Los Angeles, police work is one of the most difficult and hazardous professions a man can select for a career, particularly in view of the rising crime rate within the city.

A report released by the Federal Bureau of Investigation following the riot notes that murder, rape and robbery were on the increase in Los Angeles. The latest figures contained in the Uniform Crime Statistics report compiled by the FBI show that there were 102 murders committed in the city during January-June, 1965—14 more than the number counted in the first half of 1964. Forcible rapes totaled 602, robberies 4,062, up 884. Aggravated assaults totaled 4,546; burglaries and breaking-and-entering crimes came to 24,629; there were 14,818 larcenies, and 10,806 automobiles were reported stolen.

A police officer faces danger from the moment he reports for duty each day, whether he is on a motorcycle pursuing a speeding driver on the freeways, apprehending a criminal suspect or in some cases answering a simple house call about a domestic disturbance. He may ring the doorbell and be greeted by gunfire. Many cases can be cited in recent years where crazed citizens have barricaded themselves within their homes, firing at police sent to subdue them. Officers have been wounded and even killed trying to prevent normally law-abiding citizens, suddenly gone berserk, from harming innocent people.

There is the criminal element, even more ruthless and dangerous. Scan the list of fatalities among LAPD officers in the past few years, and it is readily apparent that an officer must possess more than a combination of courage and intelligence. He has to be dedicated to the cause of protecting the people of his community.

Chief Parker, after seeing his men killed and viewing the grim crime statistics across the country, believes that disrespect for the law imperils the nation. He considers his officers as the front line of defense against a creeping moral jungle that threatens to ensnare the city. He told an interviewer in 1962: "It is hard for me to believe that our society can continue to violate all the fundamental rules of human conduct and expect to survive. I think I have to conclude that this civilization will destroy itself as others have before it."

Again, he has stated that "man is the most predatory of all the animal kingdom. He must have restraints." These restraints, as he repeatedly asserted, were withering away "under a widespread explosion of liberalism without restraint. Individual freedom without regard for the law is sweeping the world."

The chief also spoke out against "liberalized" rulings by the state and federal courts that have placed the police officer in a straitjacket. Commenting in May, 1961, on the federal court McNabb-Mallory rule which holds that a confession obtained during a period of illegal detention is invalid, Parker declared: "Our free society would be in danger and our international enemies could possibly destroy us if the judiciary continues to spell out the rules of a criminal investigation."

In a speech which Chief Parker gave before an American Legion gathering in Portland a few days following the riot, he warned: "It is but a short step from minor infractions to mob violence and widespread disorder. Those who advocate the violation of laws that have neither been repealed nor declared unconstitutional advocate anarchy."

Later, at a news conference Parker said that demands for police review boards to investigate charges of brutality were an attempt to break the will of the police and get them out of the way of the social evolution that civil rights leaders choose to call civil disobedience. He said that if the citizens of Los

Angeles haven't learned from the riot that they must support strong law enforcement, "next time they'll burn up the whole city."

The sincerity of Chief Parker's convictions is undebatable. As is the case with many dedicated men, he is impatient with his critics and is often outspoken in his beliefs. Some of his remarks expressed during and after the riot had an inflammatory effect upon the Negro community. "They have no leaders," he rasped at one interview, implying that no Negro political or religious groups exerted any influence over the Watts-southeastern section of the city. His words did little to soften the sting felt by Negroes who had labored to improve the lot of the poverty-stricken residents and who were now doing considerable soul-searching to determine where their efforts had failed. But Chief Parker in his blunt appraisal had spoken the truth. Those who participated in the rioting recognized no leadership among their own people. Even Dr. Martin Luther King, Jr., who visited Los Angeles following the riot, was jeered by fellow Negroes when he attempted to address a meeting in Watts.

"Burn, baby, burn!" someone in the audience chanted, and as *Newsweek* commented: "The Negro leadership scarcely needed the evidence of King's pilgrimage to confirm a single shattering fact of the Los Angeles riot—the orthodox civil rights movement of the South simply has not reached the black masses in the wilderness of the urban north."

Parker touched off a new furor when, in describing how the riot started, he observed caustically, "One person threw a rock, and then, like monkeys in a zoo, others started throwing rocks."

This was undoubtedly an innocent remark, but enraged Negroes drew the inference that Parker was saying they were not far removed from the animal kingdom. The chief dropped another ill-timed comment when, as the rioting was finally being brought under control, he said, "We're on top and they are on the bottom."

This caused Roy Wilkins, executive director of the National

Association for the Advancement of Colored People, whose syndicated column appears in the *Los Angeles Times,* to write: "Negroes in America know this too well. The Chief Parker reminder is salt in the wound because it reflects the whole of the Negro-white picture in the United States . . . the truth is that the philosophy behind the 'we're on top' expression was the tinder under the Watts explosion. . . ."

Less than two weeks after the riot Chief Parker appeared on a nationwide television broadcast, NBC's "Meet the Press." A brilliant man when it comes to law and its enforcement, he is by no means overly articulate. Dour-faced when asked to discuss the problem of crime confronting the nation, he repeated the dogmas he has been voicing over the years. However, the chief's tenacity in face of critics and his obvious knowledge and experience in crime prevention command respect. Even his detractors accord him this.

To the white citizens of Los Angeles, who had lived six days in fear, wondering if the violence would engulf the entire city, Bill Parker was the one man they looked to for leadership during the crisis. Mayor Yorty, as has been noted, left Los Angeles during the riots for a speaking engagement in San Francisco. The mayor's over-all performance contributed little toward alleviating the tense situation. The Los Angeles City Council, usually a garrulous and argumentive body, whose 15 members represent economically and socially diverse districts within the city, was strangely silent.

Before millions of viewers, the Los Angeles police chief made an accusation that disappointed and angered many of his most staunch supporters. He accused another law enforcement agency, which had aided his own officers in suppressing the riots, for being responsible for the outbreak of violence. The object of his criticism was the California Highway Patrol.

Parker told the nationwide audience that California Highway Patrolmen do not have the training and experience to handle cases such as the one that touched off the rioting—the arrests of the three Fryes. He said that he had concluded, after studying reports on the incident, that if city police, who have handled hundreds of arrests in that area, had made the arrests on August 11, the rioting would have been averted.

"I sat back a long time before I said anything," he later told a reporter. "I've had a chance now to study the reports from my men."

When asked what reaction he expected from his statement, the chief replied: "It will probably make me a bigger s.o.b. than I've ever been in my life . . . for being a traitor to fellow police officers . . . and not taking the heat off the riots."

In the wake of Parker's speech, Mayor Yorty concurred with Chief Parker that the Highway Patrolmen lacked training in riot control. He wrote a letter to District Attorney Evelle J. Younger, urging him to make an investigation into the actions of the CHP.

August 28, 1965

The Honorable Evelle Younger
District Attorney
County of Los Angeles
Hall of Justice
211 West Temple Street
Los Angeles, California 90012

Dear Mr. Younger:

The Los Angeles Police Department has kept itself fully appraised for the potential for riots and violence in the area of the recent riots where it has the difficult responsibility of maintaining order and protecting law-abiding citizens from irresponsible and criminal elements twenty-four hours per day, every day in the year.

The "big lie" technique has long been used in the area to label all police "brutes." Communists, fellow travelers, dupes, and demagogues have drummed the charge of "police brutality" into the ears of the people of the area, deliberately fomenting antagonism to law enforcement officers, inciting the residents to resent and resist officers in the proper professional performance of their always difficult and often dangerous duty to protect the right of law-abiding citizens to be secure in their persons and property. This campaign against the police has fostered a highly charged atmosphere into which our policemen must go to perform their duties.

Originally the charge of "police brutality" was made only when an officer used physical force. As charges of excessive force were time after time proved to be unfounded, a new stratagem was used to accuse the police of "verbal brutality." This has now been changed to accuse the police of "attitude brutality."

No matter how correct and restrained the police are, so long as they perform their duties, they will continue to be subjected to false, exaggerated, and malicious charges and rumors deliberately calculated to create tension and increase the difficulty of their work.

While this insidious campaign against them has been going full steam, the police have also had their rights, authority, and powers curtailed and made extremely complex by a series of very technical decisions of the courts expanding the rights and defenses of persons accused of crime. In the meantime, the crime rate soars, and more peaceful citizens are victimized by the criminal element of our society.

In the face of the foregoing it is not easy to sustain police morale; to give them the desire and the courage to continue to do their job—a job upon which the whole fabric of our society is dependent.

As Mayor, I have felt it my duty to defend our policemen from unfair attacks and to try to arouse law-abiding citizens to recognize their responsibility to support the policemen they call when their lives or property are endangered. What would law-abiding citizens do if they called and there were no policemen willing to answer the call? We had better think about this because already there are too few police officers and they are getting harder to recruit.

Law enforcement faces a crisis, and I do not believe the magnitude of the crisis is generally understood. The recent destructive riots may serve some useful purpose if they awaken the nation to the dangers inherent in the deteriorating ability of law enforcement agencies to function effectively.

Mr. District Attorney, the foregoing is all well known to you and is a prelude to a request which is the purpose of this letter.

Obviously we must be as eager to protect the citizen against police misconduct as we are to protect the police from unfounded charges of misconduct. When charges are made against Los Angeles police officers these charges are thoroughly investigated, and if substantiated, the officers are disciplined. If warranted, they are discharged, prosecuted or both.

Our Los Angeles police officers are required to adhere to high professional standards. They are carefully trained to do their job; to avoid inciting hostility by crowds; to restrain themselves under extreme provocation; and to use especial care in areas of tension, so as not to give lawless elements an excuse to incite mob violence. Our training and tactics have made it possible for our officers to continue to police the riot area and yet avoid riots where very often the potential for mob action was present.

On August 11, 1965, at 7:15 P.M. our Police Department responded to an "Officer needs help" call from officers of the California Highway Patrol. When our policemen arrived, members of the Patrol were already using shotguns—

apparently to keep a crowd back from a Patrol car in which our officers observed a young male Negro in the front seat. An elderly female Negro and another male Negro were in the back seat. The suspect in the front seat had a large gash on his forehead.

At this time the crowd appeared to be getting unruly, and in accordance with our department's procedure in such cases a Los Angeles officer requested the Patrol to take the suspect away from the vicinity as soon as possible. This admonition was ignored. It had to be repeated at three intervals while a further force was used to subdue the suspect in the front seat. A Patrolman punched him in the stomach with a sap. The crowd was now cursing all the police.

Our officers estimate it was 20 or 25 minutes from the time they arrived until they were able to convince the Patrol officers to leave the scene. Previous to this time, what had started as a pursuit into Los Angeles of a drunk driving suspect had been permitted to get so out of hand that the suspect's brother and their elderly mother were in custody. The car driven by the suspect belonged to the mother, and she had, I am informed, originally come to the scene and requested that her son, who was with the suspect, be permitted to drive the car home. Whatever happened afterwards resulted in her being arrested along with both of her sons and she stands charged with interfering with the Patrol officers.

I understand that both of the young men pleaded guilty to some charges on advice of the Public Defender and that the mother pleaded not guilty. As far as I can ascertain at this time none of these persons has ever been convicted of a crime, and the brother of the original suspect has, I believe, just completed four years of military duty. He had been in Los Angeles only two days when the events occurred which led to his arrest.

To go back to the scene, when the Patrol officers were finally induced to leave with the suspects, and our units were ordered out, a woman in the crowd spit on a Patrol officer and then jumped back into the now unruly crowd. Patrol officers plunged into the crowd after her and placed her under arrest. All the officers left the scene.

I am told that after these events the situation continued to deteriorate into the full blown riot of Wednesday night, during which nineteen Los Angeles Police officers were injured in the performance of their duties.

It seems apparent that the least one can say is that the Patrol officers appear to have used bad judgment, which could be the result of inadequate training. Their conduct in such an area under such circumstances indicated a lack of awareness of the dangerous potentialities inherent in the situation.

Persons who do not know the difference between Los Angeles Police officers and Highway Patrol officers, and some who do not care, have raised the usual cry of "police brutality" against our officers and, as usual, are demanding the discharge of Chief Parker and the establishment of a "Police Review Board."

They ignore the fact that the California Highway Patrol was primarily involved in the incidents which appear to have triggered the devastating and disastrous riots. They also ignore the fact that our Police Department is already headed by a civilian Board on which racial and religious minority members constitute a majority.

If our police officers were involved as described above, we would already be conducting a thorough inquiry as to the propriety of their actions, the judgment used, and the amount of force justified from the time the first suspect was stopped until all were discharged from custody.

Because the Highway Patrol is not under the jurisdiction of this city, and because of the magnitude of this whole matter, I respectfully request that you, as chief law enforcement officer of the County, conduct a full and complete inquiry, and if you deem it advisable, that you request the United States Attorney General to order the Federal Bureau of Investigation to assist in said inquiry.

Sincerely,
Sam Yorty
MAYOR

SWY/m

There are several points in the mayor's letter which his critics would take issue with. A Highway Patrolman did not punch one of the Fryes in the stomach with a sap. To be specific, it was a riot baton. This is made from wood, and is often referred to as a nightstick. There is considerable difference between the two weapons. An officer can rap a suspect over the head with a riot baton, if necessary, and the most damage it will generally do is to knock the adversary senseless. Most of the time, the baton is more effectively employed as a prod. The sap is far more lethal, being a short leather-wrapped cudgel that is weighted on the end with lead shot. A sharp blow on the top of a man's head with a sap can split his skull wide open like an eggshell. For this reason, few California Highway Patrolmen carry them.

It would also have been easy for Mayor Yorty to ascertain before writing this letter that Marquette Frye did have a prior police record—a background of juvenile arrests. It would have been equally simple for him to investigate the training program the California Highway Patrol has for its officers before he concurred with Chief Parker's accusations that they lacked adequate training in riot control. Yorty has a capable staff of investigators, and if one of them would have taken the trouble to visit the CHP headquarters in Gardena, which was the central operating base for all of its officers during the riot, he could have examined records of the training schedule in race relations and riot prevention and control, for which classes have been held in that building for the past three years. All officers attend them, and the instruction is generally given by watch commanders at roll call before the men go out in the field on patrol. Some of the topics covered in the discussions relate to their contacts with minority races, specifically Negroes. This included the Muslims and stressed courtesy and diplomacy.

Two hours in four sessions at roll call were devoted to racial relations in the Watts and Willowbrook areas. In these lectures, watch commanders re-emphasized the safety of officers, calling for back-up when necessary, the importance of being alert and watchful of crowds gathering at accidents when arrests are being made, and especially dealing with making physical arrests in this area, and the importance of removing the prisoner from the area immediately. Additional lectures covered: mob and riot control—a total of seven hours per man given in ten sessions on this subject—and the psychology of the Negro in the Watts area, and the Black Muslims. These sessions were conducted by a CHP captain with the aid of intelligence furnished by the Los Angeles Sheriff's Department, as well as from an officer detailed by the Los Angeles Police Department to aid the CHP in its training program. Many more hours were devoted to studying the laws and methods of control in civil disturbances and civil rights demonstrations, instructions and application in the use of the police baton in riot squad formations, procedure on physical arrest in the Watts area, and a review of physical arrest of minority groups and of juvenile violators in the Watts community.

For Mayor Yorty to imply that because Highway Patrol officers were involved in the events which appeared to have triggered the riots, and thus affix the responsibility for the outbreak upon their organization alone, would be to refute the growing signs of unrest that had been evident within Watts and the entire depressed Negro community of south-central and southeastern Los Angeles for a considerable period. As Murray L. Schwartz, professor of law at the University of California, Los Angeles, expressed it in the *Saturday Review* (November 13, 1965): ". . . to attribute the riots to the arrest of one or two individuals by the State Highway Patrol is like attributing World War I to the assassination of the Archduke Ferdinand. Catalyst it may have been; cause it was not. . . ."

The underlying reasons for the rioting had much deeper roots than hostility for law and order. For years these people had known discrimination, poverty and utter frustration. Public apathy was apparent, and this did little toward contributing any feeling of hope for a better way of life to those who have long lived on the fringe of an affluent society, performing menial tasks when they could find employment.

And so, in days of anger, the feelings of futility and resentment of a great many people relegated by economic circumstances to a subservient, substandard mode of living were finally fused into a lethal atmosphere. The fumes of hate were easily detectable on that heat-charged August night. They required but a spark of provocation to ignite, and the riot was on.

32

AN ANGERED California Highway Patrol Commissioner Bradford M. Crittenden was quick to rally to the defense of his officers following the televised remarks of Los Angeles Police Chief Parker. He termed the charges against his men unwarranted and bitterly denounced accusations by Mayor Yorty and Chief Parker that CHP officers caused the riot. At a press conference held in his Sacramento office, he declared: "I have 3,000 men who are the best-trained law enforcement officers in the world and they were down there getting shot at the same as Parker's men and in fairness to them I thought I should say something. . . . I have been deeply shocked and disturbed by Chief Parker's statements. During the period of the riot I was in and out of the chief's office. At no time did he indicate to me his presently expressed feelings.

"Particularly is it difficult for me to understand why, if my men are so poorly trained and qualified, as he now states, he continually asked for and received during the period of the riot the assistance of 60 or more Highway Patrolmen. If he has so little confidence in my men, why then did he knowingly risk their lives?"

In answer to charges that the CHP officers used improper procedures in facing the crowd, Crittenden said the officers acted properly, displaying shotguns when it became necessary, but keeping them unloaded.

Later, at another press conference in Los Angeles, following his appearance before the McCone Commission probing the cause of the riot, Commissioner Crittenden defended the arresting officers in the Frye incident, and the policy of CHP arrest procedures. In response to a question about Chief Parker's allegation that delay in removing the prisoners touched off the riot, he said: "I have great admiration for Chief Parker, but I say that my officers followed correct procedures and made these arrests as expeditiously as possible under the circumstances. It took 40 minutes from the time the automobile was stopped by a motorcycle officer until the transportation car with the suspects left the scene. We must remember there were several different incidents which occurred during this 40 minutes and that this was not a peaceful arrest. Before we arrest anybody, we must be certain that a crime has been committed. It takes time to establish this certainty."

On August 12, 1965, the Highway Patrol performed a task which in light of the many catastrophic events that followed seems to have gone unnoticed. It was, however, what most rankled all CHP officers who had been on duty in the riot zone, when they learned of Chief Parker's criticism of the actions of the Patrol.

At approximately 9:45 P.M. 16 California Patrol cars containing 31 officers responded to a radio call from the Los Angeles Police Department in the vicinity of 110th and Avalon. As the convoy drove through the area, their cars were subjected to a bombardment of rocks, bricks and, in some instances, gunfire. Arriving at the scene, where Los Angeles police officers were pinned down, the CHP officers got out of their vehicles under a rain of hurled objects. Several of them were hit. There were less than a dozen LAPD officers trying to hold back a savage mob of more than 1,000 jeering rioters. The CHP officers were armed with shotguns. The LAPD officers were not. CHP Commissioner Bradford C. Crittenden later stated: "A shotgun is a terrific leveler in crowd control, causing tremendous respect, but it should be used very carefully."

His officers put them to good use that sultry, angry night. They charged into the crowd, which fell back, scattered and fled. "I don't want to be in front of one of them shotguns when it goes off," one of the Negroes who had been at the scene said later. "A blast from one of those guns can tear a man to shreds. I seen what happened to a guy once who tried to hold up a liquor store. A manager let him have it from a second-floor balcony. The guy didn't have no face left."

A CHP officer later wrote in his report that a Los Angeles police inspector told him: "You saved our butts."

This rather crude but effective expression of appreciation may be the only accolade the California Highway Patrol will ever receive from the Los Angeles Police Department for aid rendered during a crucial period of the rioting.

Governor Brown appointed an eight-member commission to investigate the causes of the riot. John A. McCone, sixty-two, former director of the Central Intelligence Agency, was selected to head the panel. McCone, a successful businessman, had held various government appointments, among them the chairmanship of the Atomic Energy Commission. The other members of the commission represented a cross section of interests and professions in the community. They included a judge, an attorney, a leading businessman and several educators. For three months the panel interviewed several hundred witnesses. Some 90 persons arrested during the riot were questioned, and the commission's consultants conducted written surveys of 10,000 persons, before the final report was written for the governor. The study cost $250,000. Of this amount, $150,000 came from a Ford Foundation grant, and the balance was paid for by the state. The voluminous record of the hearings covered some 6,000 pages of testimony and exhibits.

The Los Angeles district attorney's office, in response to Mayor Yorty's letter blaming the "bad judgment" of California Highway Patrol officers at the scene of the Fryes' arrest, began an eight-week investigation which included interviews with 74 witnesses to determine the cause of the outbreak. When District Attorney Evelle J. Younger released the report, it consisted of 1,315 pages of testimony, in which witnesses described what had occurred during those tension-filled minutes preceding the violent explosion of hate and terror.

"It is our conclusion," he wrote to Yorty, "that there is insufficent evidence to justify the institution of criminal proceedings against any of the officers involved."

When Governor Brown viewed the riot area along Central Avenue and in Watts, he expressed his shock and surprise by saying, "Here in California, we have a wonderful working relationship between whites and Negroes. We got along fine until this happened. . . ."

The governor was expressing an almost universal naïveté found among city, state and county public officials. The truth is that racial tensions have long existed in cities throughout California from San Diego to San Francisco. In the Bay area, Oakland has the greatest potential for racial violence, where 34 per cent of the city's residents are Negroes. Twenty-five per cent of Oakland's adult Negro males are without jobs. Berkeley with a 20-per-cent Negro population, and Richmond with 22-percent share with the neighboring Negroes in San Francisco similar conditions of poverty and substandard housing. San Francisco has a population of 775,000 and 12 per cent are Negroes.

Oakland has been far more progressive than Los Angeles in its successful operation of anti-poverty programs. The city received an initial grant of $2,000,000 from the Ford Foundation. A variety of experiments were inaugurated covering a wide range of welfare projects, including job training, education and health. When this program was augmented by federal funds, there was no bickering over who would have the authority to dispense the money.

Racial tension in Los Angeles has been far more evident than in any other California city. There have been instances of violence, and there have been other situations where outbreaks of hostility were averted only by quick action upon the part of police officers. The South Central Avenue-Watts district has long been overdue for the explosion that occurred on the fateful August night. A number of people recognized the warning signs, but their words of advice went unheeded. One of them was former Assistant Attorney General Howard Jewel.

In 1963, following demonstrations at San Francisco's Palace Hotel, Jewel drafted a report which he sent to his chief, State Attorney General Stanley Mosk, now a State Supreme Court Justice. In his report, he predicted the riot that was to take place in Los Angeles 15 months later. Jewel placed the blame for racial unrest in that city on its chief of police, William H. Parker. It reads in part:

6000 State Building
San Francisco 2
May 25, 1964

Howard H. Jewel
Racial Situation—Los Angeles

This month these incidents happened in Los Angeles: Loren Miller's paper* headlined: "Fight blamed on cops." The lead paragraph of this story read as follows: "Tensions between the Negro community and the police department erupted in two new outbreaks this past weekend and in a flood of charges, counter charges and demands."

The Los Angeles CORE demanded the resignation of Chief Parker and commenced a campaign to make that demand a reality. The campaign included the picketing of

* *The California Eagle,* a Negro newspaper. Miller was editor and publisher until his appointment as a Los Angeles Municipal Court judge.

the Los Angeles Police Station by James Farmer, National Director of CORE.

Station KNX carried an editorial accusing the three Negro councilmen of Los Angeles of encouraging violence in the Negro community, accusing them of a lack of respect for law and order.

A mob formed in Pacoima which almost transformed an insignificant incident into an ugly racial disturbance.

The Governor and the Attorney General have had requests from at least two organizations for a "public hearing" of the racial situation in Los Angeles.

Soon the "long hot summer" will be upon us. The evidence from Los Angeles is ominous.

Negro leaders in San Francisco and Los Angeles do not materially differ in their outlook or in their tactics. The demonstrators do not differ materially—the attitudes of the white communities of San Francisco and Los Angeles do not differ materially. What does differ is the attitude of the respective police departments.

Chief Cahill* of San Francisco has bent every effort to convince San Francisco and his own police department that the civil rights struggle is not between the demonstrators and the police, but that in fact the police department is a third and neutral force. Chief Parker, by contrast, has made it clear that the struggle *is* between the police department and the demonstrators.

The chief feels, correctly I suppose, that he can "handle" the demonstrators. He has a well trained and efficient force, skilled in the police techniques of crowd dispersal, etc. I believe the chief is right when he says that

* Police Chief Thomas Cahill has worked hard at developing a friendly relationship with minority groups. The San Francisco Police Department established a community relations bureau several years ago. It works with citizens' groups in minority neighborhoods, seeking better understanding and discussing police problems.

he can "handle" the demonstrators. But I think he is missing the point. For the true danger in these civil rights disturbances does not arise simply from the demonstrators themselves but from the possibility that the demonstrators will be joined by the Negro community generally. In San Francisco this did not happen. There was some rumor that the longshoremen would join but they did not. There was never, so far as I can tell, a real danger that Negroes would pour out of the ghettoes of Hunter's Point or Fillmore Street to join in with demonstrators at the Palace or on Van Ness Avenue. If they had done so, of course, the dimensions of the danger would have been multiplied many fold.

In Los Angeles if demonstrators are joined by the Negro community at large the policing will no longer be done by the Los Angeles Police Department, but by the State Militia. If violence erupts millions in property damage may ensue, untold lives may be lost and California will have received an unsurpassed injury to her reputation.

One cannot contemplate the personalities and the emotional makeup of the chief antagonists in this struggle—the civil rights leader on the one hand and Chief Parker on the other—without being struck by the similarities.

Each is intelligent and strong willed. Each regards himself as a champion of a beleaguered minority. Each has almost Oriental regard for "loss of face." Each is determined to prevail, no matter what the cost to the community generally. Each is currently embarked upon a course of conflict which is designed not to *avoid* violence but to place the blame for violence upon the opposing party. Neither is willing to take any steps to reduce the possibilities for violence. Each has his motto: "not one step backward."

Chief Parker does not deserve the reputation for bigotry which clings to him. Chief Parker does not dislike Negroes because they are Negroes, but because they dislike the police department. This, in Parker's book, is the only unforgivable sin.

Parker thinks his department is unprejudiced and efficiently administered. I agree with him. But Parker must convey this fact to the Negroes of Los Angeles. Somehow he must be convinced that showing his department in its true light to the Negroes of Los Angeles is not demeaning, not submitting to the enemy.

To put the problem another way. In San Francisco there was no way for the civil rights leaders to personify their irritations. They could not attack the mayor for they had campaigned for him two months previously. Chief Cahill removed himself as a target. . . . But in Los Angeles Chief Parker personifies the frustrations of Negroes and gives focus to their activities. I am not saying that this is fair or justified, but I am saying that it is a fact. . . .

The Attorney General forwarded a copy of Jewel's report to Governor Brown's office, but little further action was taken. The governor never saw it. He commented: "My people didn't regard it of significant importance to pass it along to me. Perhaps they should have."

The first serious disturbance involving many Los Angeles Negroes took place on Memorial Day, May 30, 1961. The setting was the city's vast recreational area, Griffith Park, which has ample room for three golf courses, miles of bridle trails, a zoo and plenty of woodland trails for hikers. There were 30,000 persons in the park that day and the majority were Negroes.

Adjacent to the zoo is a refreshment stand. Nearby is a merry-go-round. A seventeen-year-old Negro boarded the carousel without paying. The operator of the concession, Ross R. Davis, seventy-five, attempted to remove him, but the belligerent youth refused to leave. Several companions, who had been drinking beer, berated Davis. He summoned police.

Officer J. D. Calderwood and A. H. Dunn answered the call. After a brief scuffle, they arrested the boy, but as they tried to lead him to their car, a throng of 200 Negroes blocked their way. There were approximately 3,000 people in the immediate vicinity of the merry-go-round.

Officer Calderwood later said: "The crowd took our prisoner from us, and he escaped in the disturbance that followed."

When a white citizen attempted to aid the officer, he was knocked down by Negroes, beaten over the head and his nose was smashed. The Negroes attacked the police officers with baseball bats, hurling rocks and bottles. Seventy-five officers were rushed to the scene.

"I could feel the crowd getting ugly," one witness related. "Then an officer was hit on the head by a vacuum jug. Police swarmed in. It was an ugly crowd. Some of them muttered, 'This is not Alabama.' "

As the mob closed in on a small group of policemen, Officer Michael Seybert fired one shot into an embankment above him that caused the crowd to disperse sufficiently for the officers to gain temporary refuge in a foreman's office until reinforcements arrived. Police cars entering the park were stoned. One was overturned. Four police officers were injured before the park was cleared and order restored. Twenty-two persons were arrested. Fifteen were juveniles.

On September 2, 1961, one of the earliest incidents of violence involving the anti-white Black Muslim cult took place in Los Angeles, when six of its members were arrested in a supermarket at Western Avenue near Venice Boulevard after a disturbance which drew 40 officers to the scene. Two store detectives were beaten and stomped when they tried to stop distribution of a Muslim newspaper in the market.

One of the store detectives, Fred Prendergast, reported that the market had been having trouble for ten months, as groups of Muslims blocked the market doorways, trying to sell their papers to the customers. The publication, *Mr. Muhammad Speaks,* carried a headline in large type which stated: "Muslims Set for Christian Attack."

According to the paper's masthead, it was printed at 113 Lenox Avenue in New York's Harlem. Prendergast said two of the paper sellers jumped him when he tried to oust them from the store. "Next thing I knew they were on me from all directions, and I don't recall what happened after that."

When police officers arrived, they found Prendergast on the ground trying to defend himself against the attacks of the two Negroes, and attempting to draw his gun. His partner was pinned against the wall by three others. Prendergast, who sustained a cut face and bruises in the battle, said, "The market is private property, and time and again we've asked them to stop bothering customers and preaching their doctrine in there. This isn't the only store that's having trouble. Others around here are getting the same treatment."

A far more violent eruption involving cult members occurred in April, 1962. It received nationwide notoriety and left Los Angeles residents concerned, probably for the first time, about the strange all-Negro sect which spewed out hate for whites under the guise of religion.

Officers Frank Tomlinson and Stanley Kensic had stopped to investigate a car containing a large amount of clothing, which was parked in front of the Muslim Temple at 5606 South Broadway. The officers separated the two suspects for questioning. There had been a number of burglaries in the neighborhood. The loaded car had aroused the suspicion of the officers. Tomlinson took one man to the rear of the car, while Kensic had the other in front of the vehicle. Suddenly, this suspect began to choke him. As Tomlinson ran to assist his partner, a number of Muslims charged from the temple. Tomlinson was knocked to the sidewalk. A band of some eight or ten Negroes kicked and beat him, chanting, "Let's get them, brothers, let's kill them, brothers."

Tomlinson later told a Superior Court jury trying his attackers: "I heard a gunshot and saw a man with a gun and heard him say, 'Leave those officers alone.'" This man was later identified as Special Officer William Trible. Tomlinson said Trible fired one shot into the air because he was being rushed by some of the Muslims.

"Then a group started toward me and this time one of the men had a revolver. He fired three times. One of the bullets hit me. The impact knocked me down. This time I stayed down. Kensic was on the sidewalk. There were ten or twelve men kicking or beating me."

Tomlinson had been shot in the elbow. The gun his Negro assailant used had been taken from his partner, Stanley Kensic. As police reinforcements arrived, a Muslim came out of the temple firing a rifle. Police officers returned the fire. Two Muslims fell to the street. Members of the sect dragged them into the building. By the time the battle ended, one Muslim, Ronald T. Stokes, twenty-nine, was dead, and six were wounded. Fourteen others were arrested. It required 75 officers to restore order. Several were injured. One was hit on the head with a five-gallon water bottle.

Chief Parker testified before the criminal complaints committee of the grand jury on May 2, 1962, regarding the gunfight. He warned them that full-scale clashes could break out at any moment between the white-hating Muslim sect and police or any other segment of the community.

"This is real dynamite," he said. "It was the most brutal conflict I've seen since I've been in Los Angeles. . . . The Muslims have a trained muscle squad of strong young men called the FOI—Fruits of Islam. I feel this sect should be exposed like any threat to the community. People should realize this is a racial situation which can be alleviated only by proper exposure, such as any other problem. Their teachings are of the nature that such clashes as occurred the other night are bound to re-occur and will become more frequent."

The Muslim movement had it origin in 1933, when it was

founded by Wallace Fard. The basic philosophy of his teachings was based on the Moslem religion and a fanatic hatred for the white race. Leadership passed into the hands of Elijah Poole, his six sons and his son-in-law, Raymond Sharrieff. Poole devoted his energies to the organization of the Negro Muslims with considerable success. Temples were established in Los Angeles, San Francisco, Sacramento, New York, Detroit, Boston, Philadelphia and Miami. As the list of recruits grew, so did the funds in the Muslim treasury. Extensive real estate holdings were acquired and schools were established to teach the young. Many criminals serving time in penal institutions were enlisted, and upon their release the Muslims demonstrated remarkable success in rehabilitating even those with lengthy past records as felons. They were put to work in gainful occupations. Significantly, there is little unemployment among members of the sect.

Poole adopted the name of Muhammad, the Messenger of Allah, and his followers were required to discard their family names and substitute simply the capital letter "X." Members of the faith are required to follow many of the dictates of the Muslim religion. They can consume only one meal a day, are required to pray five times daily as they kneel facing Mecca, the first prayer commencing at 5 o'clock in the morning. The women members may not use cosmetics of any kind, nor can the members use tobacco, alcohol or any form of narcotics. They are forbidden to engage in any act of sexual infidelity. The violation of any of these rules results in immediate expulsion.

Prominent Negro leaders throughout the country have condemned the Muslim movement, but most of them concede that it has exerted a great appeal to many Negroes. It has given them a purpose, a hope and something to work for. It has bound them together with ties of religion and anti-white fanaticism. A report made in 1961 by the California State Senate Fact-Finding Committee on Un-American Activities pointed out that "every real or fancied act of discrimination drives more Negroes into the Muslim ranks—and our survey discloses considerable sympathy among Negroes who have no connection with the movement, but who are being stirred by the fact that this group is implementing its resentment with action. . . ."

In his study of the Black Muslims, C. Eric Lincoln writes: "The Black Muslims have made a science of black nationalism. They have made *black* the ideal, the ultimate value; they have proclaimed the Black Man to be the primogenitor of all civilization, the Chosen of Allah, 'the rightful ruler of the Planet Earth.' And their extreme racist doctrine has attracted more than a hundred thousand adherents—a vivid warning of the deep resentment American Negroes harbor for their status in our society and the futility they feel about the likelihood of a genuine and peaceful change. . . ."*

It is difficult to state how many Muslims were involved in the August riots of 1965, and whether as an organization they were responsible for initiating any of the mass burning and looting. There were Muslims arrested, who were quickly released from jail on bail. The Muslims were active in circulating inflammatory literature within the riot area from the beginning of the outbreak, an activity which during any civil disorder increases the fury of the malcontents.

The Muslims have little patience with other leading Negro organizations. The National Association for the Advancement of Colored People (NAACP) as well as the Urban League are dominated by white men, according to those who preach the Muslim doctrine. They deplore the philosophy of passive resistance advocated by Reverend Martin Luther King, Jr. They have no use for a creed that stresses loving one's oppressor, and he, in the eyes of all Muslims, is the white man.

* *The Black Muslims in America* (Boston: Beacon Press, 1961), pp. 25–34.

33

HOSTILITY TOWARD law and order continued to increase within the Negro community in the southern section of Los Angeles. On April 11, 1964, a policeman was knocked unconscious and windows of two patrol cars were smashed by a mob of youths following a track meet at Jefferson High School, 1319 E. 41st Street. Officer Joe G. Northey, twenty-six, was rushed to the Central Receiving Hospital after being struck in the face by a brick. Other police officers were showered with sticks and stones by spectators objecting to the arrest of a youth who had been ejected from the track meet. More than 100 officers were summoned before the crowd, estimated at 600 persons, was dispersed. While several officers drew their guns, no shots were fired. One of the officers reported that the riot started when they ejected a nineteen-year-old spectator who had been drinking. Six juveniles were arrested at the scene, including the Negro youth who had hurled the brick at Officer Northey.

Nine Negroes were arrested on Saturday night, April 25, 1964, and many more escaped pursuing officers after police rushed into the Central Receiving Hospital to battle an unruly crowd of Negroes rioting through its halls and operating rooms, as surgeons and nurses were trying to treat a number of injured persons who had arrived in ambulances.

There had been a collision between two autos earlier at 50th Street and Ascot Avenue. One of the drivers was critically injured. The three occupants of the other vehicle received lesser injuries. A crowd collected after the accident. Two Los Angeles police officers arrived at the scene. They could not get through the pressing mob to aid the injured. The officers were taunted by the crowd, most of which was composed of women. Ambulances managed to remove the injured and left for the hospital. A number of the Negroes followed in private cars. When they reached Central Receiving Hospital, members of the caravan began shouting complaints about poor treatment, roamed into emergency rooms and disregarded orders to leave. One of the drivers involved in the earlier accident knocked down a police officer attempting to question him, and then kicked a nurse.

When the sirens of the approaching police cars were heard, the Negroes attempted to flee. Some of them, including George N. Washington, twenty-two, the driver who had assaulted a police officer in the hospital, were cornered in the parking lot.

Hollywood, a section of Los Angeles far removed from the Negro community, and which has often been described in guidebooks and magazines as a land of tinsel and make-believe, was jolted shortly after midnight on December 26, 1964. A mob of jazz fans, comprised mainly of Negroes, smashed the plush interior of the Hollywood Palladium when they became infuriated over a musical company's failure to complete a performance.

The mob was composed of members of an audience of 3,000 who had paid about $5 per person to view a performance of "New Perspectives for '65." The promoter of the one-night show had apparently neglected to pay his entertainers. The show had been scheduled to start at 8 P.M., but the first singer did not appear until more than an hour later. There was another 45-minute lapse, and a second singer named Gloria Lynne came out on the stage. She sang a few numbers, then the program came to a halt. The curtain kept going up and down. Musicians walked off the stage. The crowd began to shout, pushing and shoving. A woman jumped up on the stage, shouting for the performers to appear. Others went out to the box office, demanding their money back. Entertainer Bobby Blue Bland finally came out to the microphone and announced: "Man, there isn't enough bread to sing for. I'm getting out."

The crowd went wild. Three liquor bars that had been set up for intermission breaks were overturned. Liquor bottles were hurled at plate glass mirrors in the lobby. Potted plants were trampled, draperies torn from the walls and a fire set in a backstage trash can. It was extinguished before causing damage. As the rioters came rushing from the building onto Sunset Boulevard, 200 police officers met them at the front door.

Many of the rioters were carrying liquor bottles they had taken from behind the bars. Officers grabbed a man clutching four bottles of vodka as he ran from the dance hall with a bartender in pursuit. Negroes jumped the policemen and slugged the Palladium employee. The shouting mob showered the officers with cocktail glasses, while others stood across the street hurling bottles and other projectiles, which smashed against the walls of the Palladium, shattering windows. Remarkably, only a few persons were injured in the melee. Several were taken into custody. The charge: suspicion of disturbing the peace.

And so the pattern of disorder, unrest and violence gained momentum, escalating toward its inevitable climax. It was evident that the white society wasn't getting along with "these people," as the state's chief executive had been mistakenly led to believe. In August, 1965, the social fabric of the city of Los Angeles finally came apart at the seams.

In the aftermath of the riot, a stunned community demanded to know why this violent outbreak had occurred. Many views were advanced for the basic causes. Opinions were expressed by learned men whose backgrounds covered a broad range of experience with sociological problems. There were also voices from within the affected area which, while not as articulate, were often more eloquent in their directness and simplicity.

All seem in agreement—the contributing factors were poverty, lack of employment and the frustrations of a racial minority relegated to a substandard way of living, while surrounded and ignored by a prospering community, both white and black.

The issue of police brutality became the most bitter source of contention from within the Negro community of Watts and the south-central section of Los Angeles. But the argument also found support among affluent Negroes living in prosperous areas of the city. However, the primary concern is with the attitudes of those living in the depressed neighborhoods—those who became so enraged by an accumulation of real or imagined grievances that a single incendiary provocation impelled them to put their community to the torch.

It is apparent that within the social structure of those who inhabit Watts and other blighted sections of south-central Los Angeles, the police officer is hated. Even worse, he is feared. A contempt and disregard for law and order are synonymous with such an attitude. This attitude is of course in complete antithesis to the feelings of the white community, and, it should be stated, to the feelings of thousands of Negroes residing in Los Angeles who deplored the violence and disregard for constituted authority and the rights of those who own property.

Hostility against the police must certainly be regarded as one of the primary causes for the riot. The McCone report pointed out the necessity for improving police-community relations when it recommended that law enforcement agencies "place greater emphasis on their responsibilities for crime prevention as an essential element of the law enforcement task, and that they institute improved means for handling citizens' complaints and community relationships."

Evidence of "a deep and long-standing schism between a substantial portion of the Negro community and the Police Department" was noted by the McCone Commission when its report was finally released on December 6, 1965. "'Police brutality' has been the recurring charge," the commissioners wrote. "One witness after another has recounted instances where in their opinion, the police have used excessive force or have been disrespectful and abusive in their language or manner."

Police officers currently engaged in trying to combat an ever-growing crime rate in the Watts, Central Avenue and southeastern section of Los Angeles categorically deny these charges, and as the McCone Commission pointed out: "The police have explained to us the extent to which the conduct of some Negroes when apprehended has required the use of force in making arrests. Example after example has been recited of arrestees, both men and women, becoming violent, struggling to resist arrest, and thus requiring removal by physical force."

In Watts, as well as in the other areas affected by the riot, the battle against crime is a constant one. Here, the police must wage a continuous struggle to control the spread of criminal activities embracing narcotics, vice, robbery and even murder. These are indigenous to any community where poverty incubates the pestilential germs of moral decay.

A report prepared by the U.S. Labor Department contains some dismal statistics regarding the breakdown in family life among Negroes. It states that more than five out of every ten Negro children have lived in broken homes by the time they are eighteen. This figure is compared to one out of ten white children. Almost one out of four Negro women living in the city who has been married is now divorced or separated—three times the number of white women. One Negro family out of four is fatherless and one Negro baby out of four is illegitimate. The Labor Department report says that with a 40-per-cent-higher birth rate, the crowded Negro urban ghettos are getting more crowded, so that their descending spiral of poverty and frustration is getting worse.

These broken families present a growing problem for Los

Angeles welfare agencies. In Los Angeles County, nearly one out of every 20 residents is receiving some sort of financial assistance. The Bureau of Public Assistance handles about 40,000 cases a month involving 130,000 children in broken homes, and many of them are Negroes. Of these, 85 per cent are father desertion cases.

Public assistance funds being expended in the South Los Angeles riot area now total a staggering $5,500,000 per month. The recipients of all types of aid in the Watts area receive more than 20 per cent of the total county welfare budget, but represent less than 10 per cent of the county population. The increase in illegitimate children is another problem in the riot zone. Young mothers of illegitimate children become permanent recipients of relief, and the more children they have, the more money they receive. The tragic result of broken homes in the low-income groups is that the wives and children, deserted by their fathers, must turn to welfare for help. The mothers, usually unskilled, have little opportunity to become productive job holders.

Some 2,000 Negroes arrive in Los Angeles each month. Most of these represent unskilled labor. While Los Angeles industry has been continually expanding, its needs are for highly skilled and technical workers. The newly arrived Negroes, lacking these qualifications, settle largely in the Watts area, or its environs—thus adding to the growing unemployment rate. Roughly 60 per cent of the Watts residents are on relief. This army of Negro unemployed within the city is but a small but significant segment of the ever-growing Negro population in Los Angeles.

The statistics show that the city's population was 2,479,015 in 1960, including a Negro community numbering 334,916. The population of Los Angeles, according to a July 1, 1965, census, is 2,738,375. Of that figure, Negroes comprise around 400,000. The total Negro population in city and county is estimated at more than 650,000—less than 10 per cent of the present city-county figure of 6,885,794.

The Negro population is growing at a rate about four times that of the white population. Almost all Negro families settle in the Central district (roughly the area which embraces Central Avenue and other parallel thoroughfares extending south to Watts). It has been estimated that by 1970 Negroes will constitute 45 per cent of the metropolitan population, exclusive of the San Fernando Valley.

The face of Watts had changed little six months after the rioting. The scars were still visible—burned-out buildings, others boarded and locked. Much of the rubble had been cleaned away, leaving barren and deserted lots. On some of these, Negroes were employed chipping mortar from bricks, piling them into neat stacks, which were hauled away by contractors. Used brick is much prized for decorative construction in California homes. The Negroes received a penny a brick for their efforts. A fast worker could earn $20 in a day's time. Many of the men, however, were old. Their hands moved slowly and they tired easily. These men were lucky if they could clean and stack a little more than 100 bricks in a day's time. They sat in the sun, patiently hammering away at all that remained of the walls of their community, which had either been destroyed by the flames or flattened by wrecking crews which leveled the buildings damaged beyond repair.

A white passer-by approached one of the workers. "Where do I see about buying a load of these bricks?" he asked.

The Negro gestured toward the foreman with his hammer.

"I'm building a barbecue in my patio," the white man explained, as though it might be of interest to the Negro chipping away with his hammer. "That seems like a fitting place for these bricks to end up. That barbecue will be burning every night." He laughed at what he considered a joke and started walking cautiously through the wrecked building to where the foreman was supervising the loading of a truck. The Negro chipped at a mortar-crusted brick. It broke in two. He cursed.

There has been little rebuilding. Many of the burned-out merchants will not return. Insurance rates for business establishments within the entire district affected by the riots have soared. *Times* reporter Art Berman interviewed one white merchant, Solle Goldman, who was opening a new store in Watts, which was surrounded by burned and boarded-up buildings. As Berman later quoted Goldman in the story he wrote: "I thought if I came down here, I could give the neighborhood a place they'd be proud to shop in. It just takes one to lead and the others to follow."

Goldman had the floor of his men's wear store carpeted. The interior was tastefully decorated. An inventory of $5,000 in men's suits, sport coats and slacks was draped on hangers. Other items of apparel were displayed in showcases. Four days before Solle Goldman's new "Leed's Men's Wear" on East 103rd Street in the heart of Watts was scheduled to open, burglars bored a hole through the rear of the building. They removed Goldman's entire stock of goods. He had no insurance on the merchandise.

Leonard Rhodes owned a variety store at 4411 S. Central Avenue. During the August riots it was burned to the ground. In January, 1966, when *Times* reporter Ray Rogers interviewed him, Rhodes was rebuilding his store. It would be the first of the completely destroyed business concerns to be reestablished in the riot zone. Rhodes was encountering problems. An insurance man had informed him he couldn't even get him insurance with Lloyds of London. The Small Business Administration loaned him $15,000 of the $35,000 it will cost to rebuild, but otherwise he has seen little cooperation. Rhodes told Rogers: "The Chamber of Commerce has been having meetings, and we have drawn up a plan for this whole area. The merchants in this area have approved the plan. We tried to meet with the mayor and we got nowhere. All they want to do is study the area. These people want action, they're tired of standing around waiting for them to study the problem, and I don't blame them."

The construction of the building had not gone without incident. Negro youngsters threw rocks at the cement finishers, bringing a temporary halt to the work. The contractors took an additional precaution in the construction of the building with an eye on possible future needs. The outside walls are heavily lined with asbestos.

A tall, slender Negro leaned against the wall of a burned-out store building not far from Goldman's store. He was thirty, employed in a meat-packing plant in the not too distant industrial community of Vernon. Married, the father of two small children, he lived in a neat frame house within walking distance of the Watts business district which was virtually destroyed.

It was a January day. He and the writers were discussing what lay ahead for Watts, and if there were any visible signs of conditions being improved.

"Nothing much has happened," he said. "We hear a lot of talk. All kinds of white people come poking around down here asking questions. They go back uptown and write reports. I guess they file them away some place in City Hall. Everybody knows that what these people need here is something to do." He pointed to a small cluster of men gathered on a corner across the street. "Those are workingmen, only they ain't working. They can't find jobs. They hang around that saloon, drinking a little beer when they got the price of a glass. Sure, maybe some of them are lazy, but I think the majority would rather be out earning bread. Man, you've got to make it to eat.

"I'm lucky. I got a high school education and I'm working. Sure, maybe it's the kind of a job they can only get Negroes and Mexicans to do. Did you ever think of what it's like to spend the whole day in a goddamn icebox? Well, shit, man, I don't care. I belong to a union. I make pretty good money and my boss treats me fair. He's a white man."

He paused to light a cigarette, then grinned. "Working in a packinghouse has its compensations. My family eats well. So what if some of the steaks don't go out of the plant on a truck. Everybody knocks down a little no matter what he's doing. Them sharp business guys have their expense accounts. They figure they're grafting a little off the company. So what? The owner then writes it off on his income tax. He figures he's screwing Uncle Sam.

"But getting back to what has been done down here. I got one answer: nothing. Ask any of the people around here. Knock on any door. They'll tell you the same thing. The city officials don't know how to deal with these people. Sometimes they're not too careful who they pick out in the Negro community to work for them. Just because a Negro guy's a minister, it ain't going to stop him from busting out with a shiny new Cadillac once he gets his hands on some of that poverty dough.

"They opened up some center up on Central Avenue recently. It's supposed to be a place where the poor can go for help. It's run by Negroes, and I hear they got a good chunk of dough from the mayor's office. Someone told me it was around forty grand, so they could get things started. A guy I know went up there. He was just curious, you know, like he just wanted to see what they were doing.

"He says they put wall-to-wall carpeting in the place, and there were paneled offices and a lot of guys sitting behind desks looking important and shuffling papers. He saw one guy sitting in an office clipping pictures out of a magazine. I guess you can't blame them. Negroes are so tired of being crapped on that if you put them in a suit with a tie and a clean shirt, and then stick them in a fancy office behind a desk, why, they feel important. They is big men. They look down on a nigger like me who works in a slaughterhouse. Sometimes maybe I don't smell so good when I come home at night. But I bet I have more money in my pocket than they have.

"The other day I seen an article in a downtown newspaper about what this place is doing with all their dough. It said that they had opened a toy lending library for kids. If that's the poverty program, man, you can shove it."

The release of the McCone Report in early December after 100 days of exhaustive inquiry and research was a disappointment to many observers. It contained nothing that most people who had studied the Negro problem in Los Angeles were not already aware of.

The report delved deeply into educational, employment and police problems of the disadvantaged areas, as well as health, welfare, housing and transportation. Some of the "aggravating events" which took place in the year prior to the riots were cited:

1—"Publicity given to the flowing promise of the federal poverty program was paralleled by reports of controversy and bickering over the mechanics to handle the program here in Los Angeles, and when the projects did arrive, they did not live up to their press notices."

2—"Throughout the nation, unpunished violence and disobedience to law were widely reported, and almost daily there were exhortations here and elsewhere to take the most extreme and even illegal remedies to right a wide variety of wrongs, real and supposed."

The Commission urged reforms in police procedures to ease racial tension. It interpreted the fact that Police Chief William H. Parker was the focal point of Negro complaints "as evidence that the Board of Police Commissioners is not visibly exercising the authority over the department vested in it by the City Charter."

The report also found deficiencies in the present responsibility for investigating police misconduct charges, which in the vast majority of cases was left to the division commander of the individual officer involved. The commissioners found inequalities in public schools and libraries in the poverty sections of the city. They concluded "that the schools in the disadvantaged areas do not provide a program that meets the unique educational needs of culturally disadvantaged children."

The report found little hope for any immediate improvement in the employment situation among Negroes, but it stressed the importance of aiding the thousands of idle workers: "The most serious immediate problem that faces the Negro in our community is employment—securing and holding a job that provides him an opportunity for livelihood, and a chance to earn the means to support himself and his family, a dignity, and a reason to feel that he is a member of our community in a true and a very real sense."

The commission could not pinpoint any one circumstance as the single reason for the outbreak, but rather found it was a "spiral of failure" brought on by ". . . The economic and sociological condition in our city that underlay the gathering anger which impelled the rioters to escalate the routine arrest of a drunken driver into six days of violence." The McCone Report described the riot as a "formless, quite senseless, all but hopeless violent protest, engaged in by a few but bringing great distress to all."

In Los Angeles, people wonder what the future will bring. They are aware that the underlying causes of the August rioting have not been eliminated. Tension still exises in Watts and its environs. Aid programs have been initiated. Some, like an ambitious project undertaken by the Los Angeles Chamber of Commerce, have shown significant gains. The Chamber, which is supported by local business concerns, has found jobs for 4,000 Negroes, and these were not in menial capacities, but in department stores, savings and loan institutions, and other leading concerns. The largest number of placements were in the aerospace industry. Requirements were not lowered. The applicants hired had the necessary qualifications in both experience and training. The perplexing question is where to place those lacking any skills in gainful employment.

This problem is not confined to adults. The statistics reflect an ever-growing number of unemployed youths. Many have failed to complete a high school education, and among those attending classes in Negro areas, there is a tendency to minimize the value of a diploma as a passport to economic success. It has been among these youths that a continued attitude of belligerence has been most evident. While educators and social workers intensified their efforts toward creating an atmosphere of understanding, police officers increased their vigilance. Unrest continued in Watts. There were minor altercations and an ever-present undercurrent of growing hostility, fear, and the possibility of renewed violence.

It came in March. Two young Negroes were wounded by shotgun slugs fired from a car in front of a liquor store at 2066 E. 103rd Street. Their assailants, identified as Mexican-Americans, were later taken into custody. The ambush had been in retaliation for a fight that had taken place earlier in the store, when a Mexican-American youth had been assaulted by Negroes. The following day, March 15, 1966, there were rumors at nearby Jordan High School that there would be a "rumble" between Negroes and Mexicans. Racial hatred had been mounting between the two groups in Watts.

A Negro youth, Thomas Lee Galloway, hurled a rock at a passing car driven by a white schoolteacher, Robert Hyder. Detectives picked up Galloway in a barber shop near the school. As they led him away, the youth shouted "police brutality" to a crowd of youths which had gathered. Police officers blamed Galloway for the violence which followed.

Maurice Michels, thirty-three, was behind the wheel of his beer truck at 103rd and Grape Streets, stopped in traffic. Suddenly, he was surrounded by a mob of young Negroes. Michels is white. A brick shattered the front window of his truck. The door opened. He was dragged from the seat and hurled to the ground, where he was kicked and beaten. Someone slashed his trouser pocket, robbing him of nearly $200 in delivery receipts. Michels didn't lose consciousness. Bottles crashed in the street, as the enraged Negroes tossed cases from his truck. He could hear the sirens of approaching police cars. The mob fled. Later, as doctors stitched up his scalp, he recalled the words of the youths who tried to kill him. "You white bastard," they chanted.

Events quickly followed the same pattern of the previous summer, but with far less momentum. Marauding gangs roamed the streets of Watts, overturning automobiles. Twenty-five people were either stabbed or beaten. Molotov cocktails ignited numerous fires. Only fast action by firemen prevented these from becoming another conflagration. Store windows were smashed, and once again the looters were at work. More terrifying, some of the rioters were armed. As snipers exchanged shots with police officers, Joseph Lee Crawford, twenty-eight, a Negro, fell dead on the sidewalk in front of a liquor store at 10367 S. Wilmington Avenue. He had been an innocent bystander. A bullet from a 9-mm. automatic pistol struck him over the left eyebrow. Los Angeles police officers do not carry weapons of this caliber.

Larry Gomez, thirty-five, was a deliveryman for the Sparkletts Drinking Water Corp. Married, he was the father of five children, ranging from ages 1 to 11. He was a hard worker. In 1965, his firm had selected Larry as "Man of the Year." As a Caucasian, he felt no fear in working in a Negro neighborhood. He was an ardent champion of civil rights. Parking his truck near 101st and Grape Streets, Larry shouldered a five-gallon bottle and carried it to a house on his route. As he walked back to his truck, a gang of Negro boys jumped him. Gomez started to run.

"Let's get the waterman," they shouted.

One of the attackers was a seventeen-year-old youth, Sam Henry Fullerton. He was carrying a .22-caliber single shot derringer in his pocket, which he had borrowed from a friend. A derringer is a palm-sized weapon, lethal, and so easily obtainable from mail-order firms that among young hoodlums it is replacing the homemade zip gun. Fullerton drew the pistol and fired. Gomez staggered from doorway to doorway, begging for help. He had been shot in the chest. No one came to his aid. He collapsed and died in the street.

The riot was soon brought under control by swift mobilization of the Los Angeles Police Department. Young hoodlums were dispersed by squads of officers before they had an opportunity to assemble in large mobs, which had been able to defy police during the August riots. The National Guard was alerted, but it did not become necessary to summon Guardsmen for aid. In contrast to what happened in August, a sobered adult Negro community gave no encouragement to the young hoodlums. Ever further, responsible Negro youth groups, mindful of what had happened the previous summer, went into the streets, beseeching others of their own age to return to their homes. Police cars with shotgun-carrying officers raced through the streets, quelling disturbances and averting others by a strong show of force. There were a number of arrests. Among these was Sam Henry Fullerton, who fired the fatal bullet that struck Larry Gomez. Detectives apprehended him on an informant's tip.

"Why did you shoot him?" Fullerton was asked by officers.

The youth shrugged. "I wanted to be the big man."

Once again the streets were silent. Along East 103rd, the heart of the Watts business community, debris littered the gutters. Broken glass covered the sidewalks, where store windows had been knocked out by looters. One furniture store was going out of business. They were selling merchandise at half price. Solle Goldman had remained in Watts, operating his Leed's Men's Wear, even after burglars had robbed him of a $5,000 inventory prior to opening his store the previous December. The cost of insurance still remained prohibitive. Despite the setbacks he had suffered, Goldman remained confident. He had faith in the future of the community. On Tuesday, during the riot, looters ransacked his shop. They removed $25,000 in men's clothing. Suits were even stripped from mannequins. Goldman is bankrupt.

In Watts, the sickness still prevails.

Addressing a symposium on urban problems in December, 1965, Vice-President Hubert H. Humphrey predicted that massive riots would erupt unless America settles the plight of the poor in the cities. He said that there is a "simmering, smoldering explosion ready to go off" in overcrowded areas. "Like nuclear power itself it can be used either for destruction or peace. City after city will explode in violence that would make last summer's riots in Los Angeles look like an afternoon picnic."

The conclusion of the FBI's manual, *Prevention and Control of Mobs and Riots,* contains a somber evaluation of the aftermath of a riot and the possibility of its recurrence:

"The exercise of violence during a riot does not result in a purification of the atmosphere, leading to peace. It is not a situation in which excess energy is worked off, leaving the decks cleared for cooperation. Deep scars are left on both sides through this failure of law enforcement to control people. The rioters, especially the more active ones, take pride in their accomplishments regardless of the outcome of the riot. They do not feel guilty and tend to justify their actions on the basis of 'moral reasons.' One of the immediate consequences of a riot is a stimulation of determination to prepare for the 'next time.' Far from eliminating the differences which caused the violence in the first place, they are consolidated, reinforced and deepened. . . ."

The McCone Report is hardly any more optimistic, when it says: "As a Commission, we are seriously concerned that the existing breach, if allowed to persist, could in time split our society irretrievably. So serious and so explosive is the situation that, unless it is checked, the August riots may seem by comparison to be only a curtain-raiser for what could blow up one day in the future."

A city and a nation hope that this will not take place.

STATISTICS

THE MCCONE COMMISSION report contained the following statistics on the riot: "In the ugliest interval, which lasted from Thursday through Saturday, perhaps as many as 10,000 Negroes took to the streets in marauding bands. They looted stores, set fires, beat up white passersby whom they hauled from stopped cars, many of which were turned upside down and burned, exchanged shots with law enforcement officers, and stoned and shot at firemen. The rioters seemed to have been caught up in an insensate rage of destruction. By Friday, the disorder spread to adjoining areas, and ultimately an area covering 46.5 square miles had to be controlled with the aid of military authority before public order was restored. . . .

"The final statistics are staggering. There were 34 persons killed and 1,032 reported injuries, including 90 Los Angeles police officers, 136 firemen, 10 national guardsmen, 23 persons from other governmental agencies, and 773 civilians. 118 of the injuries resulted from gunshot wounds. Of the 34 killed, one was a fireman, one was a deputy sheriff, and one a Long Beach policeman. . . .

"It has been estimated that the loss of property attributable to the riots was over $40 million. More than 600 buildings were damaged by burning and looting. Of this number, more than 200 were totally destroyed by fire. The rioters concentrated primarily on food markets, liquor stores, furniture stores, clothing stores, department stores, and pawn shops. Arson arrests numbered 27 and 10 arson complaints were filed, a relatively small number considering that fire department officials say that all of the fires were incendiary in origin. Between 2,000 and

3,000 fire alarms were recorded during the riot, 1,000 of these between 7:00 A.M. on Friday and 7:00 A.M. on Saturday. . . .

"There were 3,438 adults arrested, 71% for burglary and theft. The number of juveniles arrested was 514, 81% for burglary and theft. Of the adults arrested, 1,232 had never been arrested before; 1,164 had a 'minor' criminal record (arrest only or convictions with sentence of 90 days or less); 1,042 with 'major' criminal record (convictions with sentence of more than 90 days). Of the juveniles arrested, 257 had never been arrested before; 212 had a 'minor' criminal record; 43 had a 'major' criminal record. Of the adults arrested, 2,057 were born in 16 southern states whereas the comparable figure for juveniles was 131. Some of the juveniles arrested extensively damaged the top two floors of an auxiliary jail which had been opened on the Saturday of the riots. . . .

"The police and Sheriff's Department have long known that many members of gangs, as well as others, in the south central area possessed weapons and knew how to use them. However, the extent to which pawn shops, each one of which possessed an inventory of weapons, were the immediate target of looters, leads to the conclusion that a substantial number of the weapons used were stolen from these shops. During the riots, law enforcement officers recovered 851 weapons. . . ."

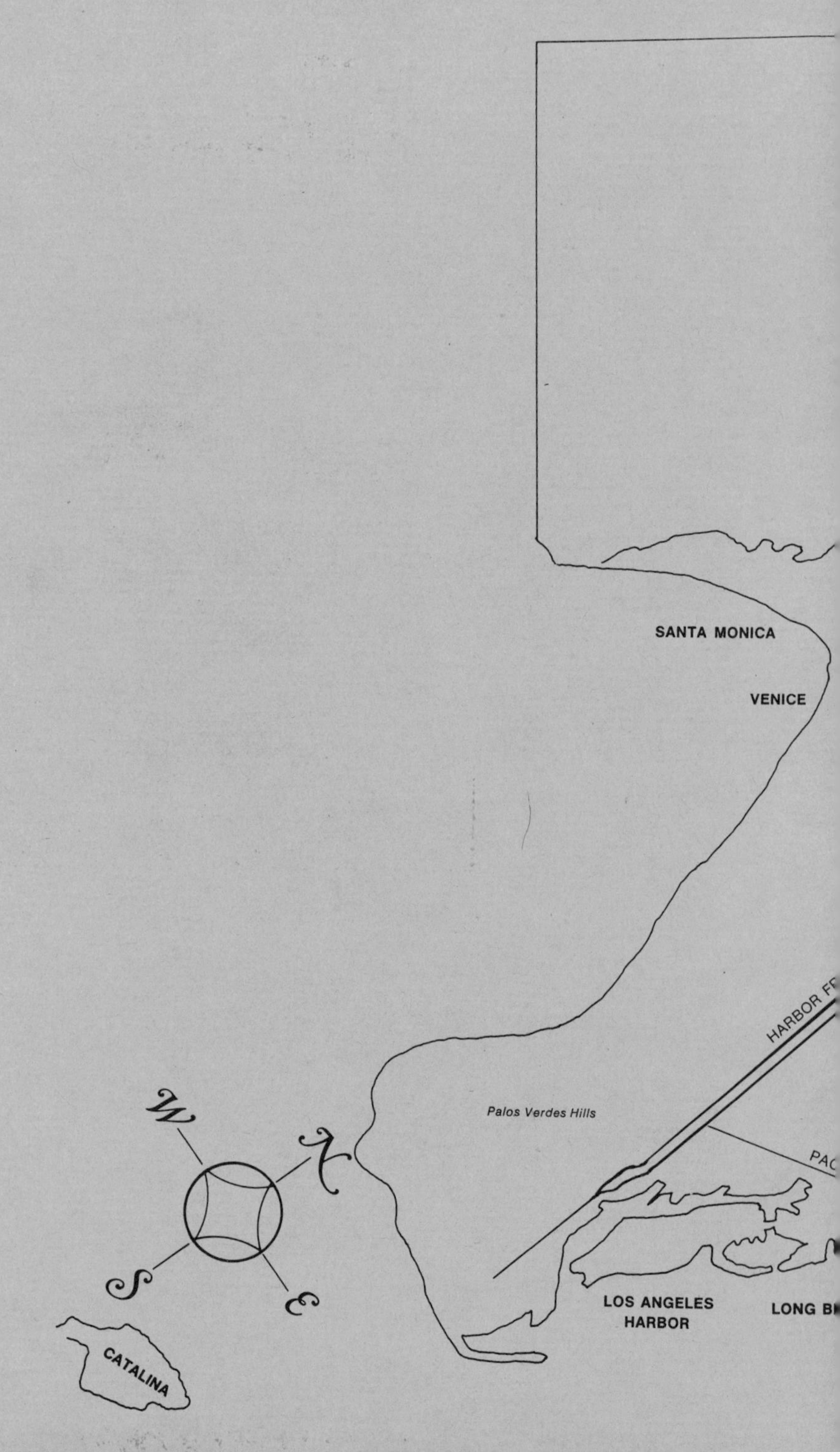

SANTA MONICA
VENICE
HARBOR
Palos Verdes Hills
W
N
S
E
LOS ANGELES
HARBOR
CATALINA